STUDY GUIDE TO ACCOMPANY
LIBERTY, EQUALITY, POWER
A HISTORY OF THE AMERICAN PEOPLE
THIRD EDITION

VOLUME II: SINCE 1863

John M. Murrin
Paul E. Johnson
James M. McPherson
Gary Gerstle
Emily S. Rosenberg
Norman L. Rosenberg

Prepared by
Mary Jane McDaniel
University of North Alabama

WADSWORTH

THOMSON LEARNING

Australia   Canada   Mexico   Singapore   Spain   United Kingdom   United States

0-15-506098-8

Cover Credit: *On the Steps* by George Luks
(1867–1933). David David Gallery,
Philadelphis/SuperStock.

For more information about our products,
contact us at:
Thomson Learning Academic Resource Center
1-800-423-0563

For permission to use material from this text,
contact us by:
Phone: 1-800-730-2214
Fax: 1-800-730-2215
Web: www.thomsonrights.com

Asia
Thomson Learning
60 Albert Complex, #15-01
Albert Complex
Singapore 189969

Australia
Nelson Thomson Learning
102 Dodds Street
South Melbourne, Victoria 3205
Australia

Canada
Nelson Thomson Learning
1120 Birchmount Road
Toronto, Ontario M1K 5G4
Canada

Europe/Middle East/South Africa
Thomson Learning
Berkshire House
168-173 High Holborn
London WC1 V7AA
United Kingdom

Latin America
Thomson Learning
Seneca, 53
Colonia Polanco
11560 Mexico D.F.
Mexico

Spain
Paraninfo Thomson Learning
Calle/Magallanes, 25
28015 Madrid, Spain

PREFACE

Liberty, equality, and power are themes that have been interwoven throughout the events in American history. The relative position of these concepts varies considerably over the centuries, with many ups and downs and forward and backward steps. If, however, a student follows American history from the earliest times to the present, he or she should be able to see a growth of liberty, equality, and empowerment for both individuals and groups of people. Despite the fact that American society still has a way to go in these matters, students should realize that this transformation is an ongoing process that they can carry forward during their lifetime.

This Study Guide is designed to help students in their study of American history and to complement, but not replace, the basic textbook. The chapters correspond with those in the text regarding material covered and the basic emphasis. Each chapter relates to the overall theme of liberty, equality, and power. It is followed by a basic chronology of the important events covered in each chapter, which gives the student a better sense of the span of time involved. A number of very different activities could have happened at the same time in history.

The glossary of important terms permits the student an opportunity to master key terms and concepts covered by the text chapter. The basic definitions deal with the terms as they were used in the period covered, but some attempt was made to develop definitions that also could be useful to the student today.

The Who? What? Where? sections should help students develop a sense of the important people, places, and events of the period. The multiple-choice questions test basic knowledge gained by a thorough study of the chapter. Students should also learn to evaluate maps, charts, and illustrations. Many of the questions dealing with these seem minor, but they are designed to encourage careful study of the visual material offered in the text.

Essay question responses develop writing, organizational, and analytical ability. They also encourage a broad overall view of events of the American past. Most of all, they are designed to encourage students to think, compare, and understand the significant events of each time period. Hopefully, some comparison can be made with modern times and the reality of life today. The What If? section, added to each chapter, encourages students to identify with groups and individuals in American history. It should help them to understand important decisions of the past.

Many people supported me in this work, especially my friends in the Department of History and Political Science at the University of North Alabama. Students in some of my classes were exposed to many of the questions and ideas developed in this Study Guide. Special thanks to Amy Calvert and Laura Watson, who typed the revisions for the third edition. I appreciate their work and encouragement very much.

Mary Jane McDaniel
University of North Alabama

CONTENTS

CHAPTER 17

RECONSTRUCTION, 1863–1877

Reconstruction was a traumatic period of transition for many Americans. Concerns focused on the identity of the newly reconstructed union and the roles of the various groups in it. Significant controversy surrounded which branch of the government, the presidency or Congress, would control Reconstruction and the new union. Each president of the period, Abraham Lincoln, Andrew Johnson, and Ulysses S. Grant, handled the issues differently. Their actions, along with their respective struggles with members of Congress, had lasting effect.

Another controversy surrounded the rights of former slaves, now freedpeople, and the role of their former owners in the postwar South. National discussions about African Americans focused on race in both the former Confederate and former Union areas. These discussions often ended in violence or confusion, ultimately leading to the drafting and ratification of constitutional amendments that defined citizenship and its rights. State governments could not abridge the rights of citizens without due process; and African Americans legally were entitled to vote in all states. In practice, however, they often were intimidated and lacked the financial resources to maintain their new position successfully.

Gradually, the public shifted its attention to other controversial issues, including civil service reform, currency, labor unrest, and corrupt elections. Reconstruction ended as a result of the disputed election of 1876, during which a compromise was reached. Rutherford B. Hayes was inaugurated as president and acted quickly to remove federal troops from the South, leaving white southerners in control of the former Confederate states. In other parts of the country, most people reacted with indifference. They wanted to move on to other matters, leaving behind the issues of Reconstruction and race. African Americans were left without a protector, and they gradually lost most of the rights they gained during Reconstruction.

LIBERTY, EQUALITY, POWER

Power is often the critical variable in determining which contending group gets what, and it is often necessary to ensure liberty and equality. This is reflected in the Reconstruction era, with systems of patronage, including the spoils system. To provide conditions for the liberty and equality of former slaves to thrive, for example, the federal government had to assert new powers to combat Black Codes and bulldozing. The powers the federal government adopted ranged from martial law to constitutional amendments (the Thirteenth, Fourteenth, and Fifteenth Amendments) to the creation of the Freedmen's Bureau.

Though Reconstruction was a qualified success, the idea of the strong state as a guarantor of liberty and equality lived on, as we shall see, in the social movements of farmers, workers, feminists, and minorities, and in the politics of liberal reform (Populism, Progressivism, the New Deal, the Great Society) from the 1890s through the 1960s.

OBJECTIVES

After studying this chapter, a student should be able to

1. Compare presidential Reconstruction under Lincoln and Johnson with congressional Reconstruction.

2. Describe life and labor in the South after the Civil War for whites and African Americans.

3. Discuss the purposes, provisions, and results of the three Reconstruction amendments to the Constitution.

4. Analyze the Grant administration.

5. Examine Reconstruction in the South from both the southern and northern point of view.

6. Describe the election of 1876 and compromise of 1877.

CHRONOLOGY

1862–1863	Lincoln advocated that freedpeople emigrate to all-black countries, such as Haiti, where they could advance their lives without experiencing the prejudice of whites.
1863	Lincoln issued his Proclamation of Amnesty and Reconstruction in **December,** which offered a presidential pardon to most southern whites who took an oath of allegiance to the United States.
1864	Union troops controlled considerable portions of the Confederate states of Louisiana, Arkansas, and Tennessee.
	Both houses of Congress approved the Wade-Davis Reconstruction bill in **July.** This bill levied such strict loyalty requirements on southern whites that few of them could take the required oath. Lincoln vetoed it.
	Andrew Johnson of Tennessee was nominated as Lincoln's running mate to procure support from War Democrats and border-state Unionists.
1865	General William T. Sherman issued a military order in **January** setting aside thousands of acres of abandoned plantation land in Georgia and South Carolina for settlement by freed slaves. However, President Johnson's Amnesty Proclamation restored most of the property to pardoned ex-Confederates.

In **March**, Congress established the Freedmen's Bureau to supervise relations between former slaves and owners. The bureau established posts throughout the South to oversee wage contracts and to circulate food rations.

Lincoln was assassinated by John Wilkes Booth in **April**, and Andrew Johnson succeeded him as the seventeenth president of the United States.

In **May**, President Johnson issued two proclamations that exposed his intentions of excluding both blacks and upper-class whites from the Reconstruction process and establishing yeomen whites as the backbone of the new South.

Republicans began public criticism of President Johnson's special pardons, which restored property and political rights to 13,500 ex-Confederates.

Individual southern states enacted Black Codes.

1866

Congress passed two laws to protect the economic and civil rights of freedpeople, but Johnson vetoed the laws.

In **February**, Johnson denounced Republican leaders as traitors who did not want to restore the Union except on terms that would degrade white southerners.

Congress passed the Freedmen's Bureau and Civil Rights bills, with more than a two-thirds majority in both houses, over the president's vetoes.

The Fourteenth Amendment was proposed.

1867

Congress enacted two laws, over Johnson's vetoes, directing new procedures for the full restoration of the former Confederate states. These acts divided the southern states into five military districts, ordered army officers to register voters for the election of delegates to the new constitutional conventions, and enfranchised males twenty-one and older (including blacks) to vote in those elections.

President Johnson tried to stop the Reconstruction process by placing Democrats in command of southern districts, interpreting the acts contrary to the intention of Congress, and encouraging southern whites to use tactics to defer the registration of voters and the election of convention delegates.

1868

Johnson ensured his impeachment in **February** by removing from office Secretary of War Edwin M. Stanton, who had operated the War Department in support of the congressional Reconstruction policy. This removal appeared to violate the Tenure of Office Act.

In **May**, Republican senators fell one vote short of the necessary two-thirds majority required to remove Johnson. Several moderate Republicans were apprehensive that such a precedent might tip the balance of powers.

The Ku Klux Klan made its initial political appearance during the 1868 elections.

1870   Missionary societies concentrated heavily on making higher education accessible to African Americans.

The Fifteenth Amendment was ratified, which prohibited states from denying individuals the right to vote on the basis of race, color, or previous condition of servitude.

1870–1871   Congress enacted three laws intended to enforce the Fourteenth and Fifteenth Amendments. These laws made interference with voting rights a federal offense.

1871   Secretary of State Hamilton Fish negotiated the Treaty of Washington, which settled the Alabama Claims and the status of Canada.

1873   A Wall Street panic plunged the economy into a five-year depression.

1874   Democrats made large gains in congressional elections, winning a majority in the House of Representatives for the first time in eighteen years.

1875   The Mississippi Plan, using economic pressure, threats, and violence to influence elections, was introduced.

Congress passed a civil rights act banning racial discrimination in public transportation and accommodations. In 1883 the Supreme Court declared the act to be unconstitutional.

1876   The Supreme Court ruled that parts of the 1870–1871 laws for enforcement of the Fourteenth and Fifteenth Amendments were unconstitutional because the federal government could not prosecute individuals.

As a reaction to widespread corruption, both Democrats and Republicans selected reform governors as their candidates for president. There was extensive economic coercion, threats, and violence. The very close elections produced disputed returns in three states and caused questions about which party won the presidency.

1877   The electoral commission issued its ruling regarding the 1876 disputed election results and declared Rutherford B. Hayes president in **February**.

Hayes was inaugurated as president peacefully in **March** as a result of a compromise between northern Republicans and some southern Democrats.

In **April**, the withdrawal of federal troops constituted both a symbolic and actual end of the twelve-year postwar era known as Reconstruction.

GLOSSARY OF IMPORTANT TERMS

amnesty   A general pardon granted to a large group of people.

appellate   A court with the power to hear appeals and review decisions of other courts.
jurisdiction

Black Codes   Laws passed by southern states that defined the rights of former slaves and addressed black-white relationships. In general, these laws executed blacks from juries and the ballot box and generally discriminated on racial grounds.

bulldozing   Using force to keep African Americans from voting.

carpetbaggers   A term that referred to northerners who settled in the South during Reconstruction.

Crédit Mobilier   The construction company for the Union Pacific Railroad. It gave shares of stock to some congressmen in return for favors.

Era of Good   A term used to describe the explosion of corruption in the years after the
Stealings   Civil War.

felony   A major crime.

Fenian   An Irish-American secret society that believed an invasion of Canada would
Brotherhood   help bring independence to Ireland.

filibuster   Congressional delaying tactic involving lengthy speeches that prevent legislation from being enacted.

forty acres and   The dream of many former slaves that they would receive free land from
a mule   the confiscated property of ex-Confederates. Only a few areas gave them land. Most ex-Confederates got their plantations back through general amnesty programs, or they received a special pardon from President Johnson.

franchise   The right to vote. **Enfranchise**: To give or allow a group the right to vote. **Disfranchise**: To take away the right to vote.

Freedmen's Bureau   A federal agency created in 1865 to supervise newly freed people. It oversaw relations between whites and blacks in the South, issued food rations, and supervised labor contracts.

habeas corpus   The right of an individual to obtain a legal document as protection against illegal imprisonment.

impeach   To charge government officeholders with misconduct in office. In the case of the president, the House of Representatives brings the charges; the Senate serves much like a jury, and the members of the Supreme Court preside. The removal (impeachment) of a president requires a two-thirds vote by the Senate.

levee	An earthen dike or mound, usually along the banks of rivers, used to prevent flooding.
martial law	Government by a military force rather than by civilians. Most often, it was used in emergency situations.
monopoly	An individual or company having exclusive control of a service or item sold in the marketplace or having enough control to establish the price of the item.
patronage	Government jobs given out by political figures to their supporters, regardless of ability.
quasi slavery	A position that resembled slavery. Some northerners thought the Black Codes created a type of quasi slavery.
rolling stock	Locomotives, freight cars, and other types of wheeled equipment owned by railroads.
scalawags	Term used by southern Democrats to describe southern whites who worked with the Republicans.
share wages	The payment of workers' wages with a share of the crop rather than with cash.
sharecropping	Working land in return for a share of the crops produced instead of paying cash rent. Shortage of currency in the South made sharecropping a frequent form of land tenure. African-American families preferred it because it eliminated the labor gangs used in the days of slavery.
southern yeoman	A farmer who owned relatively little land and few or no slaves.
spoils system	A system by which the victorious political party rewarded its supporters with government jobs.
union leagues	Organizations that informed African-American voters and mobilized them to support the Republican Party.
universal male suffrage	A system that allows all adult males to vote without regard to property, religious, or race qualifications or limitations.
vagrant	A person who wanders from place to place and has no occupation or visible means of support.

WHO? WHAT? WHERE?

WHO WERE THEY?

Complete each statement that follows (questions 1–12) by writing the letter preceding the appropriate name in the space provided. Use each answer only once.

    a. Adelbert Ames
    b. Alexander H. Stephens
    c. Charles Sumner

  d. David Key
  e. Edwin M. Stanton
  f. George W. Curtis
  g. Hamilton Fish
  h. Jay Cooke
  i. Nathan Bedford Forrest
  j. Thaddeus Stevens
  k. Thomas Nast
  l. Samuel J. Tilden

_____   1. Congressman from Pennsylvania and leader of the Radical Republicans.

_____   2. One of the principal exponents of the Radical Republicans in the Senate and a leading advocate of civil rights for blacks.

_____   3. Secretary of War, under whose leadership the War Department supported congressional Reconstruction. He was removed from office by President Johnson.

_____   4. High-ranking Confederate general who became an official in the Ku Klux Klan.

_____   5. Important reformer who was appointed by President Grant to head a civil service commission.

_____   6. Secretary of State under President Grant who negotiated with Britain to end the Alabama claims dispute.

_____   7. Prominent political cartoonist who could influence national elections with his incisive cartoons.

_____   8. Leader of the banking firm that helped finance the Civil War and the building of the Northern Pacific Railroad.

_____   9. Reconstruction governor of Mississippi who asked for federal troops to control the violence in his state and was refused by Grant for political reasons.

_____   10. Vice president of the Confederacy who was elected to Congress in Georgia during the first days of Reconstruction.

_____   11. Democratic governor of New York who was the unsuccessful candidate for president in the disputed election of 1876.

_____   12. Ex-Confederate from Tennessee who became postmaster general as part of the Compromise of 1877.

WHAT WAS IT?

Complete each statement that follows (questions 1–10) by writing the letter preceding the appropriate response in the space provided. Use each answer only once.

  a. American Equal Rights Association
  b. Civil Rights Cases
  c. Fifteenth Amendment

    d. Fourteenth Amendment
    e. Mississippi Plan
    f. Proclamation of Amnesty
    g. Reconstruction Acts of 1867
    h. spoils system
    i. Tenure of Office Act
    j. Thirteenth Amendment

_____ 1. Bill passed over presidential veto that required the consent of the Senate before removing officeholders approved by the Senate. President Johnson was accused of violating this act.

_____ 2. Prohibited states from denying the right to vote on the grounds of race, color, or previous condition of servitude.

_____ 3. Organization working for both black and woman suffrage.

_____ 4. Bill that divided the ten southern states into five military districts, directed army officers to register voters, enfranchised males of both races that were over age twenty-one, and disfranchised certain ex-Confederates.

_____ 5. Gave United States citizenship to all native-born or naturalized persons and prohibited states from depriving any person of life, liberty, or property without due process.

_____ 6. This document offered a presidential pardon to southern whites, with a few exceptions, who took an oath of allegiance to the United States and accepted the abolition of slavery.

_____ 7. Combination of economic pressure and physical intimidation (from the threat of violence to actual violence) to force black and white supporters of the Republican Party in southern states to vote Democratic or stay away from the polls.

_____ 8. Glue that kept the party faithful together when a party was out of office.

_____ 9. Decision by the Supreme Court that declared the civil rights law of 1875 unconstitutional because the Fourteenth Amendment applied only to states and not to individuals.

_____ 10. Abolished slavery everywhere in the United States.

WHERE WAS IT?

Complete each statement that follows (questions 1–7) by writing the letter preceding the appropriate response in the space provided. Use each answer only once.

    a. Florida
    b. Hamburg
    c. Louisiana
    d. Memphis
    e. Promontory Point
    f. South Carolina
    g. Tennessee

_____ 1. One of the states with disputed returns in the 1876 presidential election.

_____ 2. City where race riots took place during Reconstruction.

_____ 3. First ex-Confederate state readmitted to the Union.

_____ 4. Place where the Union Pacific and Central Pacific railroads met to form the first transcontinental railroad.

_____ 5. First area to reorganize under Lincoln's moderate plan for Reconstruction.

_____ 6. Only state where African Americans made up the majority of elective officials.

_____ 7. Small village where a battle took place between a black militia unit and white southerners.

CHARTS, MAPS, AND ILLUSTRATIONS

1. According to the map on the Hayes-Tilden election (p. 625), from which former slave states did disputed election returns come in 1876? _____

2. One state in the military district commanded by General Philip Sheridan was

_____.

3. One of the illustrations (p. 604) shows the desperate poverty of the South after the Civil War. Which illustration was it and how does it indicate this poverty?

_____

4. The generic name for the secret groups that terrorized the southern countryside was the _____. Part of their purpose was _____.

MULTIPLE CHOICE

Circle the letter that best completes each statement.

1. Some northerners wanted more advances over slavery than just the recognition of freedom and a minimal provision for education. They were known as
   a. scalawags.
   b. Radical Republicans.
   c. freethinkers.
   d. Whigs.

2. All of Lincoln's expectations for the reconstructed government in Louisiana were not realized because of all of the following except
   a. The new government would not grant literate blacks the right to vote.
   b. The new government would not grant black Union soldiers the right to vote.
   c. The new government authorized planters to enforce restrictive labor policies on black plantation workers.
   d. The new government provided a school system for blacks.

3. The Wade-Davis reconstruction bill of 1864
    a. liberated blacks—a policy that commanded a majority of Republicans.
    b. was supported by Lincoln in every aspect.
    c. was passed in the House of Representatives, but not in the Senate.
    d. imposed such strict loyalty requirements on southern whites that few were able to take the required oath.

4. To attract the votes of War Democrats and border-state Unionists in 1864, Republicans adopted the name
    a. Whig Party.
    b. Reconstruction Party.
    c. Union Party.
    d. Representative Party.

5. All of the following statements are true of Andrew Johnson except
    a. He denounced planters as "stuck-up aristocrats."
    b. He became a self-appointed spokesman for southern yeomen.
    c. He was a Democratic senator from a Confederate state who refused to support the Confederacy.
    d. His background of upper-class privileges assured him of political success.

6. Political ambitions motivated President Andrew Johnson to
    a. issue special presidential pardons for ex-Confederates, which restored their property and political rights.
    b. establish new state constitutions that prohibited ex-Confederates from holding state offices.
    c. establish new policies excluding ex-Confederates from holding national offices, such as congressional seats.
    d. issue special presidential pardons for ex-Confederates that restored all their property but not their political rights.

7. The Black Codes of 1865 did all of the following except
    a. exclude blacks from juries, voting, and testifying in court.
    b. ensure blacks were not punished more severely than whites were for crimes.
    c. ban interracial marriages and provide for the apprenticing to whites of black youths who did not have adequate parental support.
    d. exclude blacks from leasing land and, in some states, define unemployed blacks as vagrants who could be hired out to planters.

8. All but one of the following conditions describe the postwar South:
    a. Its landscape was marked by burned-out plantations, fields overgrown with weeds, and railroads without tracks.
    b. Half its livestock and most of its other tangible assets, except the land, had been destroyed.
    c. Many people, both whites and blacks, literally did not know from where their next meal would come.
    d. An increase in the numbers of marshals and other officials was necessary to prevent a collapse of law and order.

9. The Freedmen's Bureau did all of the following except
    a. establish posts throughout the North.
    b. supervise and enforce free-labor wage contracts between landowners and freed-people.
    c. become the principal agency for overseeing relations between former slaves and former owners.
    d. issue food rations to 150,000 people daily, one third of whom were white, during 1865.

10. The Fourteenth Amendment did all of the following except
    a. define all native-born or naturalized persons as American citizens and prohibit states from denying them their rights as citizens.
    b. increase the number of congressional seats and electoral votes for each state by 2 percent.
    c. disqualify a number of ex-Confederates from holding federal or state offices.
    d. empower Congress to enforce the Fourteenth Amendment by appropriate legislation.

11. Never had a president and Congress been so bitterly at odds as in 1867 when Johnson put every roadblock he could in the way of the Reconstruction process. President Johnson took all of the following actions except to
    a. remove several Republican generals from command of southern military districts and appoint Democrats in their place.
    b. have his attorney general issue a ruling that interpreted the Reconstruction Acts narrowly, and thereby force a special session of Congress to pass a supplementary act in July 1867.
    c. encourage southern whites to engage in obstructive tactics to delay the registration of voters and the election of convention delegates.
    d. encourage the Democratic Party to accept black leaders into the party with the hope that this would increase black support for the upcoming election.

12. The underlying cause of Andrew Jackson's impeachment trial was
    a. his defiance of the will of Congress on Reconstruction.
    b. his secret dealings with foreign governments, which some interpreted as treason.
    c. his public behavior, refusal to be held accountable to the American people, and rumors of bribery.
    d. his severe punishment of ex-Confederate military officers, government officers, and government officials.

13. The purpose of the Fifteenth Amendment was
    a. to grant Congress the power to lay and collect taxes on income.
    b. to extend suffrage to women.
    c. to prevent any further revocation of black suffrage by reconstructed states and to extend equal suffrage to the border states and to the North.
    d. to prohibit the manufacture, sale, or transportation of intoxicating liquors.

14. The radical wing of the suffragists opposed the Fifteenth Amendment because
    a. it required all voters to be literate.
    b. it failed to ban discrimination on the grounds of sex as well as race.
    c. it allowed all southern men to vote.
    d. it allowed all veterans to vote.

15. The increase of corruption during the period after the Civil War was due in part to all of the following factors except
    a. an increase in bureaucracy during the war, which created new opportunities for unethical individuals.
    b. the decrease of government contracts during the war.
    c. a relaxation of tensions and standards following the intense sacrifices of the war years.
    d. rapid postwar economic growth, which encouraged greed and get-rich-quick schemes.

16. Ulysses S. Grant
    a. openly supported Johnson's Reconstruction policy.
    b. was a great success as president, owing to his political experience.
    c. was a great military leader, who, by 1866, commanded greater authority and prestige than anyone else in the country.
    d. worked to cultivate supporters in the area of foreign policy.

17. "Scalawags" was a term given to individuals who participated in Reconstruction and were from the
    a. South.
    b. East.
    c. West.
    d. North.

18. The Wall Street Panic of 1873 was caused by the widespread actions of men such as Civil War financier
    a. Horace Greeley.
    b. Jonathan Gibbs.
    c. Orpheus C. Kerr.
    d. Jay Cooke.

19. During the Mississippi election of 1875, the Republican majority of 30,000 changed to the Democratic majority of 30,000. This outcome was the result of all but the following:
    a. economic pressures, social ostracism, and persuasive threats, which convinced the 10 to 15 percent of white voters who still called themselves Republicans to switch their allegiance to the Democratic Party.
    b. intimidation of black voters, who represented a 55 percent majority.
    c. the use of economic coercion and violence to keep black voters away from the polls.
    d. widespread bribery to entice black voters to join the Democratic Party.

20. In 1876, the term "bulldozing" came to describe Democratic techniques of intimidation. It meant to
    a. intimidate white Republican voters into voting Democratic.
    b. bribe black voters to support Democratic candidates.
    c. trample black voters or keep them away from the polls.
    d. burn down the homes of Republican candidates.

21. All of the following were part of the Compromise of 1877 except
    a. federal appropriations to rebuild war-destroyed levees.
    b. a guarantee of voting rights for all males in the South.
    c. the appointment of a southerner to the cabinet.
    d. the removal of federal troops from two southern states.

ESSAY

Description and Explanation (one- to two-paragraph essay)

1. Explain the difference between moderate and radical views on African Americans' voting.

2. Describe the destruction of the South during the Civil War.

3. Explain why President Johnson was not removed from office.

4. Explain the role of violence in the election of 1868.

5. Explain why there was so much corruption in the postwar decades.

6. Describe the African-American experience in holding office.

7. List and explain the motives of northerners who moved to the South.

8. Which presidential candidate should have won the election of 1876? Explain why.

Discussion and Analysis (class discussion or one- to two-paragraph essay)

1. Compare the Reconstruction policies of Presidents Lincoln and Johnson, and analyze the possibility that either of their respective sets of policies might have been successful.

2. Study the provisions of the Fourteenth Amendment carefully. Discuss which provisions are operative at the end of the twentieth century and why this amendment is considered so important in American history. Develop at least one example of how you might use or benefit from it.

What If (include an explanation of your position)

1. If you were either an ex-Union soldier, a white southerner, or an African American living in the South, how would you view the events of the Reconstruction period?

2. If you were a senator during the impeachment trial of President Johnson, would you vote guilty or not guilty?

Crossword Puzzle: Reconstruction, 1863–1877

DOWN

1. What Andrew Johnson wanted to make odious
2. The 1876 presidential election returns from this state were disputed
3. Civil service reformers advocated this as a way of finding competent government workers
4. Patronage program entrenched in government since Jacksonian era
5. Arbitrators awarded $15.5 million to the U.S. in _____ claims
6. Ku Klux Klan to freedpeople
10. Trademark luggage of northerners who moved to the South
11. Implement of those carrying out the Mississippi Plan
15. Illumination for KKK
17. _____ Mobilier was a scandal involving construction of Union Pacific Railroad
18. Sharecropper's tool
19. Compromise of 1877 was the _____ act of Reconstruction
20. This vice was satirized by Twain and Warner in *The Gilded Age*

ACROSS

1. "Winner" who lost election of 1876
4. Jury at Johnson's impeachment trial
7. Reconstruction constitutions provided for this for both races in the South
8. Baba or Muhammad
9. White southern republican
12. Home of Hayes
13. Wet dust
14. Immigrant turned Fenian
16. Short for reconstructed state
19. Sharecroppers and others
20. Ben Wade's plea to Johnson
21. 1866 act of Congress didn't provide this for Edwin M. Stanton
22. Thaddeus Stevens was a _____ _____ (2 wds.) of the House of Representatives

ANSWER KEY

WHO? WHAT? WHERE?

Who Were They?

1. j. Thaddeus Stevens, p. 599
2. c. Charles Sumner, p. 599
3. e. Edwin M. Stanton, p. 609
4. i. Nathan Bedford Forrest, p. 612
5. f. George W. Curtis, p. 613
6. g. Hamilton Fish, p. 614
7. k. Thomas Nast, pp. 618–619
8. h. Jay Cooke, p. 619
9. a. Adelbert Ames, p. 621
10. b. Alexander H. Stephens, p. 602
11. l. Samuel J. Tilden, p. 623
12. d. David Key, p. 626

What Was It?

1. i. Tenure of Office Act, p. 609
2. c. Fifteenth Amendment, p. 611
3. a. American Equal Rights Association, p. 611
4. g. Reconstruction Acts of 1867, p. 607
5. d. Fourteenth Amendment, p. 607
6. f. Proclamation of Amnesty, p. 598
7. e. Mississippi Plan, pp. 620–621
8. h. spoils system, p. 613
9. b. *Civil Rights Court Cases*, p. 623
10. j. Thirteenth Amendment, p. 602

Where Was It?

1. a. Florida, p. 624
2. d. Memphis, p. 607
3. g. Tennessee, p. 607
4. e. Promontory Point, p. 619
5. c. Louisiana, p. 598
6. f. South Carolina, p. 615
7. b. Hamburg, p. 624

CHARTS, MAPS, AND ILLUSTRATIONS

1. Louisiana, South Carolina, and Florida, p. 625
2. Louisiana or Texas, p. 614
3. the lack of a work animal, p. 604
4. Ku Klux Klan; control of the black population; p. 618

MULTIPLE CHOICE

1. b (p. 599)
2. d (p. 599)
3. d (p. 600)
4. c (p. 600)
5. d (p. 600)
6. a (p. 602)
7. b (p. 602)
8. d (p. 603)
9. a (p. 603)
10. b (pp. 606–607)
11. d (p. 608)
12. a (p. 609)
13. c (p. 611)
14. b. (p. 611)
15. b (p. 613)
16. c (p. 613)
17. a (p. 616)

18. d   (p. 619)

19. d   (pp. 620–622)

20. c   (p. 624)

21. b   (pp. 625–626)

ESSAY

Description and Explanation

  1. pp. 597–598

  2. pp. 603–604

  3. p. 609

  4. pp. 611–612

5. p. 613

6. p. 615

7. p. 616

8. pp. 624–625

Discussion and Analysis

  1. pp. 598–602

  2. p. 606

What If

  1. pp. 597–610 Chapter 17 *passim*

  2. p. 609

Crossword Puzzle

CHAPTER 18

FRONTIERS OF CHANGE, POLITICS OF STALEMATE, 1865–1898

While many Americans were preoccupied with Reconstruction, others were involved in the growth of the West and the expansion of agriculture. European Americans exploded throughout the West, and in twenty-five years occupied more land than had been claimed in America previous to the Civil War. The mining frontier propelled settlers into the gold, silver, and copper mining regions. The ranching frontier, with its cowboys, became the dominant symbol of the Old West. Farmers greatly increased the agricultural production of the United States. In the process of this expansion, the once powerful Plains Indians were pushed aside onto reservations and pressed into adapting English culture. Mexican Americans were forced to adjust to a new social order and consequently often found themselves the victims of discrimination.

Despite a spirit of enterprise in the New South, and the growth of some industries, the region remained primarily agricultural. The downward economic spiral of the rural South caused frustration and bitterness; subsequently, African Americans became the scapegoats for white rage. Southern state constitutions disfranchised most blacks, and Jim Crow laws legalized racial segregation in public facilities.

The presidential elections from 1867 to 1892 were the most closely contested elections in American history. The government as well as the two national political parties themselves seemed divided on economic and social issues, producing a political stalemate. Neither party had the power to enact a bold legislative program; both concentrated on the past rather than the present. Their members were involved in the passionate partisanship of the past.

LIBERTY, EQUALITY, POWER

In the late nineteenth century, power was concentrated in the hands of a few, in contrast to the discrimination encountered by most minority groups. The West saw the decline of the powerful Plains Indian tribes, with the deliberate killing of the buffalo a demonstration of naked power by whites. Most of the Hispanic population were displaced to separate barrios. In the South, blacks lost any political influence as state constitutions and court cases upheld their disfranchisement.

Yet many European Americans believed the frontier meant opportunities and more liberty and equality for them. The official ending of the frontier in 1890 followed by a severe economic depression caused many of them to believe that their future was in trouble. This outlook caused a serious uprising in the 1890s.

OBJECTIVES

After studying this chapter, a student should be able to

1. Describe the settlement of the West by the farmers, miners, and cattlemen.

2. Discuss the decline of the Plains Indians.

3. Describe the problems of southern agriculture and the declining position of African Americans in the region.

4. Compare the presidential and vice presidential candidates from both major parties in the age of political stalemate.

CHRONOLOGY

1862	For the massacre of approximately five hundred Minnesotans, thirty-eight Sioux Indians were hanged in the largest mass execution the country had ever seen.
1864	The Sand Creek Massacre of Cheyenne Indians in Colorado set a pattern for several similar attacks on Indian villages over the next decade on the southern Plains **(November)**.
1865	The Cherokee leader Stand Watie, who rose to brigadier general in the Confederate army, was the last Confederate commander to surrender **(June)**.
1866	Cowboys hit the trail with 260,000 head of cattle in the first of the great drives **(spring)**.
	Treaties with the five civilized tribes required them to grant tribal citizenship to their freed slaves and reduced tribal lands by half. The government then settled Indians who had been displaced elsewhere on the lands it had taken from the five tribes.
1869	President Grant announced his new "Peace Policy" toward Indians, which demanded their acceptance of white culture, the English language, Christianity, and individual ownership of property. He also established a Board of Indian Commissioners and staffed it with humanitarian reformers.
	The first transcontinental railroad was completed, foreshadowing the eradication, almost to extinction, of the millions of buffalo that had once roamed the continental United States.
1870s	The development of refrigerated rail cars provided the means for Chicago stockyards to ship dressed beef all over the country.
1871	The century-long policy of negotiating with Indian "nations" ended, and Indians became "wards of the nation to be civilized."

1874   The invention of barbed wire allowed the treeless prairies and plains to be fenced.

1876   Alexander Graham Bell invented the telephone.

At the Battle of the Little Big Horn in Montana Territory, Sioux warriors, led by Sitting Bull and Crazy Horse, along with their Cheyenne allies, wiped out George A. Custer and 225 men (**June**). In retaliation, General Philip Sheridan carried out a relentless winter campaign, crushing the Sioux and Cheyenne.

1879   Thomas A. Edison invented the incandescent light bulb.

1880   The presidential election, with the closest popular vote in American history, saw James A. Garfield defeat Winfield Scott Hancock. Garfield had a plurality of only ten thousand votes out of nine million cast.

The South produced only 5 percent of the country's textiles; by 1900 it produced 23 percent.

1881   President Garfield, shot by Charles Guiteau at the railroad station in Washington, died in **September**. Guiteau was viewed by the public as the symbol of the spoils system at its worst. This incident greatly increased interest in civil-service reform.

Helen Hunt Jackson's *A Century of Dishonor* was published. This helped to publicize the plight of Indians.

1883   Congress passed the Pendleton Act, which set up a category of civil-service jobs that were to be filled by competitive examinations.

A scientific expedition counted only two hundred buffalo in the West. With the extinction of the buffalo herds, Indians were forced to move to the reservations. By the 1880s, nearly all of them had done so.

1885   A record winter of cold temperatures and blizzards plagued the southern plains, followed by even worse weather on the northern plains two years later. Hundreds of thousands of cattle froze or starved to death. This tragedy heralded the end of the open-range grazing frontier.

James B. Duke installed cigarette-making machines in Durham, North Carolina.

1886   Southern railroads with five-foot gauges shifted to the national standard of four feet, eight and one-half inches, thus integrating them with the national network. The integration symbolized northern domination of the nation's railroads.

1887   The Dawes Severalty Act was passed; it called for the dissolution of Indian tribes as legal entities, offered Indians the opportunity to become citizens, and allotted each head of a family 160 acres of farmland or 320 acres of grazing land. In 1889, the federal government threw open parts of the Indian Territory to white settlement.

1890s

Race relations in the South reached a new viciousness. Lynching rose to an all-time high, averaging 188 per year. During this period of serious problems in the southern economy, many whites took out their rage on African Americans.

1890

By this time, there were 72,473 miles of railroad west of the Mississippi. At the end of the Civil War, there had been only 3,272 miles.

Republicans failed by one vote in the Senate to enact a federal elections law to protect black voting rights.

The McKinley Tariff raised duties on a large range of products to an average of almost 50 percent.

A confrontation between the U.S. Army and American Indians took place at Wounded Knee, in the Dakota badlands. This symbolized the death of 19th-century Plains Indian culture.

The superintendent of the census announced that there was no longer a frontier line in the West.

1892

The Johnson County War in Wyoming, the most notable of the range wars, took place.

1893

The Western Federation of Miners was founded, becoming one of the most militant American labor unions.

1895

Booker T. Washington, a prominent black educator, gave a speech at the Atlanta Exposition accepting segregation as a temporary accommodation between the races in return for white support of black education. This launched a debate over means and ends in the black struggle for equality that continued for a century.

1896

In *Plessy* v. *Ferguson*, the Supreme Court sanctioned racial segregation so long as separate facilities for blacks were equal to those for whites, which, in practice, they never were.

1898

The Supreme Court upheld disfranchisement clauses of many southern state constitutions on the grounds that they did not discriminate, on their face, against blacks.

Thorstein Veblen's book *The Theory of the Leisure Class* was published.

1900

Six million farms existed in the United States, up from the 2.5 million by the end of the Civil War. Between 1865 and 1900, white Americans claimed title to 430 million acres of land.

GLOSSARY OF IMPORTANT TERMS

Anglos   English-speaking people.

barrios   Spanish-speaking urban areas. Usually separate districts in southwestern towns and cities.

bonanza farms   Huge wheat farms financed by eastern capital and cultivated with heavy machinery and hired labor.

crop lien system   A system of credit used in the poor rural South. Merchants in small country stores provided necessary goods on credit in return for a lien, or mortgage, on the crop.

Grangers   Members of the Patrons of Husbandry, a farmers' organization. Also a contemptuous name for farmers used by ranchers in the West.

hydraulic mining   Use of high-pressure streams of water to wash gold or other minerals from soil.

Jim Crow laws   Laws passed by southern states mandating racial segregation in public facilities of all kinds.

lintheads   A term used by wealthier whites to describe poor whites who labored in southern cotton mills.

longhorn   Breed of cattle introduced into the Southwest by the Spanish. It became the main breed of livestock on the cattle frontier.

placer mining   Mining where the minerals, especially gold, were found in glacial or alluvial deposits. Gold nuggets and dust were washed from the rivers and creeks or dried stream beds.

rail head   The end of a railroad, or the farthest point on the track.

railroad gauge The distance between the rails on which wheels of railroad cars fit. The national standard gauge adopted in 1886 was four feet, eight and one-half inches.

"rainfall follows the plow"   The erroneous belief that settlement and cultivation somehow changed the weather. Evolved due to heavier than normal precipitation during the 1870s and 1880s.

sodbuster   A small farmer in parts of the West who adapted to the treeless plains and prairies. One of these adaptations was the construction of homes out of sod.

Texas fever   An infectious cattle disease transmitted by ticks.

WHO? WHAT? WHERE?

WHO WERE THEY?

Complete each statement below (questions 1–8) by writing the letter preceding the appropriate name in the space provided. Use each answer only once.

a. Booker T. Washington
b. Charles Guiteau
c. Frederick Jackson Turner
d. Grover Cleveland
e. Helen Hunt Jackson
f. Henry Grady
g. Philip Sheridan
h. Stand Watie

_____ 1. Cherokee leader who rose to the rank of brigadier general in the Confederate army and was the last Confederate commander to surrender.

_____ 2. Commander of the winter campaign that crushed the Sioux.

_____ 3. Author of a best-selling novel romanticizing Indian cultures.

_____ 4. Editor of the *Atlanta Constitution* and one of the leading spokesmen for the New South.

_____ 5. Prominent black leader who gave a speech accepting segregation as a temporary accommodation between the races in return for white support of black education.

_____ 6. Only Democratic president in the late nineteenth century and the only one that did not serve in the Union army.

_____ 7. Former government clerk who shot President Garfield at the Washington railroad station, and who was viewed by the public as a symbol of the spoils system at its worst.

_____ 8. Author of an important essay emphasizing the role of the frontier in American history.

WHAT WAS IT?

Complete each statement that follows (questions 1–11) by writing the letter preceding the appropriate response in the space provided. Use each answer only once.

a. buffalo
b. cowboy
c. Dawes Severalty Act
d. Ghost Dance
e. Grandfather Clause
f. Jim Crow laws
g. Morrill Land-Grant Act
h. Sioux
i. sodbuster

      j. water law
     k. waved the bloody shirt

_____ 1. Congressional bill that granted land to states for agricultural and mechanical colleges.

_____ 2. Small farmer in parts of the West who adapted to the treeless plains and prairies.

_____ 3. Dominant symbol of the Old West.

_____ 4. Animal on which the Plains Indians survival depended.

_____ 5. Religious revitalization movement among the Sioux Indians.

_____ 6. Largest and most warlike tribe of the Plains Indians.

_____ 7. Landmark act that called for the dissolution of Indian tribes as legal entities and offered Indians an opportunity to become citizens.

_____ 8. Most important legacy of Spanish-speaking people in the West.

_____ 9. Laws passed by many southern states that mandated segregation of the races in public places.

_____ 10. One of the ways that whites who could not meet voting requirements were allowed to register to vote in southern states.

_____ 11. Political technique used by Republicans to keep alive the memory of the Civil War.

WHERE WAS IT?

Complete each statement below (questions 1–6) by writing the letter preceding the appropriate response in the space provided. Use each answer only once.

     a. Chicago, Illinois
     b. Durham, North Carolina
     c. New Mexico
     d. Red River Valley
     e. Sand Creek, Colorado
     f. Sedalia, Missouri

_____ 1. One of the regions where bonanza farms were located.

_____ 2. Westernmost point of the Missouri Pacific Railroad and the first cowtown.

_____ 3. Location of a notorious massacre of a group of Native Americans by a territorial militia.

_____ 4. Territory where Hispanics outnumbered Anglo-Americans, allowing Hispanics to retain some influence.

_____ 5. Early center of the cigarette industry.

_____ 6. Stockyard center for the meat-packing industry.

CHARTS, MAPS, AND ILLUSTRATIONS

1. According to the map on reservations (p. 642), the largest Indian reservation belonged to _____.

2. The town nearest to the beginning of the cattle trails was _____, Texas.

3. The region where the highest percentage of black cowboys worked was

    _____.

4. One use of buffalo skulls was _____.

5. The language used in the government-sponsored schools on Indian reservations was

    _____.

6. One reason the settlers built their first houses of prairie sod was _____

    _____.

MULTIPLE CHOICE

Circle the letter that best completes each statement.

1. In the arid prairies and plains of the West,
    a. fencing was not used.
    b. fencing was made primarily of wood.
    c. fencing was made primarily of barbed wire.
    d. fencing was made primarily of interwoven wire.

2. In the eighteenth century, longhorn cattle were introduced into south Texas by
    a. Spaniards.
    b. Canadians.
    c. Europeans.
    d. Australians.

3. *Granger* was a contemptuous term for a
    a. politician.
    b. rancher.
    c. farmer.
    d. law man.

4. Siding with the Confederacy proved to be a costly mistake for the "civilized Indian tribes" because the U.S. government
    a. took more time and consideration in reconstructing Indian territory than it did in reconstructing the southern states.
    b. reduced tribal lands by half.
    c. allowed tribes to keep their slaves.
    d. required the establishment of segregated schools for Indian children aged 12 and younger.

5. The Civil War added to problems between the U.S. government and Indians in all of the following ways except
   a. the Union army was forced to pull many units out of frontier posts to fight against the Confederacy.
   b. the drain on the Union treasury to finance the war compounded the usual corruption of Indian agents.
   c. the depletion of the Union treasury to finance the war delayed annuity payments to tribes that had sold their land to the government.
   d. the Union army forced literate Indian males over the age of 20 to fight.

6. At the Battle of the Little Big Horn on June 25, 1876, Sioux warriors were led by
   a. Sitting Bull and Crazy Horse.
   b. Little Crow and Black Hawk.
   c. Tecumseh and the Prophet.
   d. Black Kettle and Joseph.

7. Which of the following was not included in President Grant's "peace policy" in 1869?
   a. Indian acceptance of the white culture and the English language
   b. Indian acceptance of Christianity and individual ownership of property
   c. Indian allegiance to the United States rather than to a tribe
   d. Indian agreement to a nomadic lifestyle in the West

8. Like the American Indians, Mexican Americans were forced to adjust their lifestyles for all the following reasons except
   a. They lost their land.
   b. They lost political influence.
   c. Their culture was suppressed.
   d. They were not allowed freedom of worship.

9. By the late 1880s, the "Pittsburgh of the South" was
   a. Atlanta, Georgia.
   b. Birmingham, Alabama.
   c. Memphis, Tennessee.
   d. Jacksonville, Florida.

10. Which of the following factors did not contribute to the weakness of southern agriculture?
    a. one-crop specialization
    b. overproduction
    c. increasing prices
    d. an exploitative credit system

11. The competitive advantage of southern textile mills came from
    a. proximity to the cotton, the leading raw material.
    b. abundance of local capital.
    c. cheap, nonunion labor.
    d. good transportation to foreign markets.

12. Booker T. Washington accepted segregation as a temporary accommodation in return for
    a. official opposition to lynching of African Americans.
    b. southern support for the convict leasing system.
    c. financial aid for his college in Georgia.
    d. white support for black education and economic progress.

13. In the case of *Plessy* v. *Ferguson* (1896), the Supreme Court
    a. outlawed racial segregation.
    b. sanctioned segregation laws so long as separate facilities were equal.
    c. mandated racial segregation in all educational settings.
    d. mandated racial segregation in all public facilities except for schools.

14. Which of the following was not a faction within the Republican Party?
    a. Mugwumps
    b. Stalwarts
    c. Half-Breeds
    d. Gold Bugs

15. The most prominent issue of national politics in the early 1880s was
    a. civil-service reform.
    b. prohibition.
    c. education reform.
    d. interstate commerce.

16. In 1887, which political party asserted that low tariffs would flood the country with products from low-wage industries abroad, thereby forcing American factories to close and throwing American workers out on the streets?
    a. Whig
    b. Republican
    c. Democratic
    d. Socialist

17. The region that sent a million immigrants to the West in the late nineteenth century was
    a. Great Britain.
    b. Scandinavia.
    c. Greece.
    d. Russia.

ESSAY

Description and Explanation (one- to two-paragraph essay)

1. Describe the life of the cowboy.
2. Compare the way Indians and Hispanics were treated by European Americans in the West.

3. Describe the problems in southern agriculture.
4. Describe the purposes and weaknesses of the convict-leasing system.

Discussion and Analysis (class discussion or one- to two-paragraph essay)

1. Discuss the decline of the Plains Indians, including how the use of the reservation system, destruction of the buffalo, and suppression of native cultures and religion hurt them.
2. Discuss the presidential and vice presidential candidates in the age of political stalemate. Do any of them seem distinctive and outstanding?

What If (include an explanation of your position)

1. If you were an eighteen-year-old male in Texas, would you have been a cowboy?
2. If you were a registered voter in the late nineteenth century, how would you have viewed the presidential candidates?

Crossword Puzzle: Frontiers of Change, Politics of Stalemate, 1865–1898

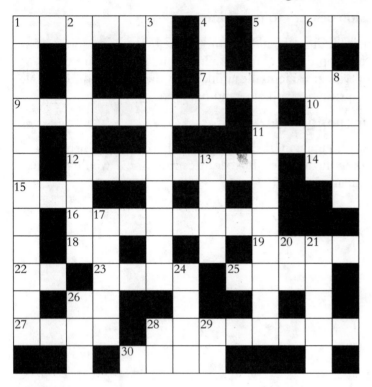

DOWN

1. Henry Grady's publication
2. Site of Chivington Massacre (2 wds.)
3. Word for a Mugwump, Half-breed, or Stalwart
4. Tobacco tycoon
5. Indians at Wounded Knee (2 wds.)
6. ___ convicts were worked like slaves in southern states.
8. Birmingham commodity
13. Pivotal state that was home to many candidates during Gilded Age
17. Hang without a trial
20. Short for southern state
21. ___ South voted Democratic for decades following the Civil War.
24. Freedom from labor
26. Catch
28. Short for Tuskegee's state
29. Short for Wounded Knee's state

ACROSS

1. Name at Battle of the Little Bighorn
5. Pike's Peak attraction
7. Santana's followers
9. Prairie home (2 wds.)
10. Part of MN capital
11. Rare sight on Great Plains
12. Engine of change for western growth
14. Short for Dover's state
15. Rail support
16. Event that caused bloody shirt to be waved
18. Neighbor of 13 Down
19. Shortage of ___ created crop-lien system in South.
22. Short for 13 Down neighbor
23. Number of survivors in Seventh Cavalry after 1876 fight
25. Number of states in South that voted Republican
26. Short for 4 Down's state
27. Biblical boater
28. Charles Guiteau for one
30. Winter vehicle

ANSWER KEY

WHO? WHAT? WHERE?

Who Were They?

1. h. Stand Watie, p. 635
2. g. Philip Sheridan, p. 638
3. e. Helen Hunt Jackson, p. 642
4. f. Henry Grady, p. 644
5. a. Booker T. Washington, p. 646–647
6. d. Grover Cleveland, p. 648
7. b. Charles Guiteau, p. 649
8. c. Frederick Jackson Turner, p. 650

What Was It?

1. f. Morrill Act, p. 629
2. i. sodbuster, p. 630
3. b. cowboy, pp. 633–634
4. a. buffalo, p. 640
5. d. Ghost Dance, p. 638
6. h. Sioux, p. 636
7. c. Dawes Severalty Act, p. 643
8. j. water law, p. 644
9. f. Jim Crow laws, p. 647
10. e. grandfather clause, p. 646
11. k. waved the bloody shirt, p. 648

Where Was It?

1. d. Red River Valley, p. 630
2. f. Sedalia, Missouri, p. 633
3. e. Sand Creek, Colorado, p. 639
4. c. New Mexico, p. 644
5. b. Durham, North Carolina, p. 645
6. a. Chicago, Illinois, p. 644

CHARTS, MAPS, AND ILLUSTRATIONS

1. Navajo, p. 642
2. San Antonio, p. 632
3. Texas, p. 635
4. Fertilizer, p. 640
5. English, p. 643
6. Lack of trees or woods, p. 631

MULTIPLE CHOICE

1. c   (p. 630)
2. a   (p. 633)
3. c   (p. 634)
4. b   (p. 635)
5. d   (p. 636)
6. a   (p. 638)
7. d   (p. 643)
8. d   (p. 643)
9. b   (p. 645)
10. c   (p. 645)
11. c   (p. 645)
12. d   (p. 647)
13. b   (p. 647)
14. d   (p. 649)
15. a   (p. 649)
16. b   (p. 649)
17. b   (p. 629)

ESSAY

Description and Explanation

1. pp. 633–634
2. pp. 638–644
3. pp. 645–646
4. p. 647

Discussion and Analysis

1. pp. 638–643
2. pp. 647–649

What If

1. pp. 633–634
2. pp. 648–650

Crossword Puzzle

CHAPTER 19

ECONOMIC CHANGE AND THE CRISIS OF THE 1890S

During the late nineteenth century, the economy grew at one of the fastest rates in American history. The value to the economy of manufacturing passed that of agriculture for the first time in the early 1880s. The expanded railroad system played an especially important role in the developing economy. The power of the railroads and the way it was unfairly wielded led to one of the first federal attempts to regulate business.

In the increasingly urban society, labor became a commodity to be bought and sold, and many workers felt a loss of independence and status. Worker dissatisfaction led to the creation of several national labor organizations and produced labor radicalism, resulting in some incidences of violence. The situation was only exacerbated by a severe four-year depression beginning in 1893. To wealthier Americans, labor protests seemed a threat to the social order. To lower-class Americans, the power wielded by the new business leaders was to be feared.

The election of 1896 marked a crucial turning point in American political history, moving the country away from the stalemate of the previous two decades. The Democratic Party adopted many of the issues favored by discontented rural America and nominated William Jennings Bryan of Nebraska for president. Bryan launched an unprecedented whistle-stop campaign but was countered by his Republican opponent, William McKinley, who initiated "front-porch speeches." Soon after McKinley took office, the economy pulled out of the depression and entered another long period of growth. The nation seemed embarked upon a placid sea of plenty, but, below the surface, the currents of protest and reform still ran strong.

LIBERTY, EQUALITY, POWER

The biggest shift in power in America was seen in the increasing size and wealth of large businesses and their owners. There was an increasing sense of class inequality. In general, business leaders showed little or no concern for the rights of their workers or of the general public. At the time, efforts to legislate control over big business were weak and poorly supported by labor rights advocates.

The decline in the working class's sense of liberty and equality helped produce urban violence. Labor woes, along with the failing economic climate for western and southern farmers, led to increased interest in political activities, such as with organizations like the Populist Party. There was a growing feeling that liberty and equality could no longer be taken for granted. Liberty, equality, and power for many Americans would have to wait until another time.

OBJECTIVES

After studying this chapter, a student should be able to

1. Explain the importance of labor violence to America.

2. Compare the Knights of Labor and the American Federation of Labor.

3. Analyze the effects of the depression on American life.

4. Describe the basic issues in the currency problem and why it became a major question.

5. Describe the problems of southern and western farmers, their organizations, and their political activities.

6. Discuss the election of 1896, including the issues, candidates, and outcome. Why was this a major election?

CHRONOLOGY

1866	National Labor Union was formed.
1867	Farmers organized cooperatives to sell crops and buy supplies. The umbrella organization for many of these cooperatives was the Patrons of Husbandry, or the Grange.
1869	The Knights of Labor was founded in Philadelphia. At first very small, it began to grow after it abandoned secrecy in 1879.
1870	For the first time in American history, the census reported that a majority of employed persons worked for wages paid by others rather than worked for themselves.
1873	Congress enacted a law demonetizing silver. This measure, which eliminated silver coins except for small ones, was later labeled the Crime of 1873. Some considered it a conspiracy to destroy silver.
1875	Specie Resumption Act enacted by Congress.
1877	In *Munn* v. *Illinois*, the Supreme Court ruled that states could regulate businesses clothed with a "public interest," such as railroads, millers, and innkeepers.
1879	Henry George published his book *Progress and Poverty*, exposing the contrast between wealth and poverty.
1880	The Standard Oil trust was formed.
1883	The railroads created four standard time zones for the United States, an outstanding example of the railroads' impact on everyday American life.
1884	Congress created the Bureau of Labor. It was elevated to cabinet rank in 1903.

1886 The American Federation of Labor, an affiliation of unions that were organized by crafts or skills, was founded. It shunned radical crusades, accepted capitalism and the wage system, and worked for better conditions, higher wages, shorter hours, and occupational safety within the system.

A strike took place at the McCormick farm machinery plant in Chicago, the hotbed of labor radicalism. In response to violence, a protest meeting was called at the Haymarket Square in **May**. A bomb was thrown at police, who then fired into the crowd. This set off a wave of hysteria against labor radicals. Eight men were tried for conspiracy to commit murder, and all were convicted despite the lack of evidence. This case divided the country; the majority of Americans applauded the oppression of un-American radicalism.

1887 Congress passed the Interstate Commerce Act, which was a compromise reflecting viewpoints of several pressure groups.

1888 Edward Bellamy's utopian romance *Looking Backward* was published.

1890 Congress passed the Sherman Anti-Trust Act to regulate big business.

The Farmers' Alliance evolved into the National Farmers' Alliance and Industrial Union, reaching out to two million farm families. In **December**, it held a national convention in Ocala, Florida, and set forth its many goals.

The Sherman Silver Purchase Act, which increased the amount of silver currency, was passed. President Cleveland called a special session of Congress to repeal it in 1893, because he thought it was a cause of the Panic of 1893.

1892 A major strike took place outside Pittsburgh at the Homestead plant of the Carnegie Steel Company. A full-scale gun battle between strikers and Pinkerton detectives left nine strikers and several Pinkertons wounded. It also severely crippled the workers' union.

The People's Party, known as Populists, became the first "third party" to win any electoral votes since the election of 1860. It held its first nominating convention in Omaha, Nebraska, in **July** and nominated James B. Weaver for president. He received nine percent of the popular vote and twenty-two electoral votes.

1893 The United States entered a severe four-year economic depression.

1894 Congress established the first Monday in September as an official annual holiday, Labor Day, to honor working people.

After the depression began, there was a sharp drop in orders for Pullman rail cars, so the company laid off one third of its workforce and cut wages but did not reduce rents or prices in the company town. The dispute over rents and prices escalated into a boycott of Pullman cars led by the American Railway Union, founded by Eugene V. Debs. The strike ended when President Cleveland sent in the army. The attorney general obtained a federal injunction against Debs under the Sherman Anti-Trust Act on the grounds that the boycott and the strike were a conspiracy in restraint of trade. This use of the Sherman Act became a powerful weapon against labor unions in the hands of conservative judges.

Jacob Coxey and his unemployed followers hit the roads and rode the rails to Washington. They hoped to petition Congress for public works jobs for the unemployed. Coxey and others were arrested for trespassing on the Capitol grounds, and the incident ended.

1895   The Supreme Court delivered a decision in *U.S. v. E.C. Knight Company*. The Court ruled that manufacturing was not commerce and therefore did not fall under the jurisdiction of the Sherman Anti-Trust Act, greatly limiting the power of the act for the time being.

1896   The national election in 1896 was the most impassioned and exciting in a generation. The Democratic nominee, William Jennings Bryan, a silver-tongued orator from the West, lost to Republican William McKinley.

1897   The economy pulled out of the depression and entered into a long period of growth.

1898   Thorstein Veblen's book *The Theory of the Leisure Class* was published.

1913   American manufacturing output equaled that of Germany, Britain, and France combined.

GLOSSARY OF IMPORTANT TERMS

anarchist   A member of a group that called for the violent destruction of the capitalist system so that a new socialist order could be built.

bank notes   Paper money, issued by banks, that circulated as currency.

collective bargaining   Negotiations between representatives of workers and employers. Issues included wages, hours, and working conditions.

cooperatives   Marketing groups established by such groups as the Farmers Alliance. They eliminated "middlemen" and reduced prices to farmers. The idea also was tried by some labor groups and included other types of businesses, such as factories.

deflation   A decline in consumer prices or a rise in the purchasing power of money.

direct election of senators   Senators would be elected by the people rather than selected by state legislatures, requiring an amendment to the Constitution.

drawbacks   As used by the railroads, drawbacks were a form of rebate offered to very special customers. Rebates were paid even on competitors' shipments.

free silver   The government would purchase all silver offered for sale and coin it into silver dollars. The preferred ratio between silver and gold was sixteen to one.

Gold Bugs   "Sound money" advocates who wanted to keep the United States on the international gold standard.

graduated income tax   A tax based on income with rates that gradually rise as the level of income rises.

greenbacks   Paper money issued by the federal government during the Civil War to help pay war expenses. They were called greenbacks because of their color.

gross national product (GNP)   The total value of all goods and services produced during a specific period.

holding company   A corporation established to own all or portions of other businesses.

lockout   The act of closing down a business by the owners during a labor dispute.

pools   One technique used by railroads to divide up traffic and fix rates, thereby avoiding ruinous competition.

real wages   The relationship between wages and the consumer price index. If wages rise more than the rate of inflation or fall less than the rate of deflation, then real wages are increasing.

rebates   Certain big businesses were given a reduction in freight rates or a refund by the railroads.

restraint of trade   An activity that prevents competition in the marketplace or free trade.

scabs   Another term for *strikebreakers*—those who were willing to act as replacements for striking workers, thus undermining the effect of strikes as leverage against company owners.

sitdown   An act of protest. Workers refused to leave their workplace during a labor dispute, preventing management's use of strikebreakers.

specie   Metal money or coins, usually made of gold or silver.

subtreasuries   Federal warehouses for crop storage that enabled farmers to wait until market prices were more favorable to sell their crops. Low-interest loans available on the crops allowed farmers to pay their annual debts. Thus, they could escape the ruinous interest rates of the crop-lien system in the South and bank mortgages in the West.

trust   Term derived from an investment strategy pioneered by John D. Rockefeller in which stockholders of several refining companies turned their shares over to Standard Oil. In return, they received trust certificates. The term came to be applied to all large corporations that controlled a substantial share of any given market.

WHO? WHAT? WHERE?

WHO WERE THEY?

Complete each statement below (questions 1–9) by writing the letter preceding the appropriate name in the space provided. Use each answer only once.

    a. Benjamin Tillman
    b. Eugene V. Debs
    c. Grover Cleveland
    d. Henry Clay Frick
    e. Jacob Coxey
    f. Jame C. Weaver
    g. Mark Hanna
    h. Terence V. Powderly
    i. William Jennings Bryan

_____ 1. Machinist by trade who became the leader of the Knights of Labor.

_____ 2. Plant manager of the Homestead plant of Carnegie Steel.

_____ 3. Reformer from Ohio who conceived the idea of sending a living petition of unemployed people to Congress to work for appropriations for public works.

_____ 4. Founder of the American Railway Union who launched a boycott of Pullman cars.

_____ 5. Union veteran from Iowa who was the Populist candidate for president in 1892.

_____ 6. President who forced the repeal of the Sherman Silver Purchase Act.

_____ 7. South Carolina senator who delivered the most abusive attack on a president ever delivered by a member of his own party when he described President Grover Cleveland.

_____ 8. Silver-tongued orator from Nebraska.

_____ 9. Skillful political leader and Ohio businessman who served as chairman of the Republican National Committee during the campaign of 1896.

WHAT WAS IT?

Complete each statement that follows (questions 1–10) by writing the letter preceding the appropriate response in the space provided. Use each answer only once.

    a. cotton
    b. cooperatives
    c. greenback
    d. Molly Maguires
    e. Pendleton Act
    f. Pinkerton Detective Agency
    g. pools
    h. Populist Party

i. railroads

j. *U.S. v. E.C. Knight Company*

_____ 1. Single most important agent of economic growth during the Gilded Age.

_____ 2. Technique used by railroads to avoid ruinous competition.

_____ 3. Supreme Court case that ruled that manufacturing was not commerce and, therefore, did not fall under the jurisdiction of the Sherman Anti-Trust Act.

_____ 4. Combination labor union and secret order of Irish-Americans that carried out guerrilla warfare against mine owners.

_____ 5. Private security force that specialized in antiunion activities.

_____ 6. One of the crops that declined in price on the international market in the late nineteenth century.

_____ 7. U.S. Treasury paper note.

_____ 8. Marketing groups established to eliminate the middleman and reduce prices to farmers.

_____ 9. The first "third party" to win any electoral votes since the election of 1860.

WHERE WAS IT?

Complete each statement below (questions 1–5) by writing the letter preceding the appropriate response in the space provided. Use each answer only once.

a. Chicago, Illinois

b. Haymarket Square

c. New Jersey

d. Omaha, Nebraska

e. Pullman, Illinois

_____ 1. State that used an incorporation law permitting holding companies to control several firms at the same time.

_____ 2. Center of labor radicalism in the late nineteenth century.

_____ 3. Location of a protest meeting where violence killed fifty people and touched off a wave of hysteria against labor radicals.

_____ 4. Company town where streets were clean and the owner punished workers for behavior of which he did not approve.

_____ 5. Site of the first nominating convention of the People's Party.

CHARTS, MAPS, AND ILLUSTRATIONS

1. The site of the first Labor Day parade was _____.

2. The region from which McKinley received the greatest number of votes in the election of 1896 was_____.

3. The Pacific Coast state that split its electoral vote in the 1896 election was

_____.

4. In the chart showing the index of wholesale commodity prices (p. 668), was the rate of deflation high or low? Was this decline good or bad?

_____

5. The first professional baseball team was

_____.

The powerhouse among early football teams was

_____.

MULTIPLE CHOICE

Circle the letter that best completes each statement.

1. The Interstate Commerce Act of 1887 did all of the following except
   a. led to strict regulation of the railroads.
   b. outlawed long-haul/short-haul differentials.
   c. created the Interstate Commerce Commisssion.
   d. required that freight or passenger rates must be reasonable.

2. One example of the railroads' impact on everyday life was
   a. the increase in the inequality of social classes.
   b. the ability to move mail across the country in three days.
   c. the creation of standard time zones.
   d. the increase in transportation costs for moving most household items.

3. Which of the following men is paired incorrectly with his business?
   a. John Pierpont Morgan—banking.
   b. James B. Duke—ranching.
   c. Andrew Carnegie—steel.
   d. Jay Gould—railroads.

4. Which of the following did not contribute to the rising tide of labor discontent in the United States?
   a. America had the world's highest rate of industrial accidents.
   b. No workmen's compensation existed.
   c. Worker autonomy was eroding in factories.
   d. The type of work performed was becoming easier.

5. The company at which the Railroad Strike of 1877 began was
   a. the Pennsylvania.
   b. the Union Pacific.
   c. the Erie.
   d. the Baltimore and Ohio.

6. The Knights of Labor
   a. gave many unskilled and semiskilled workers union representation for the first time.
   b. organized assemblies according to craft.

c. was founded in New York.

d. refused to admit women or blacks.

7. Under the leadership of Samuel Gompers, the American Federation of Labor (AFL)
   a. encouraged radical crusades.
   b. rejected capitalism and the wage system.
   c. represented company owners.
   d. worked for occupational safety.

8. The book *Progress and Poverty* dealt with
   a. economics.
   b. poetry.
   c. utopian settlements.
   d. 20th-century romance.

9. Edward Bellamy preferred to call his collectivist order
   a. Nationalism.
   b. Marxism.
   c. Socialism.
   d. Utopianism.

10. Which of the following was not a cause of the depression of 1893–1897?
    a. an economic slowdown abroad, which caused British banks to call some of their American loans
    b. unlimited immigration, which flooded the labor market and forced wages down
    c. political controversy about the American monetary system and nervousness in financial circles
    d. declining farm prices and attendant rural interest

11. The combined circumstances causing the Pullman Strike of 1894 were
    a. The Panic of 1893 caused a sharp drop in orders of Pullman cars, layoffs and wage cuts were enacted, rents on company houses and prices in company stores were not reduced, and George Pullman refused to negotiate with a workers' committee.
    b. George Pullman banned liquor from the company town and punished workers whose behavior did not suit his idea of decorum.
    c. Workers and their families, who were forced to live in the company town, were inspired by Coxey's Army to fight for paved streets, clean houses, and a decent environment.
    d. The depression of 1873–1878 caused a drop in orders for Pullman cars; the company declared bankruptcy, refusing to provide unemployment pay, and workers could not afford to relocate.

12. Farmers blamed all of the following for their economic problems except
    a. local governments.
    b. banks.
    c. commission merchants.
    d. railroads.

13. After the Civil War, the Treasury's policy was to bring the greenback dollar to par with gold by reducing the amount of greenbacks in circulation. This policy caused deflation, which hurt
    a. the East and the North.
    b. farmers and debtors.
    c. farmers and factory owners.
    d. the East and the South.

14. The ratio of silver to gold wanted by free silver supporters was
    a. 12:1.
    b. 16:1.
    c. 20:1.
    d. 24:1.

15. The National Farmers' Alliance and Industrial Union, which evolved by 1890, did all of the following except
    a. set up marketing cooperatives to eliminate middlemen.
    b. served the social and economic needs of farm families.
    c. gave farmers a sense of pride and solidarity.
    d. worked against the idea of developing a comprehensive political agenda for farmers.

16. All of the following were part of the Farmers' Alliance political agenda except
    a. graduated income tax.
    b. direct election of U.S. senators.
    c. price supports for fruit crops.
    d. free and unlimited coinage of silver.

17. Southerners opposed the idea of a third party because they
    a. feared the return of Republicans and black rule.
    b. believed that the Democrats would support the price of cotton.
    c. blamed the third party for supporting voting for women.
    d. disliked the antiliquor position of the proposed third party.

18. William Jennings Bryan, the Democratic candidate for president in 1896,
    a. focused primarily on declining farm prices.
    b. had an especially well-financed campaign.
    c. covered eighteen thousand miles, giving as many as thirty speeches a day.
    d. conducted four major debates with Republican candidate William McKinley.

19. The economy pulled out of the serious depression in 1897 for all of the following reasons except
    a. the discovery of rich, new gold fields.
    b. the long deflationary trend since 1865 reversed itself.
    c. farmers entered an era of new prosperity.
    d. federal spending on important social issues doubled, which increased the amount of money in circulation.

ESSAY

Description and Explanation (one- to two-paragraph essay)

1. Compare the Knights of Labor and the American Federation of Labor.

2. Compare the ideas of Henry George and Edward Bellamy as expressed in their books.

3. Describe the issues of the People's Party, or Populist Party. How many of these issues were acted upon?

Discussion and Analysis (class discussion or one- to two-paragraph essay)

1. Discuss labor violence and how it affected the American public.

2. Discuss the election of 1896, its issues, candidates, excitement, and outcome, as well as its role as a turning point in American politics.

What If (include an explanation of your position)

1. If you were an industrial worker living in Chicago in the 1890s, would you join a union? Would it make a difference if you were a skilled or unskilled worker?

2. If you were a farmer in 1892, would you support the People's or "Populist" Party? Would it make a difference if you lived in Kansas or Georgia?

3. If you were a registered voter in 1896, which party or candidate would you support?

Crossword Puzzle: Economic Change and the Crisis of the 1890s

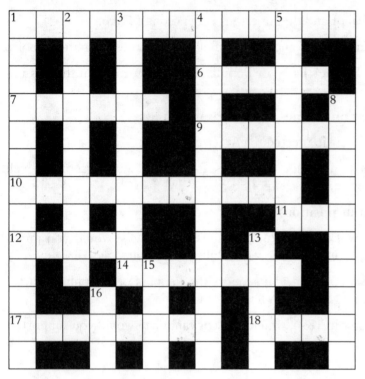

ACROSS

1. The ___ made Chicago rail yards a war zone in 1894 (2 wds.).
6. In 1869 the Public Credit Act made Civil War ___ good as gold.
7. Word for Edward Bellamy's America in 2000
9. Interstate Commerce Act required rail rates to be based on ___ and justice.
10. Follower of economic theory of Henry George
11. Desire
12. Interstate Commerce Act outlawed the ___ that some railroads had created.
14. Author of 1890 anti-monopoly law
17. One of four established by railroad consortium in 1883 (2 wds.)
18. Front porch state in 1896

DOWN

1. Group whose first convention was in Omaha during July 1892 (2 wds.)
2. Organization for Terence Powderly or Samuel Gompers (2 wds.)
3. Pictures were no longer ___ after the 1890s.
4. Federal warehouses for crops favored by 1 Down
5. Knights of Labor were organized by ___ rather than by craft.
8. Labor leader Eugene V. Debs went to jail for violating one.
13. The Gilded Age tycoon was called a robber ___.
15. Barrel or skirt part
16. South Carolina senator Tillman was known as "Pitchfork ___."

ANSWER KEY

WHO? WHAT? WHERE?

Who Were They?

1. h. Terence V. Powderly, p. 661
2. d. Henry Clay Frick, p. 664
3. e. Jacob Coxey, p. 665
4. b. Eugene V. Debs, p. 666
5. f. James B. Weaver, p. 671
6. c. Grover Cleveland, p. 666
7. a. Benjamin Tillman, p. 671
8. i. William Jennings Bryan, p. 672
9. g. Mark Hanna, p. 673

What Was It?

1. i. railroads, p. 654
2. g. pools, p. 654
3. j. *U.S. v. E.C. Knight Company*, p. 660
4. d. Molly Maguires, p. 658
5. f. Pinkerton Detective Agency, p. 664
6. a. cotton, p. 668
7. c. greenbacks, p. 669
8. b. cooperatives, p. 654
9. h. Populist Party, p. 671

Where Was It?

1. c. New Jersey, p. 660
2. a. Chicago, Illinois, p. 663
3. b. Haymarket Square, p. 662
4. e. Pullman, Illinois, p. 666
5. d. Omaha, Nebraska, p. 671

CHARTS, MAPS, AND ILLUSTRATIONS

1. Union Square, New York City, p. 662
2. Northeast, p. 674
3. California, p. 674
4. high, bad, p. 674
5. Red stockings, Yale, p. 657

MULTIPLE CHOICE

1. a (p. 655)
2. c (p. 655)
3. b (p. 656)
4. d (p. 660)
5. d (p. 660)
6. a (p. 661)
7. d (p. 663)
8. a (p. 663)
9. a (p. 664)
10. b (p. 665)
11. a (p. 667)
12. a (p. 668)
13. b (p. 669)
14. b (p. 669)
15. d (p. 670)
16. c (p. 670)
17. a (p. 671)
18. c (p. 673)
19. d (p. 674)

ESSAY

Description and Explanation

1. pp. 661–662

2. pp. 663–664

3. p. 671

Discussion and Analysis

1. pp. 662–666

2. pp. 673–674

What If

1. pp. 661–662, 664, 673–674

2. p. 671

3. pp. 673–674

Crossword Puzzle

CHAPTER 20

AN INDUSTRIAL SOCIETY, 1890–1920

With the end of the depression in 1897, the American economy embarked on a remarkable stretch of growth. From the late 1890s to the late 1920s, the gross national product (GNP) more than tripled and per capita GNP more than doubled. By 1910, the United States was the world's greatest industrial power. New corporate structures and management techniques combined with new technology created the conditions that propelled economic growth. The assembly line of the Ford Motor Company was one of the wonders of the world.

By 1920, urban population outstripped that of rural areas for the first time. In eastern and midwestern cities, the majority of the workers were immigrants drawn primarily from Europe by the promise of a better economic future. Each ethnic group established a network of institutions that gave it a sense of community and provided sources of assistance. Urban areas also attracted African Americans, who migrated to the industrial centers for a better life. The nation's worsening racial climate, however, adversely affected those who moved north. Young single women discovered in cities opportunities for work and independence.

Each of these groups—immigrants, African Americans, and women—experienced poverty, hardship, disappointment, and discrimination. But they were resourceful and creative—they strove to improve their economic circumstances, fashion a new urban culture, and alter popular conceptions of gender, race, and sexuality. They also helped shape the politics and culture of the new industrial society. However, pressure from minority groups aroused considerable anxiety in some sectors of American society.

LIBERTY, EQUALITY, POWER

Millions of immigrants arrived in the United States seeking liberty and economic freedom. Despite the problems they encountered adjusting to their new lives, most actually gained economic independence and some political power. African Americans who had migrated from the South found a deterioration in the quality of their existence in urban areas. The black middle class and skilled workforce were declining in number, and there was a marked deterioration in working and living conditions for nonwhites. In contrast, owners of big businesses found themselves wielding vast amounts of power over their workers. These men were less likely, however, to flaunt this power publicly. Instead, most simply turned a blind eye on the conditions that their employees faced daily in their urban factories. The much-vaunted new scientific management techniques that business owners favored for their efficiency and control served to lessen the self-esteem and liberty of workers.

On the other hand, women increasingly held jobs with regular wages that gave them more economic freedom. They socialized at dance halls, movies, and amusement parks, and they began to engage in sports and other activities. This led to a need for simpler clothing to allow more freedom of movement. Women demanded equality and were willing to strive for it despite the almost-intolerable working conditions many found in the cities. Overall, the early twentieth century was marked by a widespread dissatisfaction with the growing regimentation of industrial labor; society at the time found itself with a vested interest in increasing individual liberty.

OBJECTIVES

After studying this chapter, a student should be able to

1. Explain the sources of economic growth, especially the role of technology, scientific management, and new forms of corporate management.

2. Describe the growth and changes in immigration.

3. Describe the development of ethnic communities and the role of minorities in the growing cities.

4. Explain the role of unions in the early twentieth century.

5. Discuss the rise of the new woman.

CHRONOLOGY

1870	About a third of the black men in many northern cities held jobs as skilled tradesmen: blacksmiths, painters, shoemakers, and carpenters. However, by 1910, only ten percent of black men made a living in this way. The shrinking numbers of black tradesmen during these years was attributable partially to the rise of the AFL's racist policies.
1870–1910	Real wages paid to factory workers and common laborers rose, but not steadily.
1878	The first gasoline engine was patented in the United States.
1880–1900	Employment of women doubled during these years and increased fifty percent by 1920.
1880–1920	Twenty-three million immigrants came to the United States—a country that had numbered only 76 million at the turn of the century. During these years, most European immigrants came from eastern and southern Europe and were called "new immigrants" as opposed to the "old immigrants."
1880s–1890s	Urban mortality rates fell due to housing inspections, improvements in reservoirs and sewers, and newly paved roads.
1882	The U.S. government refused to admit Chinese immigrants after this year.

1890	The Sherman Anti-Trust Act declared cartel-like practices illegal, but enforcement of the law proved to be very weak.
1890s	The first "horseless carriages" appeared on European and American roads.
	Mass-production techniques became widespread in steel manufacturing and sugar refining.
	By this time, powerful and sophisticated investment bankers possessed both the capital and the financial skills to engineer the complicated stock transfers and ownership negotiations upon which mergers depended.
	This was a time of heightened enthusiasm for competitive sports, physical fitness, and outdoor recreation. Millions of Americans began riding bicycles and eating more healthful foods. In the new liberated climate, young women began to engage in sports and other activities long considered too manly for the "fragile sex."
1897	The depression ended in 1897, and the American economy made a remarkable comeback.
1898–1904	Many corporations that would dominate American business throughout the twentieth century acquired their modern form during these years.
1890–1910	Approximately 200,000 blacks left the South for the North and West.
1890–1920	The proportion of American industry powered by electricity rose from virtually none to almost one third.
1899	Andrew Carnegie advocated a "gospel of wealth." He believed the wealthy should consider all income in excess of their needs as a "trust fund" for their communities.
1899–1910	Seventy-five percent of the immigrants from southern and eastern Europe were adult men in search of economic opportunity that would enable them to improve their standing in their homeland.
1900	Railroads provided the country with an efficient transportation system that allowed corporations to ship goods virtually anywhere in the United States.
	French-Canadian immigrants and their children held one of every two jobs in New England's cotton-textile industry.
	Annual earnings of American manufacturing workers averaged only $400 to $500 a year, though there were substantial variations from region to region and skill to skill. Income in the South averaged only $300 a year; the average in the North was $460. Skilled workers could earn as much as $1,500 to $2,000 a year.
	The population density of New York City's Lower East Side reached seven hundred persons per acre, a density greater than that of the poorest sections of Bombay, India. The crisis in urban living induced city leaders to yield to

the insistence of urban reformers that cities adopt housing codes and improve sanitation.

Graft had become essential to the smooth operation of government in most large cities and was a source of economic gain for local officeholders.

early 1900s   Gangsterism was a scourge of Italian neighborhoods as Sicilian immigrants imported the notorious Mafia. Gangsters established strongholds in Irish, Jewish, Chinese, and other ethnic communities as well.

Blacks were a growing presence in the urban North, where they worked on the fringes of industry as janitors, elevator operators, teamsters, longshoremen, and servants of various kinds.

1900–1910   In the first decade of the twentieth century, immigrant men and their male children constituted 70 percent of the workforce in fifteen of the nineteen leading U.S. industries. Between 1900 and 1914, an average of one million immigrants arrived each year.

1900–1920   Virtually every major city built electric-powered transit systems to replace horse-drawn trolleys and carriages. By 1912, forty thousand miles of electrical railway and trolley track had been laid.

1901   The largest merger occurred when Andrew Carnegie and J. P. Morgan formed the U.S. Steel Corporation from 200 separate iron and steel companies.

Andrew Carnegie withdrew from industry and devoted himself to philanthropic pursuits, especially in art and education.

One in every four hundred railroad workers died on the job, and one in every twenty-six suffered injury on the job.

1904   Social investigator Robert Hunter published his book *Poverty*. In it he estimated that 20 percent of the industrial population of the North lived below the poverty line.

1905   The Industrial Workers of the World (IWW) was founded by western miners and led by the charismatic William "Big Bill" Haywood.

The Supreme Court declared unconstitutional a New York state law limiting bakery employees to a ten-hour day. This was viewed as a sign that courts were undermining gains made by organized labor.

1907   The U.S. government refused to admit Japanese male immigrants after this time.

1908   In the Danbury Hatters case, the Supreme Court outlawed labor's use of the product boycott against manufacturers who refused to accept a union on their premises.

1909   Ford unveiled his Model-T: an unadorned, even homely, car, but reliable enough to travel hundreds of miles without servicing and cheap enough to be affordable for most working Americans.

1910   By this time, America had become the world's greatest industrial power.

Twenty thousand nickelodeons dotted northern cities.

The "white slave trade" inspired passage of the Mann Act, which made the transportation of women across state lines for immoral purposes a federal crime.

1910s   Mass-production techniques established themselves firmly in the machine tools industry and in automobile manufacturing. Engineers broke down the making of an automobile into a series of simple, sequential tasks—each worker performed only one task.

1911   Frederick D. Taylor's *The Principles of Scientific Management*, which dealt with scientific management practices for manufacturing, was published.

The Triangle Shirtwaist Company, a New York garment factory, was destroyed by fire, killing 146 workers, mostly young women. There were no fire escapes and the entrances to each floor were locked to keep the women at work.

1913   Ford engineers introduced the first assembly line, a continuously moving conveyor belt that carried the car in production through each work station. By this time, the Ford Motor Company's new Highland Park plant was the most highly integrated production system yet seen in metal manufacture.

The Rockefeller Foundation was incorporated officially. By 1919, John D. Rockefeller had dispersed an estimated $500,000,000 to philanthropic causes.

1914   Ford raised the wage he paid assembly-line workers to $5 per day, double the average manufacturing wage then prevalent in America. Few manufacturers were willing to follow Henry Ford's example, so most factory workers remained in a fragile economic state.

Theda Bara emerged as the movies' first sex symbol. She was the first of the big screen's many "vamps," so-called because they acted the part of vampires who thrived on the blood (and death) of men.

Company police of the Colorado Fuel and Iron Company, a subsidiary of Rockefeller's Standard Oil, fired randomly into a group of tents occupied by evicted strikers, killing sixty-six men, women, and children.

1916   Prior to this time, no federal laws protected the right of workers to organize or required employers to bargain with the unions to which their workers belonged.

1917	Many working-class families still did not have running water in their homes.
1919	By the time of his death, Andrew Carnegie had given away or entrusted to the Carnegie Foundation ninety percent of his fortune.
	Using labor-intensive methods, Japanese farmers producing fruits and vegetables yielded $67 million in annual revenues. This was one-tenth of the total revenue generated by California agriculture, but the farmers owned only one percent of the land.
1920	Wage earners employed by corporations swelled the ranks of city dwellers until the nation's urban population outstripped that of the countryside for the first time.
1920s	Many corporations established personnel departments, instituted welfare and recreational programs for employees, and hired psychologists to improve human relations in the workplace.
	Petty extortion escalated in urban areas, and underworld crime became big business.
1923	A dramatic increase in the rate of production enabled Ford to slash the price of a Model-T from $950 in 1909 to $295 in 1923.

GLOSSARY OF IMPORTANT TERMS

antisemitism	Hostility, prejudice, or discrimination toward Jews or Arabs.
boycott	A labor group would ask supporters not to purchase any goods in an effort to use economic leverage against an antiunion employer.
bread-and-butter unionism	Union efforts concentrated on the means of a worker's livelihood or issues related directly to the job
continuous assembly line	Process of using a continuously moving conveyor belt to carry the production item through each work station. This method eliminated the time involved in moving parts from one work area to another. Usually highly efficient.
Doctrine of Separate Spheres	Asserted that there existed a male sphere: work, politics, and sexual passion. The female sphere was one of domesticity, moral education, and sexual reproduction. Men and women were to remain in their own spheres, meaning that men and women spent substantial portions of their lives apart from each other.
domestic market	Items sold within the country (the United States).
down time	The period between production steps.
heterodoxy	Early 20th-century group that held different beliefs and behavior standards from the majority of the surrounding population. Primarily women, many

of them lived in Greenwich Village, a bohemian community in Manhattan, New York. They were among the first to use the term *feminism*.

industrial union	Offered membership to all workers in an industry, irrespective of skill.
machine boss	Leader of a highly organized political group, usually in urban areas. Frequently corruption was a unifying force among the members of the group.
machine tools industry	Produced machines for industrial plants, or machines that built other machines, usually involving shaping metal.
mass production	An industrial technique requiring the coordination of machines with other machines to permit high-speed, uninterrupted production at every stage of the manufacturing process.
nickelodeons	Early movies that cost a nickel, usually lasted fifteen minutes, and required no knowledge of the English language.
padroni	A term used for Italian labor contractors.
social Darwinism	A philosophy that allegedly showed how closely the social history of humans resembled the physical evolution of animals (the biological evolution documented by English botanist Charles Darwin with his principle of "survival of the fittest"). According to this theory, human social history could be understood as a struggle among races, with the strongest and the fittest invariably triumphing.
time-and-motion studies	Every distinct motion a worker made in performing a job was recorded and studied: what was done, how long it took, and how often it was performed. The goal was to enable the human laborer to emulate the smooth and apparently effortless operation of an automatic and perfectly calibrated piece of machinery.
vamp	A female portrayed in many early movies. These women acted the part of vampires who thrived on the blood and death of men.
ward boss	The leader of the political "machine" in a particular ward of the city.

WHO? WHAT? WHERE?

WHO WERE THEY?

Complete each statement that follows (questions 1–10) by writing the letter preceding the appropriate name in the space provided. Use each answer only once.

    a. Alice Paul
    b. Amadeo P. Giannini
    c. "Big Bill" Haywood
    d. Frederick W. Taylor
    e. James Buchanan Duke

f. J. P. Morgan
g. John Francis Fitzgerald
h. Madame C. J. Walker
i. Mrs. Bradley Martin
j. Theda Bara

_____ 1. Person who almost single-handedly transformed the cigarette into one of the best-selling commodities in American history.

_____ 2. America's leading investment banker of his time.

_____ 3. One of the founders of scientific management.

_____ 4. Hostess of a New York party that cost $370,000 for one evening's entertainment. Public outrage forced her and her husband to leave for Europe.

_____ 5. San Franciscan who used his savings from a fruit and vegetable stand to launch a career in banking. He eventually made his bank, The Bank of America, the largest financial institution in the United States.

_____ 6. Child of penniless Irish immigrants who became a major political figure in the government of Boston.

_____ 7. Black entrepreneur who built a lucrative business by selling hair and skin lotions to black customers throughout the United States.

_____ 8. Leader of the Industrial Workers of the World who hoped to organize all workers into one big union.

_____ 9. First sex symbol of the movies.

_____ 10. Founder of the National Women's Party who brought a new militancy to the campaign for women's suffrage.

WHAT WAS IT?

Complete each statement that follows (questions 1–9) by writing the letter preceding the appropriate name in the space provided. Use each answer only once.

a. alternating current
b. assembly line
c. incandescent bulb
d. industrial union
e. Mann Act
f. nickelodeons
g. time-and-motion studies
h. Triangle Shirtwaist Company
i. United States Steel

_____ 1. Technological improvement that made electric lighting possible in homes and offices.

_____ 2. Technique that made transmitting electrical power over long distances possible.

_____ 3. Company formed by the largest merger in the United States up to that time.

_____ 4. Studies that strove to make human labor emulate the operation of an automatic piece of machinery.

_____ 5. Most-admired and most-feared symbol of mass production.

_____ 6. Garment factory where the doors were locked to keep the workers on the job. When a fire broke out, 146 workers, mostly young women, were killed.

_____ 7. Offered membership to all workers in a particular industry, irrespective of skill.

_____ 8. Form of early motion pictures.

_____ 9. Bill that made it illegal to transport women across state lines for immoral purposes.

WHERE WAS IT?

Complete each statement below (questions 1–7) by writing the letter preceding the appropriate name in the space provided. Use each answer only once.

   a. Fort Lee, New Jersey
   b. Greenwich Village
   c. Lower East Side
   d. Ludlow, Colorado
   e. Menlo Park, New Jersey
   f. New Orleans, Louisiana
   g. River Rouge, Michigan

_____ 1. Location of the largest industrial plant in the world at the time.

_____ 2. Location of Thomas A. Edison's research laboratory that became the model used by many businesses for their research facilities.

_____ 3. Principal area in New York City where Jewish immigrants settled and one of the most densely populated areas in the world.

_____ 4. City where black and white dock workers began an experiment in interracial unionism that flourished for several decades.

_____ 5. Location of a major strike against a Rockefeller-owned property where company police killed sixty-six men, women, and children.

_____ 6. One of the first centers of movie production in the United States.

_____ 7. Site of a bohemian community in lower Manhattan where women found a supportive environment in which to express and live by their feminist ideals.

CHARTS, MAPS, AND ILLUSTRATIONS

1. The only state that had no leading industry in the industrial society from 1900 to 1920 was _____.

2. The building known as the "Cathedral of Commerce" was _____.

3. The occupation that showed the greatest decline in workforce between 1870 and 1900 was _____.

   The occupation with the highest percentage growth at that time was _____.

4. Between 1860 and 1900, the European area from which the largest group of immigrants came to America was _____.

   Did most Europeans emigrate from the same area between 1900 and 1920? _____

5. The immigrant group that used agriculture as a route to middle-class status and income was _____.

MULTIPLE CHOICE

Circle the letter that best completes each statement.

1. Skyscrapers were made possible by the use of
   a. stone framework.
   b. fiberglass framework.
   c. concrete framework.
   d. steel framework.

2. Two of the most important new technologies of the early twentieth century were the invention of the gasoline-powered internal combustion engine and the
   a. creation of the atom bomb.
   b. invention of the cotton gin.
   c. harnessing of electric power.
   d. invention of the compass.

3. Electricity made possible the construction of the first subways in the city of
   a. Boston.
   b. San Francisco.
   c. Philadelphia.
   d. New York.

4. In 1909, Henry Ford unveiled a car that was reliable and affordable to most Americans; it was called a
   a. Model-A.
   b. Model-B.
   c. Model-T.
   d. Mercury.

5. Buyers and sellers separated by thousands of miles were able to maintain constant communications due to a national network of
   a. telegraph lines.
   b. phone lines.
   c. pony-express lines.
   d. postal lines.

6. Mass-production techniques were taken up first by industries that employed chemical, rather than mechanical, processes. Which one of the following processes did not use the techniques of mass production?
   a. refining of petroleum and sugar
   b. distilling of alcohol
   c. manufacture of iron and steel
   d. production of thread and yarn

7. Andrew Carnegie and J. P. Morgan merged two hundred separate companies and formed
   a. U.S. Steel.
   b. General Electric.
   c. DuPont.
   d. Armour and Swift.

8. Early 20th-century managers who aimed to introduce scientific theory into their companies did all of the following except
   a. create research departments and hire professional scientists to come up with new technological and scientific breakthroughs.
   b. recruit managers and workers with extensive on-the-job experience rather than those with a higher education.
   c. introduce cost-accounting methods into departments charged with controlling the inflow of materials and the outflow of goods.
   d. require college or university training in science, engineering, or accounting for entry into the echelons of middle management.

9. All of the following reasons were why the introduction of scientific management practices rarely proceeded smoothly except
   a. Studies were costly.
   b. Formulas for increasing efficiency and reducing waste were often far less scientific than developers claimed.
   c. Willingness of workers to play the mechanical role assigned to them was overestimated.
   d. Skilled workers and foremen used every means possible to convince co-workers to increase efficiency for the good of the company.

10. A dramatic increase in production enabled Ford in 1923 to slash the price of a Model-T to
    a. $1,200.
    b. $875.

    c. $465.
    d. $295.

11. Which problem was not encountered by Ford?
    a. Workers hated the assembly line.
    b. Workers refused to unionize, not wanting a voice in production matters.
    c. Workers repeated a single motion all day long, inducing mental stupor.
    d. Managerial efforts to speed production induced physical exhaustion.

12. Ford doubled the average manufacturing wage then prevalent in American history when he raised the wage of his assembly line workers to
    a. fifty cents a day.
    b. $2 a day.
    c. $5 a day.
    d. $11 a day.

13. Who was the devout Baptist who refrained from flaunting his wealth but was so ruthless in assembling the Standard Oil Corporation and in crushing his competition that he became one of the most reviled of the robber barons?
    a. Cornelius Vanderbilt
    b. W. K. Kellogg
    c. John D. Rockefeller
    d. John Simon Guggenheim

14. In the new liberated climate, young women began to engage in sports and other activities long considered too manly for the "fragile sex." Young women responded to this post-Victorian period by
    a. discarding their corsets.
    b. lengthening their skirts.
    c. adopting shirtwaists.
    d. wearing decorative skirts.

15. Which of the following groups believed that society developed according to the principle of "survival of the fittest"?
    a. muckrakers
    b. social Darwinists
    c. environmentalists
    d. Marxists

16. The working class was overwhelmingly ethnic everywhere in the United States, except in the
    a. South.
    b. North.
    c. East.
    d. West.

17. What proportion of total immigration to America was European?
    a. one quarter
    b. one third

    c. three fourths
    d. one half

18. The post-1880 "new immigrants" were regarded as all of the following, except
    a. They were racially inferior.
    b. They were culturally impoverished.
    c. They were incapable of assimilating to American values and traditions.
    d. They were politically mature.

19. Most of the mass immigration to America was propelled by
    a. religious persecution.
    b. economic hardship.
    c. political persecution.
    d. educational aspirations.

20. In 1900, the annual earnings of American manufacturing workers averaged
    a. $200 to $300 a year.
    b. $400 to $500 a year.
    c. $800 to $1,000 a year.
    d. $1,500 to $2,000 a year.

21. Who published the book *Poverty* in 1904?
    a. Robert Hunter
    b. Carey McWilliams
    c. Alexander Berkman
    d. Henry Clay Frick

22. Which of the following infectious diseases was not the result of overcrowding and poor sanitation?
    a. diphtheria
    b. typhoid fever
    c. malaria
    d. pneumonia

23. By 1900, urban leaders began to yield to the insistence of reformers that the crisis in city living could only be solved by adopting housing codes and improving sanitation. Which of the following did not occur between 1880 and 1900?
    a. Housing inspectors condemned the worst of the tenements and ordered landlords to make minimal improvements.
    b. Urban mortality rates rose.
    c. City governments built reservoirs, pipes, and sewers.
    d. Newly paved roads reduced the amount of dirt, mud, and stagnant pools of water and thus reduced the spread of disease.

24. Each ethnic group of immigrants in America quickly established a network of new institutions, such as fraternal societies, that gave them a sense of community. Which of the following was not a way that these societies aided members?
    a. making small loans
    b. providing members with death benefits

c. serving as centers of sociability

d. encouraging members to adopt American customs

25. Machine bosses used a variety of legal and illegal means to ensure victory on election day. They won the loyalty of urban voters—especially immigrants—through all of the following means, except
    a. providing poor neighborhoods with paved roads and sewer systems.
    b. helping newly arrived immigrants obtain jobs (often on city payrolls).
    c. passing laws to disfranchise immigrants.
    d. occasionally providing food, fuel, or clothing to families in dire need.

26. Bosses who ran political machines
    a. refrained from soliciting campaign contributions.
    b. engaged in widespread election fraud.
    c. prosecuted gamblers, pimps, and other entrepreneurs of urban vice.
    d. saw to it that construction contracts went to the lowest bidder who could provide the highest quality work.

27. Black farmers were exploited in all of the following ways, except
    a. They were pressured to vote for white landowners in local elections.
    b. Landowners, most of whom were white, often forced them to accept artificially low prices for their crops.
    c. Landowners charged high prices for seed, tools, and groceries at the local stores that they controlled.
    d. They risked retaliation—either physical assaults by white vigilantes or eviction from their land—for traveling elsewhere to sell their crops.

28. The American Federation of Labor (AFL) poured most of its energy into organizing craft or skilled workers, including all of the following except
    a. machinists.
    b. farmers.
    c. plumbers.
    d. carpenters.

29. The Industrial Workers of the World (IWW)
    a. supported the principle of craft organization.
    b. welcomed the notion that only a conservative union could survive in American society.
    c. readily signed collective-bargaining agreements with employers.
    d. was founded in 1905 by western miners and was led by William "Big Bill" Haywood.

30. Which of the following statements *incorrectly* characterizes early twentieth-century movies, known as "nickelodeons"?
    a. They usually were located in upper-class neighborhoods.
    b. They lasted only fifteen minutes—therefore requiring little leisure time to watch.
    c. They only cost a nickel.
    d. Moviegoers needed no knowledge of English to understand what was happening on the "silent screen."

31. Which of the following was *not* a source of the revolt against Victorianism?
    a. Middle-class men were tiring of a life devoted to regimented work with no time for indulgent play.
    b. Middle-class women, after achieving first-rate educations at elite women's colleges, were told they could not participate in the nation's economic, governmental, or professional enterprises.
    c. Immigrants, blacks, and other groups were never fully socialized into the Victorian world.
    d. Upper-class mothers and grandmothers of the post-Victorian age wanted their descendants to enjoy the unsupervised leisure activities of the new age.

ESSAY

Description and Explanation (one- to two-paragraph essay)

1. Why were skyscrapers technologically possible? What did they symbolize?

2. Explain corporate expansion in terms of the desire to avoid market instability.

3. Describe social Darwinism, its basic beliefs, and its roots in intellectual and socio-economic developments. Do you think it would appeal at any time to minority or "weak" countries?

4. Describe the social mobility among immigrants.

5. Describe big-city political machines as both a positive and negative force in American life.

6. Describe the role of the early movies in the cultural life of the cities.

7. Describe the changing role of women in the workplace and how it affected their non-working lives.

Discussion and Analysis (class discussion or one- to two-paragraph essay)

1. Compare the work of Frederick W. Taylor and scientific management with Henry Ford and his assembly line. What were the advantages of each system of management? What were the disadvantages for labor?

2. Discuss the differences between the "old" and "new" immigrants as to their points of origin, causes for increases in immigration to America, and how and why native-born Americans viewed them differently.

3. Discuss the decline of equality and opportunities for African Americans and describe the increasing racial discriminations against them.

What If (include an explanation of your position)

1. If you were an industrial worker in the early 20th century, would you work for Henry Ford?

2. If you were an immigrant arriving in the United States in 1910, would life be better in the United States? Would it make a difference if you were from Russia or Italy?

3. If you were a young female, would you enjoy city life?

Crossword Puzzle: An Industrial Society, 1890–1920

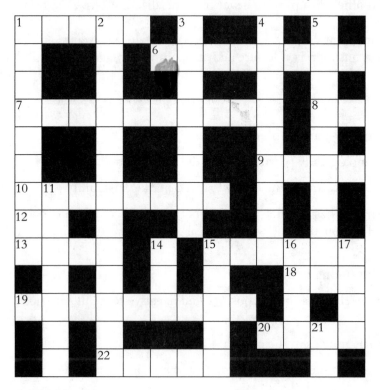

ACROSS

1. Type of war "Big Bill" Haywood called for
6. Namesake of separate spheres doctrine
7. Alexander Berkman and other radicals
8. Short for long-distance electricity
9. Deadly female like Bara
10. Part of Gompers's group
12. Injunction in a word
13. Henry Adams on immigration
15. Separate-sphere role for female
18. Gilded Age for one
19. Sears and Roebuck philanthropist
20. Triangle tragedy
22. Immigrants like Carnegie

DOWN

1. One group out of 4 million Slavic immigrants
2. Vulnerable and often victimized southern farmers
3. ___ immigrants established outposts of the Mafia.
4. He urged Americans to "boldly face the life of strife"
5. Samuel Gompers on a roll
11. Frederick W. Taylor studied the ___ of workers.
14. Followers of "Big Bill" Haywood for short
15. Japanese immigrants barred after 1907
16. 50 percent prefix
17. Railroad cartels prevented ruinous ___ wars.
21. NE state

ANSWER KEY

WHO? WHAT? WHERE?

Who Were They?

1. e. James Buchanan Duke, p. 681
2. f. J.P. Morgan, p. 682
3. d. Frederick W. Taylor, p. 683
4. i. Mrs. Bradley Martin, p. 686
5. b. Amadeo P. Giannini, p. 696
6. g. John Francis Fitzgerald, p. 697
7. i. Madame C. J. Walker, p. 701
8. c. "Big Bill" Haywood, p. 704
9. j. Theda Bara, p. 706
10. a. Alice Paul, p. 707

What Was It?

1. c. incandescent bulb, pp. 678-679
2. a. alternating current, p. 679
3. i. United States Steel, p. 683
4. g. time-and-motion studies, p. 683
5. b. assembly line, p. 685
6. h. Triangle Shirtwaist Company, p. 693
7. d. industrial union, p. 703
8. f. nickelodeons, p. 705
9. e. Mann Act, p. 708

Where Was It?

1. g. River Rouge, Michigan, p. 681
2. e. Menlo Park, New Jersey, p. 683
3. c. Lower East Side, p. 695
4. f. New Orleans, Louisiana, p. 704
5. d. Ludlow, Colorado, p. 705

6. a. Fort Lee, New Jersey, p. 706
7. b. Greenwich Village, p. 708

CHARTS, MAPS, AND ILLUSTRATIONS

1. South Dakota, p. 680
2. Woolworth Building, p. 679
3. agriculture; professional, clerical, p. 681
4. Germany; no, p. 690
5. Japanese, p. 691

MULTIPLE CHOICE

1. d   (p. 677)
2. c   (p. 678)
3. d   (p. 679)
4. c   (p. 679)
5. a   (p. 681)
6. d   (p. 681)
7. a   (p. 683)
8. b   (p. 683)
9. d   (pp. 683–684)
10. d   (p. 685)
11. b   (p. 685)
12. c   (p. 685)
13. c   (p. 686)
14. a   (p. 687)
15. b   (p. 688)
16. a   (p. 689)
17. c   (p. 689)
18. d   (p. 690)
19. b   (p. 690)
20. b   (p. 694)

21 a   (p. 694)

22. c   (p. 695)

23. b   (p. 695)

24. d   (p. 695)

25. c   (p. 697)

26. b   (p. 697)

27. a   (p. 698)

28. b   (p. 703)

29. d   (p. 704)

30. a   (p. 705)

31. d   (p. 706)

ESSAY

Description and Explanation

1. pp. 677–678

2. p. 682

3. p. 688

4. pp. 695–696

5. pp. 696–697

6. pp. 705–706

7. pp. 706–707

Discussion and Analysis

1. pp. 683–685

2. pp. 689–692

3. pp. 698–701

What If

1. pp. 683–685

2. pp. 689–696

3. pp. 705–707

Crossword Puzzle

¹C	L	A	²S	S	■	³S	■	⁴R	■	⁵C
R	■	H	■	⁶V	I	C	T	O	R	I	A
O	■	A	■	C	■	O	■	G	■
⁷A	N	A	R	C	H	I	S	T	S	■	⁸A	C
T	■	E	■	L	■	E	■	R	■
I	■	C	■	I	■	⁹V	A	M	P
¹⁰A	¹¹M	E	R	I	C	A	N	■	E	■	A
¹²N	O	■	O	■	N	■	L	■	K
¹³S	T	O	P	■	¹⁴I	■	¹⁵M	O	T	¹⁶H	E	¹⁷R
■	I	■	P	■	W	■	A	■	¹⁸E	R	A
¹⁹R	O	S	E	N	W	A	L	D	■	M	■	T
■	N	■	R	■	E	■	²⁰F	I	²¹R	E
■	S	■	²²S	C	O	T	S	■	■	I

CHAPTER 21

PROGRESSIVISM

The variety of reform initiatives and the contrast of motives during the first two decades of the twentieth century make it one of the most important reform periods in American history. Reformers sought to contain the power of the trusts, protect the rights of workers and consumers, and make life more secure for everyone. Progressives wanted to tame and regulate capitalism; they did not want to eliminate it. They wanted to improve the working and living conditions of the masses but not cede political control to them. In fact, many of their changes actually weakened the influence of workers and minority groups.

In the area of politics, reformers sought to do away with big-city machines, curb the power of political parties, and stiffen voter qualifications. They wanted to restore sovereignty to the people and to encourage honest, talented individuals to enter politics. Citizenship was a great gift that carried grave responsibilities; it was not to be bestowed lightly. Serving as the testing grounds for the Progressives, cities introduced new types of government designed to transfer power to nonpartisan experts. From the urban areas the movement quickly spread to the states, where legislation was pushed by an alliance of middle-class and working-class reformers and dynamic state governors. Overall, Progressives substantially altered the composition of the electorate and strengthened the role of government over daily lives.

As the Progressives focused more on economic justice and social matters, such as prostitution, alcohol consumption, and Americanization of immigrants, they sought to increase their influence in national politics. Certain problems demanded national solutions rather than a patchwork of state regulations. National leadership of the movement came from Presidents Theodore Roosevelt and Woodrow Wilson. They sponsored reforms that profoundly affected the lives of Americans and altered the nature of the American presidency by transforming it into a force for legislative and popular leadership.

LIBERTY, EQUALITY, POWER

The issues of liberty, equality, and power were of major importance during the Progressive period. Concern about the power of big business over workers and consumers stimulated attempts by the government to regulate businesses on the local, state, and federal levels. Assaults on the power of political machines promoted major changes in government. Progressives were proud of the efficiency they brought to the complex process of sorting out those who deserved citizenship from those who did not. On the one hand, Progressives enlarged the electorate by extending the right to vote to women, one of the great political accomplishments of American history; but, on the other hand, they either initiated or tolerated laws that barred large numbers of minority and poor voters from the polls. Asian immigrants were declared permanently ineligible for citizenship. Between 1890 and 1904, every ex-Confederate state passed laws designed to strip blacks of their right to vote. To the Progressives, the right to vote should be withheld from any person deemed racially or culturally unfit.

Various radical groups, including some socialists, emphasized protection and liberty for the weak. A new generation of African-American activists insisted that the issue of racial equality be placed on the reform agenda. Progress toward racial equality was painfully slow, and the membership of civil rights groups was not large enough to qualify as a mass movement. Most whites in America at the time accepted the practices of racial segregation and discrimination as normal.

American society and government had a long way to go to protect liberty and promote equality, much less increase the power of the weak and helpless in the United States. Despite the racial and cultural attitudes of some Progressives, many sincerely cared about people and called attention to their needs in American society. Progressives were seemingly naïve about many social problems, but they made significant attempts at solving some of them.

OBJECTIVES

After studying this chapter, a student should be able to

1. Describe the role of the muckrakers, settlement houses, and socialists in the development of the Progressive movement.

2. Explain the issues and accomplishments in local, state, and national government that were supported by the Progressives.

3. Characterize the relationship between progressivism and the Protestant churches.

4. Describe the Progressives' view of the "people" and how it helped determine which people they thought should participate in government.

5. Describe the role of women in the Progressive era and the significance of them on both the movement and how Americans viewed women.

6. Compare the domestic reforms of Presidents Theodore Roosevelt and Woodrow Wilson.

CHRONOLOGY

1860–1900	During these years, the number of students enrolled in colleges and universities rose from 30,000 to 250,000.
1870–1909	The number of daily newspapers in America rose from 574 to 2,600, and their circulation increased from less than 3 million to more than 24 million.
1870s	The tradition of investigative journalism began when newspaper and magazine writers exposed the corrupt practices of New York City's Boss Tweed and his well-oiled Tammany Hall political machine.

1885	Woodrow Wilson published *Congressional Government*, a brilliant analysis and critique of Congress that would long remain the most important work in its field.
1887	Congress established a regulatory body known as the Interstate Commerce Commission (ICC), which in theory possessed the power to set railroad shipping rates. However, the courts had so weakened the oversight and regulatory features of the ICC as to render it virtually powerless by the first decade of the twentieth century.
1889	Jane Addams and Ellen Gates Starr established the nation's first settlement house, Hull House, in Chicago.
1890s	The first states to enfranchise women were Wyoming (1890), Colorado (1893), Idaho (1896), and Utah (1896).
	Realism emerged in response to a widespread sense that prevailing attitudes were no longer relevant to the radical transformation that society was undergoing. It was a way of thinking that prized detachment, objectivity, and skepticism. Intellectuals and artists of all sorts set about creating truer, more realistic ways of representing and analyzing American society.
	Virtually every state adopted the Australian, or secret, ballot. This reform required people to vote in private rather than in public and required the government, rather than political parties, to print ballots and supervise voting.
	Launched in 1848, the campaign for woman suffrage floundered in the 1870s and 1880s, until the 1890s, when suffragists came together in a new organization, the National American Woman Suffrage Association (NAWSA), and invigorated the movement at the grass-roots level.
	People in hundreds of Wisconsin cities and towns mobilized against the state's corrupt Republican Party and the special privileges the party granted to private utilities and railroads.
1890–1904	Every ex-Confederate state passed laws designed to strip blacks of their right to vote. Because laws explicitly barring blacks from voting would have violated the Fifteenth Amendment, exclusion had to be accomplished indirectly, through literacy tests, property qualifications, and poll taxes.
1890–1920	Personal registration laws, supported by Progressives, were passed by most states. These laws established a complex set of regulations requiring voters to present proper identification and to maintain a period of residence before registering to vote.
1893	Illinois Governor John P. Altgeld named Florence Kelley of Hull House as the state's chief factory inspector. Her investigations led to Illinois's first factory law, which prohibited child labor, limited the employment of women to eight hours a day, and authorized the state to hire inspectors to enforce the law.

1899	W.E.B. Du Bois became the first African American to receive a Ph.D. from Harvard University.
1900	In the aftermath of a devastating tidal wave at Galveston, Texas, the city commission shifted municipal power from the mayor and his aldermen to five city commissioners, each responsible for a different department of city government. By 1913, more than three hundred cities had adopted the city commission plan.

Disfranchisement had some dramatic effects. For example, in 1900, only 1,300 blacks voted in Mississippi elections—down from 130,000 in the 1870s. In Virginia, voter turnout dropped from 60 percent of adult men (white and black) in 1900 to 28 percent in 1904.

Theodore Dreiser's *Sister Carrie*, a novel that re-created the sights and smells of the daily life of ordinary people of Chicago, is published.

Robert M. LaFollette, a leading reformer, was elected governor of Wisconsin and put the state in the lead as a model of progressivism.

1901   The Socialist Party of America was founded on the belief that control over industry should be transferred from a few industrialists to the laboring masses—usually defined in terms of government ownership—to make it impossible for wealthy elites to control society.

William McKinley was shot by an anarchist assassin less than a year into his second term as president. McKinley's wounds proved fatal, and he died nine days later **(September)**.

1902   Mississippi introduced the direct primary and Wisconsin followed a year later. By **1916**, all but three states (New Mexico, Rhode Island, and Connecticut) had adopted the direct primary.

Roosevelt ordered the Justice Department to prosecute the Northern Securities Company, a $400 million monopoly set up to control all railroad lines and traffic in the Northwest, from Chicago to Washington state. Never before had an American president sought to use the Sherman Anti-Trust Act to break up a concentration of wealth and power. In **1903**, a federal court ordered the company dissolved, and the next year the Supreme Court upheld the decision.

Coal miners in the eastern anthracite fields went on strike demanding recognition of their union, higher wages, and a shorter workday. In what would become a precedent for Roosevelt's "square deal," the federal government, under White House pressure, ordered employers to negotiate with their workers.

1902–1916   During these years, more than a hundred cities launched investigations into the prostitution trade. These were only one example of reform movements triggered by muckrakers, who kept the public informed with hard facts that nourished an emerging, though ill-defined, urge to reform.

1903   Roosevelt appointed a Public Lands Commission to survey public lands, inventory them, and establish permit systems to regulate the kinds and numbers of users.

1904   In his **1904** election campaign, Roosevelt promised that, if reelected, he would offer every American a "square deal." Voters felt Roosevelt identified with them and the slogan helped carry Roosevelt to a landslide victory.

1905   Black activists met at Niagara Falls to declare their independence from Booker T. Washington's leadership and to fashion their own aggressive political agenda. They demanded that blacks be given the right to vote in states where the franchise had been withheld, that segregation be abolished, and that discriminatory barriers be removed.

Gifford Pinchot, a specialist in forestry management, convinced Roosevelt to create the National Forest Service to oversee the efficient harvest of the nation's forest crop.

1906   Theodore Roosevelt achieved his goal of strengthening the ICC with congressional approval of the Hepburn Act. This legislation significantly increased the ICC's powers of rate review and enforcement and established an important precedent for future government efforts to regulate private industry.

The Pure Food and Drug Act, passed by Congress and supported by Roosevelt, protected the public from fraudulently marketed and dangerous foods and medications.

The uproar created by the publication of Upton Sinclair's *The Jungle* prompted Roosevelt to order a government investigation of conditions in the meat-packing industry. When the investigation corroborated Sinclair's findings, Roosevelt supported the Meat Inspection Act, passed that same year, which committed the government to monitoring the quality and safety of meat being sold to American consumers.

1907   A failed speculative effort by several New York banks to corner the copper market triggered a run on banks, a short but severe dip in industrial production, and widespread layoffs. Prosperity returned quickly, but the jitters caused by the depression lingered.

Charles Evans Hughes, a reform lawyer, became governor of New York and immediately established several public-service commissions to regulate railroads and utility companies.

When Roosevelt recommended the prosecution of cattlemen and lumbermen who were using federal land illegally for private gain, congressional conservatives struck back with legislation that sharply curtailed the president's power to create new government land reserves. Roosevelt responded by seizing another 17 million acres for national forest reserves before the new law went into effect.

1908	A mob in Springfield, Illinois, attacked black businesses and individuals. A force of five thousand state militia was required to restore order.
	As Roosevelt's anointed successor, William Howard Taft easily won the election—defeating Democrat William Jennings Bryan with 52 percent of the vote.
1909	Herbert Croly's progressive book *The Promise of American Life* is published. This book promoted the idea that, despite the nation's problems, life in America was still richer than that of any other nation on earth.
	Progressives had long desired tariff reduction, believing that competition from foreign manufacturers would benefit American consumers and check the economic power of American manufacturers. However, due to the efforts of the "Old Guard," the Payne-Aldrich Tariff bill was signed into law in August and did nothing to encourage foreign imports. Progressive Republicans were bitterly disappointed and held Taft responsible.
1910	Roosevelt embarked on a speaking tour, the high point of which was at Osawatomie, Kansas, where he elaborated his New Nationalism reform program.
	The National Association for the Advancement of Colored People (NAACP), a biracial political organization that made the struggle for black equality its primary goal, was founded. This establishment marked the beginning of the modern civil rights movement.
	Mann Act was enacted, which made it illegal to transport women across state lines "for immoral purposes."
1910–1912	The states of Washington, California, Kansas, Oregon, and Arizona followed the movement to enfranchise women.
1911	The Progressives joined forces with the Women's Christian Temperance Union, 245,000 members strong, and the Anti-Saloon League.
	The position of city manager was introduced in Sumter, South Carolina, and within eight years had been adopted in 130 cities.
	Those most hurt by franchise limitations were nonwhite immigrants. The Bureau of Immigration declared Chinese, Japanese, Korean, Indian, Thai, and other Asian immigrants permanently ineligible for citizenship.
	John R. Commons designed and won legislative approval for Wisconsin's Industrial Commission, which brought together employers, trade unionists, and disinterested professionals and gave them broad powers to investigate and regulate relations between capital and labor throughout the state.
	The National Urban League was founded to improve the economic and social conditions of blacks in cities. The league pressured large, private employers to open more jobs for blacks, it distributed lists of available jobs

and housing, and it developed social programs to ease the adjustment of rural black migrants to city life.

1912

At the peak of its influence, membership in the Socialist Party exceeded 115,000 members. In the same year, 1,200 Socialists held elective office in 340 different municipalities.

Despite the fact that Roosevelt swept the states with presidential primaries, the Republican convention, controlled by the "Old Guard," renominated Taft for president. The next day, Roosevelt and his supporters withdrew from the party. In **August**, they assembled as the Progressive Party and nominated Roosevelt for president.

The Democratic convention nominated Woodrow Wilson of New Jersey for president on the forty-sixth ballot. Wilson's presidential victory gave the country its first southern president in almost fifty years and restored the South to national power.

1913

The federal government established its own Industrial Relations Commission and hired John R. Commons to direct its investigative staff.

The Underwood–Simmons Tariff achieved the long-sought Progressive aim of significantly reducing protectionist barriers from approximately 40 percent to 25 percent. To replace lost revenue, an income tax was passed. This was made possible by the Sixteenth Amendment to the Constitution, which extended to the government the right to impose an income tax.

Wilson signed the Federal Reserve Act into law—the most important law passed in his first administration.

The Seventeenth Amendment was ratified, mandating the direct election of senators.

1914

In *Drift and Mastery*, Walter Lippmann theorized that ordinary people, overwhelmed by industrial and social changes, were rendered incapable of controlling their own destiny and living in the modern world. For this reason, Lippmann argued that political responsibility should be placed in the hands of experts.

Wilson swung his full support behind the Federal Trade Commission Act, which created a government agency to regulate business practices.

1915

The Supreme Court ruled that the "grandfather clauses" of the Oklahoma and Maryland constitutions violated the Fifteenth Amendment.

1915–1916

The suffrage movement regained momentum under the leadership of the strategically astute Carrie Chapman Catt, who became president of NAWSA in **1915**, and the radical Alice Paul, who founded the militant National Women's Party in **1916**.

1916	In **January**, President Wilson nominated Louis Brandeis to the Supreme Court. Not only was Brandeis one of the country's most respected Progressives, he was also the first Jew to serve on the country's highest court.

The collective efforts of Progressives, the Women's Christian Temperance Union, and the Anti-Saloon League won prohibition of the sale and manufacture of alcoholic beverages in sixteen states. Within three years, their work culminated in a constitutional amendment that made prohibition the law of the land.

Congress passed the first federal workmen's compensation law, the Kern–McGillicuddy Act, the first federal law outlawing child labor; the Keating–Owen Act; and the first federal law guaranteeing workers an eight-hour day, the Adamson Act. From this time, Democrats, rather than Republicans, became the chief guardians of the American reform tradition.

1917 The Supreme Court declared a Louisville, Kentucky, law requiring all blacks to live in predetermined areas of the city to be unconstitutional.

1920 Voter-participation rates declined from 79 percent in 1896 to 49 percent in 1920 due to growing disillusionment with the electorate and additional restrictions on the franchise. The major exception to this trend was the enfranchisement of women.

Aided by a heightened enthusiasm for democracy generated by the First World War, and by the decision to shift the movement's focus from individual states to the nation at large, suffragists achieved their goal of universal women suffrage with the ratification of the Nineteenth Amendment to the Constitution. Predictions that suffrage for women would alter politics radically proved false. Political corruption continued, government did not address the needs of women, and voter-participation rates continued to decline, although the numbers of voters increased after 1920.

GLOSSARY OF IMPORTANT TERMS

Australian ballot Also known as the secret ballot, the Australian ballot allowed people to vote in private rather than in public. In addition, it required the government rather than the political parties to print the ballots and supervise the voting.

Bull Moosers The followers of Theodore Roosevelt in the 1912 election.

city manager A form of city government under which the elected city commission set policy, but the day-to-day tasks were carried out by a hired executive.

direct primary This primary enabled the voters instead of party bosses to choose party candidates for office.

gas and water socialists A term used to describe evolutionary socialists who were interested in improving city life and government.

initiative	A process (through general elections) that allowed reformers to put measures before voters even though state legislatures had not yet approved them.
insurgent	One who rebels against party leadership.
muckrakers	A term coined by Theodore Roosevelt as a criticism of writers who wrote about scandalous situations and distasteful alliances involving money. The name became a badge of honor among "muckrakers" determined to expose the seedy, sordid side of life in the United States. They sought to shock the public into recognizing the shameful state of political, economic, and social affairs, and to prompt people into action. Much of their work was published in cheap magazines of the time.
New Freedom	The Wilsonian philosophy that called for a temporary concentration of government power to dismantle the trusts.
New Nationalism	Roosevelt's far-reaching program that called for a strong federal government to stabilize the economy, protect the weak, and restore social harmony.
Old Guard	The conservative group within the Republican Party, led by Senator Nelson Aldrich and Speaker of the House Joseph Cannon. They were closely tied to big business and were devoted to a nineteenth-century style of backroom politics.
personal registration laws	Laws passed by nearly every state between 1890 and 1920, requiring prospective voters to appear at a designated government office with proper identification in order to register before being allowed to vote.
realism	A philosophy that prized detachment, objectivity, and skepticism. It arose in the 1890s in response to a widespread sense that prevailing attitudes were no longer relevant to the radical transformation that society was undergoing. Realistic writers brought shadowy figures vividly to life.
recall	A political device that allowed voters to remove from office any public servant who had betrayed their trust.
referendum	A political device that gave voters the right to repeal an unpopular act that a state legislature had passed. Voters decided the issue directly in general elections.
settlement houses	Centers established by middle-class reformers in urban slums to help the largely immigrant poor cope with the harsh conditions of city life.
socialism	A political theory that in the early twentieth century stood for the transfer of control from a few industrialists to the laboring masses. Socialists believed that such a transfer, usually defined in terms of government ownership and operation of economic institutions, would make it impossible for wealthy elites to control society.
ticket splitting	The act of dividing one's vote between candidates of two or more parties.

WHO? WHAT? WHERE?

WHO WERE THEY?

Complete each following statement (questions 1–15) by writing the letter preceding the appropriate name in the space provided. Use each answer only once.

    a. Charles Evans Hughes
    b. Eugene V. Debs
    c. Florence Kelley
    d. Gifford Pinchot
    e. Helen Keller
    f. Ida Tarbell
    g. Jane Addams
    h. John Mitchell
    i. John Muir
    j. Lincoln Steffens
    k. Robert M. LaFollette
    l. Sam McClure
  m. Theodore Roosevelt
    n. Victor Berger
    o. Walter Lippmann

_____ 1. Writer who described the shady practices by which John D. Rockefeller transformed Standard Oil Corporation into a monopoly.

_____ 2. Author of a series on corruption in local government.

_____ 3. Very successful publisher of a cheap periodical who filled his magazine with sensational stories of ill-gotten economic power, government corruption, and urban vice.

_____ 4. Member of the group that established the nation's first settlement house.

_____ 5. Chief factory inspector of Illinois whose investigations led to the state's first law prohibiting child labor.

_____ 6. Charismatic presidential candidate of the Socialist Party of America.

_____ 7. Evolutionary socialist who abandoned talk of revolution and chose an aggressive brand of reform politics.

_____ 8. Country's leading spokesman for the disabled who traveled between the socialist and progressive camps.

_____ 9. Developer of the theory that ordinary people had been overwhelmed by industrial and social change.

_____ 10. Reform governor and leader of Progressives in Wisconsin.

_____ 11. Christian socialist, economist, and founder of the American Economic Association.

_____ 12. Reform governor of New York who established several public-service commissions to regulate railroads and utility companies.

_____ 13. Youngest chief executive in American history.

_____ 14. President of the United Mine Workers during the coal miners' strike of 1902.

_____ 15. Founder of the Sierra Club who insisted that the beauty of the land and the well-being of its wildlife should be protected from all human interference.

_____ 16. European trained specialist in forest management who led the drive for expert and scientific management of natural resources.

WHAT WAS IT?

Complete each following statement (questions 1–13) by writing the letter preceding the appropriate response in the space provided. Use each answer only once.

a. Australian ballot
b. Bull Moosers
c. The Crisis
d. direct primary
e. Federal Reserve Act
f. muckrakers
g. Mann Act
h. National Association for the Advancement of Colored People
i. National Urban League
j. Northern Securities
k. Pure Food and Drug Act
l. Seventeenth Amendment
m. Sixteenth Amendment

_____ 1. Bill which made it illegal to transport a woman across state lines "for immoral purposes."

_____ 2. Group of writers determined to expose the seedy, sordid side of life in the United States.

_____ 3. Process that enabled voters, rather than party bosses, to choose party candidates.

_____ 4. Amendment that required people to vote directly on senators.

_____ 5. Political device that allowed people to vote in private instead of in public.

_____ 6. Biracial political organization that made the struggle for black equality its primary goal.

_____ 7. Group that worked to improve the economic and social conditions of African Americans in the cities.

_____ 8. Magazine that publicized and protested the lynchings, riots, and other abuses directed against blacks.

_____ 9. Monopoly set up by leading financiers and railroad tycoons to control all railroad lines and traffic from Chicago to Washington state.

_____ 10. Bill passed by Congress to protect the public from fraudulently marketed and dangerous food and medications.

_____ 11. Followers of Theodore Roosevelt in the 1912 election.

_____ 12. Amendment that gave the federal government the right to impose an income tax.

_____ 13. Most important act passed in President Wilson's first administration.

WHERE WAS IT?

Complete each statement below (questions 1–10) by writing the letter preceding the appropriate response in the space provided. Use each answer only once.

a. Chicago, Illinois
b. Cleveland, Ohio
c. Galveston, Texas
d. Mississippi
e. Niagara Falls
f. Oklahoma
g. Oregon
h. Springfield, Illinois
i. Sumter, South Carolina
j. Wisconsin

_____ 1. Location of the country's first settlement house.

_____ 2. State where voters gave a higher percentage of their votes to the Socialist candidate in 1916 than did any other state.

_____ 3. City that was the best governed in the country, according to journalist Lincoln Steffens.

_____ 4. First city to use the city commission plan of municipal government in the wake of a devastating tidal wave.

_____ 5. City where the city manager plan first was introduced.

_____ 6. First state to use the direct primary.

_____ 7. First state to adopt the initiative and referendum.

_____ 8. Leading state in reform during the Progressive era.

_____ 9. Scene of a bloody race riot that required five thousand state militia to restore order.

_____ 10. Location of a meeting of black activists in 1905 to fashion an aggressive political agenda.

CHARTS, MAPS, AND ILLUSTRATIONS

1. The state that elected the greatest number of Socialist mayors was _____.

2. The year that voter participation in South Carolina was the highest was _____.

   The year that voter participation in South Carolina was the lowest was _____.

3. The region of the United States that did not allow voting by women before 1920 was the _____.

4. One of the two states carried by William Howard Taft in the election of 1912 was

_____.

5. The city where the Federal Reserve Bank for the Twelfth Federal Reserve District is located was _____.

MULTIPLE CHOICE

Circle the letter that best completes each statement.

1. Which of the following does not describe the age of progressivism?
   a. Progressives fought against trusts.
   b. Progressives wanted to cleanse politics of corruption.
   c. Progressives were skeptical regarding the competence of science and human beings to analyze and control their biological, economic, and social environments.
   d. Progressives wanted government to control various forms of vice.

2. What was the philosophy that emerged in the 1890s that prized detachment, objectivity, and skepticism?
   a. realism
   b. nativism
   c. transcendentalism
   d. utopianism

3. Which of the following statements incorrectly characterizes settlement houses?
   a. They were established by middle-class reformers.
   b. They were intended to help the largely immigrant poor cope with the harsh conditions of city life.
   c. They were the inspiration of young, college-educated, Protestant women from comfortable, but not particularly wealthy, backgrounds.
   d. They did not allow women and children inside.

4. Hull House offered all of the following services except
   a. a nursery for the children of working mothers and a neighborhood playground.
   b. workmen's compensation insurance and death benefits.
   c. a penny savings bank and an employment bureau.
   d. an orchestra and reading groups.

5. Which reformer used the appointment to the State Board of Charities to gain improvements in the care of the poor, the handicapped, and the delinquent?
   a. Carrie Chapman Catt
   b. Henry Demarest Lloyd
   c. Julia Lathrop
   d. John Sloan

6. Many champions of Progressive reform were cultural conservatives. Which of the following statements does not reflect this variation?
   a. Some reformers extended their conservative ideas to alcohol because drinking was a serious problem in poor, working-class areas.
   b. Some reformers endorsed efforts to limit funding to care for the poor and the disabled.
   c. Some reformers were troubled by the emergence of the "new woman" and her frank sexuality.
   d. Some reformers, such as Jane Addams, disapproved of the new working-class entertainments that gave adolescents unregulated opportunities for intimate association.

7. The prohibition movement ignored the role alcohol and saloons played in ethnic, working-class communities. Which of the following statements incorrectly portrays the role played by these so-called vices?
   a. Saloons provided thousands of packing-house workers the only decent place to eat lunch, since there were no cafeterias in meat-packing plants.
   b. Saloons attempted to Americanize ethnic groups by encouraging the speaking of English only, serving of nonethnic food and drink, and prohibiting fraternal organizations.
   c. Saloonkeepers sometimes functioned as informal bankers, cashing checks and making small loans.
   d. Alcohol was used in the Catholic communion and the Jewish Sabbath. Both groups shared wine or beer to mark the celebration of births, marriages, deaths, or other major family events.

8. The city commission and city manager plans reformed government by limiting corruption and improving services. These plans were not liked universally for the following reasons, except
   a. Poor and minority voters found that their influence in local affairs was weakened by the shift to city commissioners and city managers.
   b. Citywide elections diluted the strength of working-class and immigrant constituencies.
   c. Candidates from poor districts often lacked the money needed to run a citywide campaign.
   d. Candidates representing the "working man" enjoyed a strengthened political party and platform. The influence of radicals, minorities, and the poor was increased in elections.

9. Progressives introduced reforms designed to do all the following, except
   a. undermine the power of party bosses.
   b. gain favorable political and economic legislation for large corporations.
   c. restore sovereignty to "the people."
   d. encourage honest, talented individuals to enter politics.

10. What political device allowed voters to remove from office any public servant who had betrayed their trust?
    a. recall
    b. veto
    c. impeachment
    d. election

11. Which of the following statements incorrectly characterizes personal-registration laws?
    a. A period of residence in the state prior to registration and a certain interval between registration and actual voting was no longer required.
    b. Prospective voters were required to appear at a designated government office with proper identification before registering to vote.
    c. The laws were meant to disfranchise citizens who showed no interest in voting until election day, when a party worker arrived with a few dollars and offered a free ride to the polls.
    d. The laws excluded many hardworking, responsible poor people who wanted to vote but had failed to register, either because their work schedules made it impossible or because they were intimidated by the complex regulations.

12. The newly formed Bureau of Immigration and Naturalization (1906) made it far more difficult to become a citizen than it had been in the nineteenth century. Which of the following was not a requirement at the time?
    a. Applicants for citizenship had to prove that they had resided continuously in the United States for twelve years.
    b. Applicants for citizenship had to appear before a judge who interrogated them, using the English language, on American history and civics.
    c. Immigrants were required to provide two witnesses to vouch for their moral character and their attachment to the principles of the Constitution.
    d. Immigrants had to swear and, if necessary, prove that they were not anarchists or polygamists.

13. Which constitutional amendment extended the right to vote to women?
    a. sixteenth
    b. seventeenth
    c. eighteenth
    d. nineteenth

14. Thousands of young, college-educated women reinvigorated the suffrage movement at the grass roots by carrying out all of the following activities, except
    a. campaigning door to door.
    b. inciting violent demonstrations.
    c. holding impromptu rallies.
    d. pressuring state legislators.

15. Who designed and won legislative approval for Wisconsin's Industrial Commission, which brought together employers, trade unionists, and professionals and gave them broad powers to investigate and regulate relations between capital and labor throughout the state?
   a. John R. Commons
   b. Robert F. Wagner
   c. Robert La Follette
   d. Alfred E. Smith

16. Which of the following statements incorrectly characterizes Assemblyman Alfred E. Smith and Senator Robert F. Wagner?
   a. They converted from machine to reform politics, and their appearance in the Progressive ranks brought about a new reform sensibility.
   b. They opposed prohibition, city commissions, voter registration laws, and other reforms that seemed anti-immigrant and anti-Catholic.
   c. They fought against a minimum wage, factory safety, workmen's compensation, the right of workers to join unions, and the regulation of excessively powerful corporations.
   d. Their nationwide influence accelerated the Progressive movement's shift away from a preoccupation with political parties and electorates and toward questions of economic justice and social welfare.

17. Who was the first African American to receive a Ph.D. from Harvard University?
   a. W.E.B. Du Bois
   b. Ida B. Wells
   c. Monroe Trotter
   d. Booker T. Washington

18. Who was the first president in the 20th century to be assassinated?
   a. John F. Kennedy
   b. William McKinley
   c. Abraham Lincoln
   d. William Henry Harrison

19. Which of the following characteristics does not apply to Theodore Roosevelt?
   a. He had an insatiable appetite for high-risk adventure and confrontation.
   b. Although aggressive in his public rhetoric, he was a skilled, patient negotiator in private.
   c. He was born to a rural Texas family.
   d. He had an uncommon affection for "the people."

20. Theodore Roosevelt believed that industrial concentration brought the United States all of the following, except
   a. great wealth.
   b. moral decay.
   c. increased productivity.
   d. a rising standard of living.

21. In the 1902 coal miners' strike, George F. Baier, president of Reading Railroad and representative of employers, refused to negotiate with employees. He was shocked when Roosevelt
    a. threatened the striking workers with arrest by federal troops if they failed to return to work.
    b. refused to support a request from John Mitchell, the United Mine Workers president, for arbitration.
    c. warned the mine owners that, if they refused to go along with negotiations, ten thousand federal troops would seize their property.
    d. threatened that, with a compromise, coal production would resume under government control.

22. In his 1904 election campaign, Roosevelt promised that, if reelected, he would offer every American
    a. a "new deal."
    b. a "fair deal."
    c. an "equal deal."
    d. a "square deal."

23. In 1906, Congress passed legislation to significantly increase the Interstate Commerce Commission's power of rate review and enforcement and established an important precedent for future government efforts to regulate private industry. This bill was the
    a. Kern-McGillicuddy Act.
    b. Hepburn Act.
    c. Keating-Owen Act.
    d. Adamson Act.

24. The National Forest Service, under Gifford Pinchot's control, carried out all of the following actions, except
    a. It instituted a system of competitive bidding for the right to harvest timber on national forest land.
    b. It implemented a new policy that exacted user's fees from livestock ranchers who previously had used national forest grazing lands for free.
    c. It used new legislation and bureaucratic authority to declare vast stretches of federal land in the West off-limits to mining and dam construction.
    d. It prosecuted cattlemen and lumbermen who were using federal land illegally for private gain.

25. Sensing that he might fail to win his party's nomination, and mindful of a rash promise he made in 1904 not to run again in 1908, Roosevelt decided not to seek reelection. It was a decision that would soon come back to haunt him for all of the following reasons, except
    a. He was barely fifty and was too energetic to end his political career.
    b. His successor enjoyed unprecedented levels of popularity and support.
    c. He loved power too much.
    d. Much of his reform program had yet to win congressional approval.

26. Roosevelt thought he had found in William Howard Taft, his secretary of war, an ideal successor. To come to that conclusion, however, he had to ignore some obvious differences between Taft and himself. Which of the following statements inaccurately portrays an obvious difference between Roosevelt and Taft?
    a. Taft neither liked nor was particularly adept at politics.
    b. Taft's respect for the Constitution and its separation of powers made him suspicious of the power that Roosevelt had arrogated to the presidency.
    c. Taft's training as a jurist made him averse to risk, to public displays of emotion, and to symbolic gestures.
    d. Taft was by nature a cautious and conservative man.

27. Few would have predicted in 1908 that Woodrow Wilson would be elected to the presidency in 1912. Which of the following statements incorrectly describes Wilson?
    a. Prior to 1910, he never had run for elective office, nor had he ever held an appointed post in local, state, or federal administration.
    b. Throughout his thirty years in academe, he never had aspired to a career in politics.
    c. He was an experienced teacher of history and political science.
    d. Before running for governor in 1910, he was president of Princeton University.

28. The Federal Reserve Act of 1913
    a. established five private banks, each controlled by the federal banks of Washington, D.C.
    b. established a reserve that would be used to make loans to member banks and to issue paper currency.
    c. allowed private banks to deposit an average of 43 percent of their assets into the federal depository in Washington, D.C., on a volunteer basis.
    d. weakened the nation's financial structure.

29. Wilson supported weakening of the Clayton Anti-Trust Act, having decided that the breakup of large-scale industry was no longer practical or preferable. The purpose of the Federal Trade Commission, in Wilson's eyes, was to
    a. help business owners control workers.
    b. retain profitable industrial monopolies.
    c. dismantle large-scale industry.
    d. help businesses, large and small, to regulate themselves in ways that contributed to national well-being.

30. Who was the first Jew to serve on the Supreme Court?
    a. Louis Brandeis
    b. George Harvey
    c. William Gladstone
    d. Benjamin Disraeli

31. What was the first federal law outlawing child labor?
    a. Adamson Act
    b. Kern–McGillicuddy Act
    c. Keating–Owen Act
    d. Hepburn Act

ESSAY

Description and Explanation (one- to two-paragraph essay)

1. Describe the trend toward realism and its effects.

2. Describe the role of the muckrakers in promoting reform.

3. Describe the work of settlement-house workers in fashioning the progressive agenda.

4. Describe the evidence of conservatism among progressives as seen in their attitude toward alcohol.

5. Describe the various types of socialists and how their politics differed.

6. Compare the city-commission and city-manager plans of government and describe their political disadvantages.

7. Describe how the racial views of Progressives affected their opinions about who should or should not vote.

8. Describe Wisconsin as a leading reform state and what it was able to accomplish.

9. Describe the formation of the NAACP and its early activities.

Discussion and Analysis (class discussion or one- to two-paragraph essay)

1. Discuss the relationship between Progressivism and the Protestant spirit.

2. Discuss why the woman's suffrage movement was successful in the early twentieth century.

3. Compare political and social backgrounds, views on reform, and opinions about the role of government in the regulation of the trusts held by Presidents Roosevelt and Wilson.

What If (include an explanation of your position)

1. If you were a Progressive in the early 20th century, in which part of the movement would you have participated? Would it have made a difference if you were male or female?

2. If you were Theodore Roosevelt, how important would you consider the conservation movement? What would you do about it?

Crossword Puzzle: Progressivism

DOWN

1. Dreiser novel (2 wds.)
2. Law that limited workday for railroad workers (2 wds.)
3. Always
4. Election for senators after Seventeenth Amendment
5. Substance targeted by social hygiene campaign
6. ___ and behold
7. Roosevelt defied "___" of great wealth.
13. Suffragists' amendment
16. Short for Clark's state
17. Machine politician turned reformer in New York
18. Brandeis was first ___ member of Supreme Court
22. Pig place

ACROSS

1. Roosevelt's 1904 campaign slogan (2 wds.)
8. 6 in Roman numerals
9. Tom Johnson's level of government
10. "Uncle Joe" Cannon's title
11. A Progressive was one
12. Debs's scary scenario
14. The next state in Roman numerals
15. Hull House founder
19. Federal Reserve currency
20. Wilson wanted companies to ___.
21. Tragic event in Atlanta and Springfield
22. Coal miners in 1902
23. Last hour workers according to Roosevelt
24. Ohioan in G.O.P. guard

ANSWER KEY

WHO? WHAT? WHERE?

Who Were They?

1. f. Ida Tarbell, p. 712
2. j. Lincoln Steffens, p. 713
3. m. Sam McClure, p. 713
4. g. Jane Addams, p. 715
5. c. Florence Kelley, p. 716
6. b. Eugene V. Debs, pp. 718–719
7. o. Victor Berger, p. 719
8. e. Helen Keller, p. 719
9. p. Walter Lippmann, pp. 724–725
10. l. Robert M. LaFollette, p. 726
11. a. Charles Evans Hughes, p. 727
12. n. Theodore Roosevelt, p. 731
13. h. John Mitchell, p. 731
14. i. John Muir, p. 732
15. d. Gifford Pinchot, p. 733

What Was It?

1. g. Mann Act, p. 716
2. b. muckrakers, p. 712
3. d. direct primary, p. 721
4. l. Seventeenth Amendment, p. 721
5. a. Australian ballot, p. 722
6. h. National Association for the Advancement of Colored People, p. 729
7. i. National Urban League, p. 729
8. c. *The Crisis*, p. 729
9. j. Northern Securities, p. 731
10. k. Pure Food and Drug Act, p. 732

11. b. Bull Moosers, p. 737
12. m. Sixteenth Amendment, p. 741
13. e. Federal Reserve Act, p. 742

Where Was It?

1. a. Chicago, Illinois, p. 715
2. f. Oklahoma, p. 718
3. b. Cleveland, Ohio, p. 720
4. c. Galveston, Texas, p. 720
5. i. Sumter, South Carolina, p. 720
6. d. Mississippi, p. 721
7. g. Oregon, p. 721
8. j. Wisconsin, p. 726
9. h. Springfield, Illinois, p. 728
10. e. Niagara Falls, p. 728

CHARTS, MAPS, AND ILLUSTRATIONS

1. Ohio, p. 718
2. 1876, 1912, p. 723
3. South, p. 725
4. Utah or Vermont, p. 740
5. San Francisco, p. 742

MULTIPLE CHOICE

1. c (p. 711)
2. a (p. 714)
3. d (p. 715)
4. b (p. 715)
5. c (p. 716)
6. b (p. 716)
7. b (p. 717)

8. d   (pp. 720–721)

9. b   (p. 721)

10. a   (p. 721.)

11. a   (p. 722)

12. a   (p. 722)

13. d   (p. 725)

14. b   (p. 725)

15. a   (p. 727)

16. c   (p. 727)

17. a   (p. 728)

18. b   (p. 731)

19. c   (p. 731)

20. b   (p. 731)

21. a   (p. 732)

22. d   (p. 732)

23. b   (p. 732)

24. d   (p. 733)

25. b   (p. 736)

26. d   (p. 736)

27. b   (p. 738)

28. b   (p. 742)

29. d   (p. 743)

30. a   (p. 743)

31. c   (p. 743)

ESSAY

Description and Explanation

1. p. 714

2. pp. 712–713

3. pp. 715–716

4. pp. 716–717

5. pp. 717–719

6. pp. 720–721

7. pp. 722–724

8. pp. 726–727

9. p. 729

Discussion and Analysis

1. pp. 712

2. pp. 725–726

3. pp. 731, 740

What If

1. Chapter 21 *passim*

2. pp. 732–733

Crossword Puzzle

CHAPTER 22

BECOMING A WORLD POWER, 1898–1917

For much of the nineteenth century, most Americans showed limited interest in world affairs. They treasured their distance from Europe's corrupt societies and nondemocratic governments. International events played little role in elections, and the diplomatic corps was small and inexperienced. The American people were busy with continental expansion. The domestic market absorbed the growing American industrial production.

However, technological developments in the late nineteenth century forced this view to change. These advances brought countries of the world closer. Americans began to think about exporting the Protestant religion and their growing industrial production. Concern about the future of the country without an expanding frontier affected some; others were interested in expanding American power and influence through military buildup. Americans came to believe that the size, economic strength, and honor of their country required acceptance of the role as a world power and police officer. Americans felt they had a mission to spread American values to the farthest reaches of the world.

The United States initially wanted to oust the Spanish from Cuba, but the Spanish-American War quickly developed into a move for acquisition of a world empire. After 1898, the United States tightened control over the Western Hemisphere and projected its military and economic power into Asia. Roosevelt ensured U.S. dominance in the Western Hemisphere through the Roosevelt Corollary to the Monroe Doctrine and the acquisition of the Panama Canal Zone. He refused to use military force in Asia and concentrated on maintaining a balance of power throughout East Asia by mediating the Russo-Japanese War and the gentlemen's agreements with Japan. President Taft's administration seemed to be directed almost entirely toward expanding opportunities for corporate investment.

President Wilson cared more for morality and justice. He believed that the export of American-style democracy was a way of introducing orderly, controlled change to areas of social unrest. He feared that political unrest in Latin American could lead to violence and the installation of governments hostile to American economic interests. These ideas led to major involvement in the Mexican Revolution. Actually Wilson recognized something that Roosevelt and Taft did not. People throughout the world increasingly were determined to gain political independence and to control their own destiny. The United States had to find a way to support its democratic aspirations while, at the same time, safeguarding economic interests. World War I would make this quest for a balance between democratic principles and national self-interest urgent.

LIBERTY, EQUALITY, POWER

During this time in American history, the United States repeatedly belittled the people of the Philippines, Puerto Rico, and Guam as inferior, primitive, and barbaric. In choosing to behave like the imperialist powers of Europe, the United States abandoned its long-standing claim that it was a different kind of nation, one that valued liberty more than power. American treatment of Filipinos demonstrated absolutely no respect for their life or liberty. Forcing Cuba to include the Platt Amendment in its constitution was a display of the might of U.S. foreign policy over that of a weak country. Little patience was shown with small countries or human-rights issues abroad.

Thus the United States was capable of using its power to force its will on weaker nations, while continuing its efforts to guarantee subjugated people the right to self-determination and self-government. After 1900, America acted in ways that were increasingly offensive: seizing land, over-turning governments it did not like, forcing its economic and political policies on weaker neighbors. Not all Americans approved, however. The raw pursuit of power concerned at least a few Americans, and U.S. rule was less severe than that of some countries.

OBJECTIVES

After studying this chapter, a student should be able to

1. Understand the leading groups interested in expanding America's role abroad and their motivations.

2. Describe the causes and effects of the Spanish-American War.

3. Analyze how racism affected foreign affairs, including how the United States viewed some groups and how it influenced the military abroad.

4. Compare the different approaches of the presidents during this period and how this affected American activities abroad.

5. Understand the role of American leaders in Central America and the Caribbean and why that area was considered so important to the United States.

6. Explain the differences between the activities of Roosevelt, Taft, and Wilson in Asia.

CHRONOLOGY

1867	Secretary of State William Seward purchased the vast territory of Alaska from Russia for $7.2 million, or two cents an acre. Seward hoped that this acquisition would strengthen the Northwest against incursions from European and Asian powers, as well as stimulate interest in annexing British Columbia, the westernmost Canadian province that stood between Alaska and the rest of the United States.
1870–1900	Overseas missionary activity grew quickly, most of which was directed toward China. Convinced of the superiority of the Anglo-Saxon race,

Protestant missionaries considered it their Christian duty to teach the gospel to the "ignorant" Asian masses and to save their souls.

The United States added 125,000 square miles to its empire, while Great Britain, France, and Germany enlarged their empires by 4.7, 3.5, and 1 million square miles, respectively, in the same period.

1878   In order to establish service bases for the navy, the U.S. secured rights to Pago Pago, an excellent deep-water harbor in Samoa.

1880s   A French company obtained land rights and began construction of a canal across Panama. Even though only forty miles of land separated the two oceans, the company was plagued by technical difficulties, high financial costs, and disease—eventually bankrupting the endeavor in 1901.

Exports of American manufactured goods rose substantially after 1880, and by 1914 American foreign investment already equaled 7 percent of the nation's gross national product.

1880–1900   Every presidential administration from the 1880s on committed itself to a "big navy" policy. By 1898, the U.S. Navy ranked fifth in the world, and by 1900 it ranked third.

1885   The U.S. leased Pearl Harbor from the Hawaiians.

1889   Attempts to project U.S. power overseas quickly deepened the government's involvement in the affairs of distant lands, as in 1889 when the United States established a protectorate over part of Samoa—forestalling German and British efforts to weaken American influence on the islands.

1890   Admiral Alfred Thayer Mahan laid out a program to transform the United States into a great world power in *The Influence of Sea Power upon History*. This plan would include the construction of a first-class navy with enough ships and firepower to make its presence felt everywhere in the world.

1890s   President Grover Cleveland's administration increasingly was drawn into Hawaiian affairs, and U.S. involvement deepened as tensions between American sugar plantation owners and native Hawaiians upset the island's economic and political stability.

The appeal of foreign markets was intensified by the U.S. census report of 1890, which announced that the frontier had disappeared. In the 1893 publication of "The Significance of the Frontier in American History," Frederick Jackson Turner pronounced that the frontier had been essential to the growth of the economy and to the cultivation of democracy.

By this time, the islands of Cuba and Puerto Rico were virtually all that remained of the vast Spanish empire in the Americas. Relations between Cubans and their Spanish rulers continued to deteriorate. American journalists kept American readers informed about the situation through lurid tales of atrocities.

1898

On **February 9**, Hearst's *New York World* published a stolen letter from Dupuy de Lome, the Spanish minister to the United States, in which he criticized McKinley's character and implied that the Spanish were not serious about resolving the Cuban crisis through negotiation and reform.

McKinley's aim was not to prompt a war, but to force Spain into concessions that would satisfy the Cuban rebels and bring an end to conflict. In accordance with this plan, he ordered the battleship *Maine* into the Havana harbor to protect U.S. citizens and their property. However, the ship mysteriously exploded on **February 16**, setting off waves of suspicion that led to war with Spain.

On **March 8**, U.S. forces began to mobilize for war and, on **April 11**, McKinley asked Congress for authority to go to war. Congress complied three days later with a war resolution. On **April 24**, Spain responded with a formal declaration of war against the United States.

The main reason for the easy victory against Spain was U.S. naval superiority. In the war's first major battle, a naval engagement in Manila Harbor in the Philippines on **May 1**, Commodore George Dewey's fleet destroyed an entire Spanish fleet and lost only one sailor to heat stroke.

By **July**, Spain lost its will to fight, and the Spanish government asked for peace on **July 18**. On **August 12**, the United States and Spain negotiated an armistice to end the war.

In **October**, at the peace conference in Paris, American diplomats demanded that Spain cede the Philippines to the United States. After two months, the Spanish government agreed to relinquish the colony for $20 million. The Treaty of Paris was signed on **December 10**, ending the war.

The Hawaiian Islands were annexed.

1898–1914

In the case of Cuba, economic dependence followed closely on political subjugation. Between 1898 and 1914, American trade with Cuba increased more than tenfold (from $27 million to $300 million), while investments more than quadrupled (from $50 million to $200 million). The economic, political, and military control that the United States imposed on Cuba would fuel anti-American sentiment for years to come.

1899

The acquisition of the Philippines immediately embroiled the United States in the long, brutal American-Filipino War to subdue Filipino rebels.

On **February 6**, the Senate voted 57 to 27 in favor of the Treaty of Paris, only one vote beyond the minimum two-thirds majority required for ratification. McKinley was unsure about the outcome until the final hours.

1899–1900

Choosing a diplomatic, rather than a military, strategy to achieve its foreign-policy objectives, the United States proposed the policy of the "open door" in China to preserve American economic access to all of China.

1900	Congress passed an act extending U.S. citizenship to all Hawaiian citizens. This legislation put Hawaii on the road to statehood.
	General Arthur MacArthur was appointed commander of the Philippines. His leadership did not lessen the war's ferocity, but he understood that it could not be won by guns alone. During his administration, MacArthur offered amnesty to Filipino guerrillas who agreed to surrender and cultivated close relations with the island's wealthy elite.
	President McKinley supported MacArthur's efforts to build a Filipino constituency sympathetic to the U.S. presence. To that end, he sent William Howard Taft to the islands to establish a civilian government. By the following year, Taft became the colony's first governor-general and declared that he intended to prepare the Filipinos for independence.
	Helping the Cubans achieve independence had been one of the major rationalizations for the war against Spain. But, in 1900, when General Leonard Wood, commander of U.S. forces in Cuba, authorized a constitutional convention of Cubans to write the laws for a Cuban Republic, the McKinley administration made it clear the United States would not relinquish control of the island.
	The U.S. annexed the island of Puerto Rico outright with the Foraker Act. This act, unlike every previous annexation authorized by Congress, contained no provision for making the inhabitants citizens of the United States and, thus, Puerto Rico was designated an unincorporated territory.
	Secretary of State John Hay's open-door policy was challenged by the Chinese. From **May** through **August**, the Boxer Rebellion attempted to rid China of all foreigners and foreign influences.
1901	At McKinley's urging, the U.S. Congress attached the Platt Amendment to an army appropriations bill that outlined three conditions for Cuban independence. The Platt Amendment enjoyed little popularity and narrowly passed.
1901–1904	The Supreme Court upheld the constitutionality of the Foraker Act in a series of historic decisions known as the Insular Cases
1902	In the Philippines, the dual strategy of ruthless war against those who had taken up arms and concessions to those who were willing to live under benevolent American rule crushed the revolt. Though sporadic fighting continued until 1913, American control of the Philippines was secure.
1904	Roosevelt issued a corollary to the Monroe Doctrine, which asserted the right of the United States to prevent European powers from meddling in hemispheric affairs and the right to intervene in the domestic affairs of hemispheric nations to quell disorder and forestall European intervention.

1905   Although Roosevelt was successful in ending the Russo-Japanese War, he subsequently ignored challenges to the sovereignty of weaker Asian nations. In a secret agreement with Japan, the United States agreed that Japan could colonize Korea in return for a Japanese promise not to attack the Philippines.

1906   Roosevelt visited the Panama Canal site and became the first American president to travel overseas while in office.

Roosevelt's success in ending the Russo-Japanese War won him the Nobel Prize for Peace, the first ever awarded to an American.

1906–1907   In **1906**, a San Francisco school ordered the segregation of Asian schoolchildren so that they would not "contaminate" white children. In **1907**, the California state legislature debated a law that would bar Japanese immigrants from entering the state. These events, along with years of racism and hysterical stories in the press culminated in anti-Asian riots in San Francisco and Los Angeles.

1906–1921   The United States intervened in Cuban political affairs a total of five times during these years to protect its economic interests and those of the indigenous ruling class with whom it had become closely allied. The economic, political, and military control that the U.S. imposed on Cuba would fuel anti-American sentiment for years to come.

1907   Outraged by the treatment of its citizens, Japanese militarists began talking of a possible war with the United States. To ease tensions, Roosevelt reached a "gentleman's agreement" with the Japanese, by which the Tokyo government promised to halt the immigration of Japanese adult males to the United States in return for Roosevelt's pledge to end anti-Japanese discrimination.

1908   In the Root-Takahira Agreement, the United States tacitly reversed its earlier stand on the inviolability of Chinese borders by recognizing Japanese expansion into southern Manchuria.

1910   The Mexican Revolution broke out when dictator Porfirio Díaz, who had ruled Mexico for thirty-four years, was overthrown by democratic forces led by Francisco Madero.

1911   The inability of Taft and Knox to grasp the complexities of power politics led to a major diplomatic reversal in East Asia, as Knox's plans for a syndicate collapsed and America's open-door policy was dealt a serious blow.

1912   Knox continued his disastrous diplomatic efforts by attempting to increase American trade with China. This triggered further hostile responses from the Japanese and Russians and ultimately contributed to the collapse of the Chinese government and the onset of the Chinese Revolution.

1912–1933	Except for a brief period in 1925, U.S. troops remained in Nicaragua continuously from 1912 to 1933 to protect American investments and maintain order in Latin America.
1913	Francisco Madero was overthrown by Victoriano Huerta, a conservative general who promised to protect foreign investments. This event relieved dollar diplomats in the Taft administration and in Great Britain. Henry Lane Wilson, the U.S. ambassador to Mexico, helped to engineer the coup. However, before close relations between the United States and Huerta could be worked out, Huerta's men murdered Francisco Madero. President Wilson refused to recognize this government.
1914	In **April**, Wilson seized upon the arrest of several U.S. sailors by Huerta's troops as a reason to send marines to occupy the Mexican port city of Veracruz. The battle brought the two countries dangerously close to war, and Venustiano Carranza was able to take power.
	The Panama Canal opened to great fanfare, enhancing the international prestige of the United States and further strengthening U.S. resolve to preserve political order in Central America and the Caribbean **(August)**.
1915	The United States sent troops to Haiti to put down a revolution and remained as an army of occupation for twenty-one years.
1916	When the people of the Dominican Republic refused to accept a treaty making them more or less an American protectorate, Wilson forced them to accept the rule of an American military government.
1917	Puerto Ricans were granted citizenship in 1917 and were given the right to elect their own governor in 1947. However, they enjoyed fewer political rights than other Americans, and, throughout the century, they endured a poverty rate far exceeding that of the mainland.
	Because the United States was about to enter the First World War, Wilson could not afford a fight with Mexico. So he quietly ordered home U.S. troops in Mexico that were pursuing Pancho Villa. He grudgingly recognized the Carranza government.
1921	The United States paid the Colombian government $25 million as compensation for the loss of Panama. By the time Wilson left office, he had intervened militarily in the Caribbean more often than any American president before him.

GLOSSARY OF IMPORTANT TERMS

Boxers	A Chinese nationalist organization that instigated an uprising to rid China of all foreign influence.

dollar diplomacy	A phrase used to describe the foreign policies of Secretary of State Philander C. Knox under President William H. Taft. This type of diplomacy focused on expanding American investments abroad, especially in Latin America and China.
fueling stations	Bases used to refuel naval and commercial ships, especially coal-burning ships crossing the Pacific.
geopolitician	One who is aware of the relationship between geography and politics as they influence and relate to a country's power and position in the world.
Great White Fleet	The ships sent on a world tour by President Roosevelt to show American military power.
isolationism	A policy of avoiding or abstaining from economic or political relationships or alliances with other countries.
jingoist	A nationalist in Britain, the United States, Germany, France, or Japan in the 1890s. A jingoist thought that a swaggering foreign policy and willingness to go to war would enhance a nation's glory. Constantly on the alert for insults to their country's honor, jingoists were swift to call for military retaliation.
open-door notes	A series of diplomatic notes sent to major powers asking each to open its sphere of influence in regions inside China to merchants of other countries and to respect China's sovereignty. In the second series of open-door notes, these countries were to respect China's political independence and territorial integrity.
Rough Riders	A voluntary cavalry unit that fought in Cuba; it was made up of Ivy League gentlemen, western Indian fighters, and cowboys.
unincorporated territory	The designation given Puerto Rico when it was annexed. It meant that Congress would decide on the type of government for the island and would specify the rights of its inhabitants.
yellow journalism	A type of journalism where stories were embellished with titillating details when the true reports did not seem sensational enough. This type of writing catered to a hunger for "real-life" accounts.

WHO? WHAT? WHERE?

WHO WERE THEY?

Complete each following statement (questions 1–14) by writing the letter preceding the appropriate name in the space provided. Use each answer only once.

    a. Alfred T. Mahan
    b. Arthur MacArthur
    c. Dupuy de Lome

    d. Emilio Aguinaldo
    e. Frederick Jackson Turner
    f. George Dewey
    g. John Hay
    h. John J. Pershing
    i. Jose Santos Zelaya
    j. Philippe Bunau-Varilla
    k. Theodore Roosevelt
    l. Valeriano Weyler
    m. Victoriano Huerta
    n. Woodrow Wilson

_____ 1. Young historian who emphasized the idea that the frontier had been essential to the growth of the economy and the cultivation of democracy.

_____ 2. Most influential imperialist who was convinced that all the world's great empires had relied on their capacity to control the seas.

_____ 3. Leader of the Spanish army in Cuba who forced large numbers of Cubans into concentration camps, where 200,000 died.

_____ 4. Spanish minister to Washington whose stolen letter was published in the *New York World*.

_____ 5. Secretary of state who described the Spanish American War as "a splendid little war."

_____ 6. Commander of the American fleet that destroyed the Spanish fleet in Manila Harbor.

_____ 7. Leader of the movement for Philippine independence.

_____ 8. American commander of the Philippines in 1900 who offered amnesty to Filipino guerrillas who agreed to surrender.

_____ 9. French director of the Compagnie Universelle who encouraged the Panamanian revolt.

_____ 10. First American president to travel overseas while in office.

_____ 11. The Nicaraguan dictator who reportedly was negotiating with a European country to build a second canal. U.S. marines toppled his regime.

_____ 12. President who intervened militarily in the Caribbean more often than any American president before him.

_____ 13. Conservative Mexican general who promised to protect foreign investments in his country.

_____ 14. Commander of the American expeditionary force sent into Mexico to hunt Pancho Villa.

WHAT WAS IT?

Complete each statement that follows (questions 1–10) by writing the letter preceding the appropriate response in the space provided. Use each answer only once.

a. Boxers
b. dollar diplomacy
c. Great White Fleet
d. Hay–Bunau-Varilla Treaty
e. open-door policy
f. Roosevelt Corollary
g. Rough Riders
h. Teller Amendment
i. United Fruit
j. yellow journalism

_____ 1. Newspaper style with stories that were embellished with titillating details.

_____ 2. Part of the war resolution that said the United States would not use the war with Spain to acquire part of Cuba.

_____ 3. Voluntary cavalry unit that fought in Cuba and was made up of Ivy League gentlemen, western Indian fighters, and cowboys.

_____ 4. This was contained in a series of diplomatic notes to each of the major powers, asking each to open its sphere of influence to the merchants of other countries.

_____ 5. Chinese nationalist organization that sparked an uprising to rid China of all foreign influence.

_____ 6. Statement that the United States had the right to intervene in the domestic affairs of Western Hemisphere nations to quell disorder and forestall European intervention.

_____ 7. Treaty known in Panamanian history as "the treaty which no Panamanian signed."

_____ 8. Ships sent on a world tour by Roosevelt to show American military power.

_____ 9. Term used to describe the foreign policies of Secretary of State Philander C. Knox, who was interested in expanding American investments abroad.

_____ 10. The Boston company that established extensive banana plantations in Central America.

WHERE WAS IT?

Complete each statement that follows (questions 1–12) by writing the letter preceding the appropriate response in the space provided. Use each answer only once.

a. Beijing
b. China
c. Columbus, New Mexico
d. Danish West Indies
e. Dominican Republic
f. Hawaii
g. Pago Pago
h. Paris
i. Philippines
j. Portsmouth, New Hampshire

k. San Francisco, California

l. Veracruz

_____ 1. Area toward which American Protestant missionaries directed much of their attention.

_____ 2. Superb deep-water harbor on Samoa.

_____ 3. Location of the treaty negotiations that ended the Spanish-American War.

_____ 4. Region that American imperialists viewed as integral to the extension of American interests in Asia.

_____ 5. Only area acquired during the McKinley administration that would be allowed to follow the traditional path to statehood.

_____ 6. City where foreign legations were besieged by Boxers and had to be rescued by military expeditionary forces that included five thousand Americans.

_____ 7. Small Latin American nation where the United States assumed control of its customs collections and used the money to pay European creditors.

_____ 8. Location of negotiations led by Roosevelt that ended the Russo-Japanese War.

_____ 9. City where the local school board caused major diplomatic problems by ordering Japanese children segregated from white children.

_____ 10. Area purchased during Wilson's administration and renamed the Virgin Islands.

_____ 11. Mexican port Wilson ordered seized to prevent a German ship from unloading munitions.

_____ 12. Town attacked by Mexican rebel Pancho Villa where seventeen people were killed.

CHARTS, MAPS, AND ILLUSTRATIONS

1. The leading American export in 1875 was _____.

   Was it the same item in 1915? _____.

2. The year in which naval expenditures exceeded 20 percent of total federal expenditures was _____.

3. Two areas acquired by the United States in 1898 and 1899 in the Pacific were _____ and _____.

4. Two areas in Latin America where the United States intervened between 1898 and 1934 were _____ and _____.

5. The geographic region where the greatest amount of American capital was invested abroad was _____.

   The type of business in which the largest amount was invested was _____.

MULTIPLE CHOICE

Circle the letter that best completes each statement.

1. For much of the nineteenth century, most Americans were preoccupied with continental expansion for all of the following reasons, except
   a. Americans treasured their distance from Europe's corrupt societies, monarchical governments, and petty wars.
   b. Elections always turned on international events, and presidents often made their reputations as statesmen in the world arena.
   c. The diplomatic corps, like most agencies of the federal government, was small and inexperienced.
   d. The government possessed virtually no capacity or desire to project its limited military power overseas.

2. Which of the following groups was among the most active in promoting American interests abroad?
   a. conservationists
   b. railroad tycoons
   c. socialists
   d. Protestant missionaries

3. To construct a navy capable of transforming the United States into a world power, all of the following ingredients would be necessary, except
   a. technical support from European engineers.
   b. funding.
   c. a trans-isthmian canal in Central America through which U.S. warships could pass swiftly from the Atlantic to the Pacific.
   d. a string of far-flung service bases from the Caribbean to the southwestern Pacific.

4. Which of the following terms was coined in England in the 1890s and referred to nationalists who thought that a swaggering foreign policy and a willingness to go to war would enhance their nation's glory?
   a. carpetbaggers
   b. war hawks
   c. jingoists
   d. abolitionists

5. Who were the two publishers responsible for transforming newspaper publishing by engaging in "yellow journalism"?
   a. Andrew Carnegie and Samuel Gompers
   b. William Randolph Hearst and Joseph Pulitzer
   c. James J. Hill and Frederick Jackson Turner
   d. George Dewey and Leonard Wood

6. McKinley ordered a battleship into Havana Harbor to protect U.S. citizens and their property. However, the ship mysteriously exploded, setting off waves of suspicion. What was the name of the battleship?
   a. *Mayflower*

b. *Maine*
c. *Oregon*
d. *Alabama*

7. On March 8,1898, Congress responded to the demand for war brought about by the de Lome letter and the *Maine* incident by authorizing $50 million to mobilize U.S. forces. In the meantime, McKinley notified Spain of his conditions for avoiding war. Which of the following was not a condition cited by McKinley?
   a. Spain must pay an indemnity for the *Maine*.
   b. Spain must abandon its concentration camps.
   c. Spain must end fighting with the rebels.
   d. Spain must commit itself to Spanish domination in Cuba.

8. The main reason for the easy U.S. victory in the war with Spain was
   a. U.S. naval superiority.
   b. U.S. ground forces.
   c. bad weather.
   d. unskilled Cuban rebels.

9. On the eve of war with Spain, the U.S. Army consisted of only 26,000 troops, skilled at skirmishing with Indians but ill-prepared and ill-equipped for all-out war. Which of the following statements incorrectly characterizes U.S. forces on land?
   a. Outfitting, training, and transporting new U.S. recruits overwhelmed the army's capacities, and the army was unprepared for the effects of malaria and other tropical diseases.
   b. U.S. land forces outnumbered Spanish regulars by seven to one.
   c. The U.S. standard-issue, blue-flannel uniforms proved too heavy for fighting in Cuba and rations were very poor.
   d. Most of the volunteers had to make do with ancient Civil War rifles that still used black, rather than smokeless, powder.

10. The armistice between the United States and Spain required all of the following, except for Spain to
    a. relinquish its claim to Cuba.
    b. cede Puerto Rico and the Pacific island of Guam to the United States.
    c. make reparation payments to the United States.
    d. tolerate the American occupation of Manila until a peace conference could convene.

11. In the December 10, 1898, Treaty of Paris, the United States acquired all of the following territory except
    a. the Philippines.
    b. Guam.
    c. Alaska.
    d. Puerto Rico.

12. The Anti-Imperialist League, based in the Northeast, did not enlist support from
    a. Grover Cleveland.
    b. Andrew Carnegie.

c. Samuel Gompers.
d. Alfred Thayer Mahan.

13. At McKinley's urging, the U.S. Congress attached to an army appropriations bill the Platt Amendment, outlining three conditions for Cuban independence. Which of the following statements was not included as a condition?
   a. Cuba would not be allowed to make treaties with foreign powers.
   b. Cuba's sugar industry would no longer depend on the U.S. market.
   c. The U.S. would have broad powers to intervene in Cuban political and economic affairs.
   d. Cuba would have to sell or lease land to the United States for naval stations.

14. The relationship between Puerto Rico and the United States differed from that between Cuba and the United States in all of the following ways, except
   a. The United States did not think independence was appropriate for Puerto Rico.
   b. The United States did not follow its Cuban strategy by granting Puerto Rico nominal independence under informal economic and political controls.
   c. The United States refused to annex Puerto Rico outright; instead, Congress made provision for giving the inhabitants American citizenship.
   d. Congress dictated Puerto Rico's government, specified the rights of its inhabitants, and did not allow the people of the island to have any role in designing their own government.

15. With the Foraker Act, Congress, in effect, had invented a new authoritarian mechanism for ensuring sovereignty over lands deemed vital to U.S. economic and military security. The Supreme Court upheld the constitutionality of this mechanism in a series of historic decisions known as the
   a. Pentagon cases.
   b. Civil Rights cases.
   c. Insular cases.
   d. Foraker cases.

16. The United States was concerned that the actions of the other world powers in China would block its own efforts to open China's markets to American goods. This concern was based on the actions of Britain, Germany, Japan, Russia, and France—each coveting its own area of China, where it could do all of the following, except
   a. establish Protestant churches.
   b. monopolize trade.
   c. exploit cheap labor.
   d. establish military bases.

17. Who sent "open-door" notes to the major world powers asking them to open their spheres of influence to the merchants of other nations, to grant reasonable harbor fees and railroad rates, and to respect China's sovereignty by enforcing Chinese tariff duties in the territory it controlled?
   a. Leonard Wood
   b. James Bryce

    c. Philander C. Knox

    d. John Hay

18. Theodore Roosevelt was a driving force in the transformation of U.S. foreign policy. Which of the following statements is an incorrect characterization of him?

    a. Roosevelt was very concerned for the interests of less-powerful nations, and he exhibited patience with the claims to sovereignty of small countries and their human rights—whether or not they threatened the world order.

    b. He fervently believed that the Anglo-Saxon character of America made it destined for international supremacy in both economic and political affairs. A nation, like an individual, had to strive for greatness.

    c. He was a shrewd analyst of international relations and intended to maximize the country's advantages in the world political economy, but not at the expense of world order.

    d. He sought to bring about a balance of power among the great industrial nations through negotiation rather than through war.

19. The Panama Canal shortened the voyage from San Francisco to New York by approximately

    a. 1,000 miles.

    b. 2,300 miles.

    c. 4,000 miles.

    d. 8,000 miles.

20. Which two countries did Roosevelt perceive as the chief threats to the Open Door policy in China?

    a. Australia and Argentina

    b. Germany and Switzerland

    c. England and France

    d. Russia and Japan

21. Roosevelt entered into secret negotiations to arrange for peace in East Asia. The compromise resulted in all of the following terms, except a settlement that

    a. awarded Japan the chief prize of Korea, but also allowed Japan to control the southern part of Sakhalin Island, Port Arthur, and the South Manchurian Railroad.

    b. required Russia to pay Japan a huge indemnity and turned control of Siberia over to Japan.

    c. protected China's territorial integrity by inducing the armies of both Russia and Japan to abandon Manchuria.

    d. favored Japan by perpetuating its control over most of the territories it had won during the brief Russo-Japanese War.

22. Who was the first American to earn the Nobel Prize for Peace?

    a. Linus Pauling

    b. Henry Kissinger

    c. Theodore Roosevelt

    d. Woodrow Wilson

23. In Roosevelt's eyes, the overriding need to maintain peace with Japan justified ignoring the claims of Korea and, increasingly, those of China for all of the following reasons, except
    a. Roosevelt believed that the Japanese bid for world-power status could not be stopped.
    b. Roosevelt regarded Japanese expansion into East Asia as a natural expression of Japan's imperial ambition.
    c. Roosevelt believed the task of American diplomacy first was to allow the Japanese to build a sphere of influence in East Asia and second was to encourage them to join the United States in pursuing peace rather than war.
    d. Roosevelt was skeptical of Japan's industrial and military strength.

24. The Mexican Revolution broke out in 1910 when dictator Porfirio Díaz, who had ruled for thirty-four years, was overthrown by democratic forces led by
    a. Francisco Madero.
    b. José Santos Zelaya.
    c. Victoriano Huerta.
    d. Francisco "Pancho" Villa.

25. Who was the U.S. ambassador to Mexico who participated in an attempt to engineer Victoriano Huerta's coup?
    a. John Hay
    b. Elihu Root
    c. Henry Lane Wilson
    d. James Bryce

26. Although Huerta briefly wore the mantle of "defender of Mexico's honor," the Veracruz incident ultimately weakened and embarrassed his regime to the point where
    a. Venustiano Carranza was able to take power.
    b. Valeriano Weyler was able to take power.
    c. Emilio Aguinaldo was able to take power.
    d. Porfirio Díaz was able to take power.

27. In 1917, Wilson quietly ordered U.S. troops home and grudgingly recognized the Carranza government because
    a. under Carranza's leadership, the U.S. would lose a fight with Mexico.
    b. U.S. citizens demonstrated against Wilson's continued involvement in Mexico.
    c. the United States was about to enter the First World War and he could not afford a fight with Mexico.
    d. Carranza seemed more willing than Pancho Villa to protect U.S. oil interests.

ESSAY

Description and Explanation (one- to two-paragraph essay)

1. Describe the many problems of the United States Army during the Spanish-American War.

2. Describe the motivations of the anti-imperialists.

3. Evaluate the turn in United States foreign policy after 1898. Was it a good decision?

4. Describe Roosevelt's view of diplomacy and foreign affairs.

5. Describe Roosevelt's role in the Panamanian situation.

6. Describe Roosevelt's handling of Japan as a significant part of his foreign policy.

7. Describe American relations with Mexico under President Wilson.

Discussion and Analysis (class discussion or one- to two-paragraph essay)

1. Discuss the groups interested in extending America's business and imperialist role abroad, especially missionaries, businessmen, and imperialists.

2. Discuss how Americans' racial views of "inferior people" affected their views of black soldiers in the Spanish-American War and their view of Filipino readiness for independence.

3. Compare the activities of the United States in dealing with China under Roosevelt and Taft, including the motivations, activities, and successes or failures.

What If (include an explanation of your position)

1. If you were a young African-American male enlisted in the 10th Cavalry, would you be proud of the role of your unit in Cuba? Would you be pleased with your treatment by the American military?

2. If you were President Theodore Roosevelt dealing with the Asian situation, would you consider Japan a threat for the future? Would you deliberately work to compromise with the Japanese?

3. If you were a Mexican citizen between 1913 and 1917, what would your opinion of the United States and President Wilson be?

Crossword Puzzle: Becoming a World Power, 1898–1917

DOWN

1. U.S. ___ kept Díaz in power in Nicaragua.
2. People affected by Platt Amendment
3. Amendment that disclaimed territorial gains for U.S.
4. Leonard Wood's cavalry (2 wds.)
5. Hearst rival
7. Source of "yellow peril"
10. Key words in Mahan title (2 wds.)
14. Anti-imperialist who switched to supporting Treaty of Paris
15. De Lome's mistake
16. Invention that helped end U.S. isolation
18. Goal of open-door notes was U.S. ___ with China.
19. Great White ___ was U.S. show of strength.

ACROSS

1. Philippine conqueror
6. Pearl Harbor site
8. Adjective for Boxers in 1900
9. World War II abbreviation
10. Compass pt.
11. Island nation occupied by U.S. 1915–1936
12. Roosevelot approved Japanese sphere of influence in ____ Asia.
13. Army uniforms were better suited for northern ____ than tropical Cuba.
17. Nobel Peace Prize winner of _____, 1906
20. Black troops may have been the ___ in war with Spain.
21. Hay's department
22. ___ of Spanish fleet from Santiago ended in its destruction.

ANSWER KEY

WHO? WHAT? WHERE?

Who Were They?

1. e. Frederick Jackson Turner, p. 749
2. a. Alfred T. Mahan, p. 750
3. l. Valeriano Weyler, p. 752
4. c. Dupuy de Lome, p. 753
5. g. John Hay, p. 754
6. f. George Dewey, p. 754
7. d. Emilio Aguinaldo, p. 760
8. b. Arthur MacArthur, p. 761
9. j. Philippe Bunau-Varilla, p. 768
10. k. Theodore Roosevelt, p. 769
11. i. José Santos Zelaya, p. 773
12. o. Woodrow Wilson, p. 773
13. m. Victoriano Huerta, p. 773
14. h. John J. Pershing, p. 774

What Was It?

1. j. yellow journalism, p. 753
2. h. Teller Amendment, p. 754
3. g. Rough Riders, p. 755
4. e. Open-Door policy, p. 763
5. a. Boxers, p. 764
6. f. Roosevelt Corollary, p. 765
7. d. Hay–Bunau-Varilla Treaty, pp. 768–769
8. c. Great White Fleet, p. 771
9. b. dollar diplomacy, p. 772
10. i. United Fruit, p. 773

Where Was It?

1. b. China, p. 748
2. g. Pago Pago, p. 751
3. h. Paris, p. 756
4. i. Philippines, p. 756
5. f. Hawaii, p. 762
6. a. Beijing, p. 764
7. e. Dominican Republic, p. 766
8. j. Portsmouth, New Hampshire, p. 770
9. k. San Francisco, California, p. 771
10. d. Danish West Indies, p. 773
11. l. Veracruz, p. 774
12. c. Columbus, New Mexico, p. 774

CHARTS, MAPS, AND ILLUSTRATIONS

1. cotton; yes, p. 750
2. 1905, p. 751
3. Philippine Islands, Guam, Wake Island, Hawaiian Islands, and American Samoa, p. 757
4. Mexico, Nicaragua, Panama, Cuba, Haiti, Dominican Republic, p. 766
5. Latin American and Caribbean; mining and smelting, p. 772

MULTIPLE CHOICE

1. b (p. 747)
2. d (p. 748)
3. a (p. 750)
4. c (p. 752)
5. b (p. 752)

6. b   (p. 753)

7. d   (p. 753)

8. a   (p. 754)

9. b   (p. 754)

10. c   (p. 756)

11. c   (p. 756)

12. d   (p. 757)

13. b   (p. 762)

14. c   (p. 762)

15. c   (p. 762)

16. a   (p. 763)

17. d   (p. 763)

18. a   (pp. 764–765)

19. d   (p. 769)

20. d   (p. 770)

21. b   (p. 770)

22. c   (p. 770)

23. d   (p. 771)

24. a   (p. 773)

25. c   (p. 773)

26. a   (p. 774)

27. c   (p. 775)

ESSAY

Description and Explanation

1. pp. 754–755

2. pp. 757, 760

3. pp. 756–757

4. pp. 764–765

5. pp. 768–769

6. pp. 770–772

7. pp. 773–775

Discussion and Analysis

1. pp. 748–752

2. pp. 755–756, 760–761

3. pp. 770–771, 772–773

What If

1. pp. 755–756

2. p. 770

3. pp. 773–775

Crossword Puzzle

CHAPTER 23

WAR AND SOCIETY, 1914–1920

When war broke out in Europe in 1914, most Americans saw no reason to become involved. President Wilson announced that this was a European war that did not threaten American vital interests—the fight was not over lofty principles. As the conflict wore on, however, it became increasingly difficult to avoid taking sides or to ignore the unprecedented human carnage. Many Americans had strong cultural, economic, and political ties to Britain. Wilson, especially, was an anglophile. The use of the U-boat seemed to confirm that Germans were the aggressors, an attitude not helped by the Germans, who were less adept at manipulating American public opinion. The United States entered the war in 1917.

The United States did not suffer as much from the war as did Europe. Loss of human life was much less and, for the most part, the American civilian population was spared destruction of property, shortages of necessary items, and spread of disease. Still, the war had a profound effect on American society. The country devoted its agricultural, transportable, industrial, and human resources to the war effort. Centralized federal agencies were created to coordinate the war effort with varying degrees of success. To pay for the war, tax rates were sharply increased, and a high-pressure campaign was launched to sell war bonds. The government initiated an extraordinary effort to arouse public support for the war that promoted national unity, but it also developed an intolerant side among many Americans.

President Wilson had a vision of a democratic, just, and harmonious world order free of poverty, ignorance, and war. In the period just after Germany's surrender, Wilson was confident about achieving a just peace. Both Germany and the Allies had publicly accepted his Fourteen Points, containing his ideals of the new world order, as the basis for negotiations conducted in Paris. The Treaty of Versailles, signed with Germany in a suburb of Paris and ending the First World War, was not what Wilson expected, with its war-guilt clause and reparations. He believed that the League of Nations, which was added to the various treaties ending the war, would redeem the failures of the Paris Peace Conference. Serious problems with Republicans and a presidential failure to compromise ended with the rejection of the treaty by the Senate. When the Treaty of Versailles was voted down for the last time, Wilson's dream of a new world order died.

The end of the war brought no respite from the forces that divided American society. Workers were determined to regain the purchasing power they had lost to inflation. Employers were equally determined to halt or reverse the wartime gains labor had made. Radicals saw the possibility of a socialist revolution. Black servicemen were reluctant to return to their inferior prewar status. The "red scare" prompted government officials and private citizens alike to embark on a campaign of repression.

In many ways, the United States benefited a great deal from the war. By 1919, the American economy was the world's largest by far. Many leading corporations improved productivity and management techniques and American banks were highly influential in international finance. This combination of economic factors triggered an extraordinary burst of growth in the next decade. The war, however, exposed class, ethnic, and racial tensions that did not go away.

LIBERTY, EQUALITY, POWER

Wilson advocated a revolutionary change in world order, one that would allow each country, regardless of its size or strength, to achieve political independence and to participate as an equal in world affairs. His "peace without victory" stirred the despairing masses of Europe and inspired many Americans. Wilson gave millions around the world reason to hope that the goals of liberty and equality would be realized.

Industrial workers, women, European ethnics, and African Americans saw through the rhetoric and demanded that America live up to its democratic ideals at home as well as abroad. Women seized upon the new democratic fervor to force the issue of their fight for suffrage. African Americans thought that the war might deliver them from second-class citizenship. European ethnics believed that Wilson's support of their countrymen abroad would improve their own chances for success in America.

Despite President Wilson's hopes to the contrary, however, American society leaned further from tolerance than even before the war. German Americans became the objects of popular hatred. Foreign-language publications were required to submit all war-related stories to censors for approval. Immigrants were forced to repudiate ties to their homeland, native languages, and ethnic customs. The anti-German campaign escalated into a general anti-immigrant crusade, and immigration was limited severely by new congressional acts. Congress gave the Wilson administration sweeping powers to silence and even imprison dissenters. It was illegal to write or utter any statement that could be construed as profaning the flag, the Constitution, or the military, constituting the most drastic restriction of free speech at the national level since the enactment of the Alien and Sedition Acts of 1798. This official repression, carried out in an atmosphere of supercharged patriotism, unleashed wave after wave of persecution carried out by the people themselves. Instead of the liberty, equality, or power desired by millions, the war caused serious repression and intolerance in some areas.

OBJECTIVES

After studying this chapter, a student should be able to

1. Describe the outbreak of World War I in Europe and how the different stages evolved.

2. Explain the strong ties between the U.S. and Great Britain.

3. Analyze America's role as a neutral.

4. Explore the question of how Wilson's administration organized the economy and home front for the war and how well the various agencies worked.

5. Discuss the activities of the Committee on Public Information and the results of these.

6. Describe the role of the Republicans in the ratification of the Treaty of Versailles.

7. Analyze the "red scare" and the repression of different groups.

CHRONOLOGY

1914

In Sarajevo, Bosnia, a Serbian nationalist assassinated Archduke Franz Ferdinand, heir to the Austro-Hungarian throne (**June 28**). On **July 28**, Austria declared war on Serbia, holding it responsible for the murder of the archduke. The conflict might have remained local had not an intricate series of treaties divided Europe into two hostile camps.

Russia, part of the Triple Entente, was obligated by a treaty to defend Serbia against Austria-Hungary. On **July 30**, it mobilized its armed forces to aid Serbia. As a result, Germany was brought into the conflict to protect Austria-Hungary from Russian attack. On **August 3**, German troops struck not at Russia itself but at France, Russia's western ally. The following day, Britain reacted by declaring war on Germany, and, within the space of only a few weeks, Europe found itself inextricably involved in war.

When war broke out in Europe, most Americans at first saw no reason for involvement. Wilson declared that this was a European war.

The United States exported more than $800 million in goods to Britain and its allies, compared with $170 million to the Central Powers. The United States and Great Britain shared a prosperous economic relationship and American manufacturers and investors supported Great Britain rather than Germany.

1914–1918

The outbreak of war strengthened the power of workers; the war constricted the flow of European immigrants to America, and war orders from Europe prompted manufacturers to expand their production facilities and workforces. The number of European immigrants dropped from more than a million in 1914, to 200,000 in **1915**, and to 31,000 in **1918**. That meant that three million potential workers were lost to U.S. industry, not counting another five million workers lost to military services from **1917** to **1918**.

1915

To combat British control of the seas and to check the flow of U.S. goods to the Allies, Germany announced its intent to use its *Unterseeboot*, or U-boat, to sink any enemy ships en route to the British Isles. On **May 7**, without warning, a German U-boat torpedoed the British passenger liner *Lusitania* en route from New York to London. The ship sank in twenty-two minutes, killing 1,198 men, women, and children; 128 of them U.S. citizens. Americans were shocked and viewed the incident as cold-blooded murder.

1915–1920   Unemployment, which had hovered at around 8.5 percent in 1915, fell to 1.2 percent in 1918. Wages rose an average of 137 percent from 1915 to 1920, though post-war inflation largely negated these gains.

1916   The Allies began to arm their merchant vessels with guns and depth charges capable of destroying German U-boats. Germany considered this a provocation and renewed its campaign of surprise submarine attacks.

In **March**, a German submarine torpedoed the French passenger liner *Sussex*, causing a heavy loss of life and injuring several Americans. President Wilson demanded that Germany spare civilians from attack, and Germany once again relented. However, in the so-called *Sussex* pledge, Germany warned that it might resume unrestricted submarine warfare if the United States did not prevail on Great Britain to permit neutral ships to pass through the naval blockade.

By this time, relentless German submarine attacks forced President Wilson to conclude that America must prepare itself to fight. Between **January** and **September**, Wilson sought and won congressional approval of bills to increase the size of the army and navy and to tighten federal control over National Guard forces. In **October** the Council of National Defense was created to advise him of matters regarding war mobilization.

President Wilson did not share in the belief that war with Germany was both inevitable and desirable. Thus, he began to step up his diplomatic initiatives to forestall the necessity of American military involvement. In **January**, he sent Colonel House to London to draw up a peace plan with British Foreign Secretary Lord Grey. On **February 22**, this collaboration resulted in the House-Grey memorandum.

England brutally crushed the "Easter Rebellion" that Irish nationalists launched on Easter Monday to win their country's independence. Both the Irish in America and those in Ireland wanted to see Britain's strength reduced (and Ireland's prospects for freedom enhanced) by a long war.

In a major foreign policy address on **May 27**, Wilson formally declared his support for a League of Nations, an international parliament dedicated to the pursuit of peace, security, and justice for all the world's peoples.

The U.S. economy enjoyed a great boom during the war. Banks issued loans to the Allied powers once Wilson permitted them to do so in 1915, further knitting together the American and British economies. The British navy blockaded German ports, further limiting U.S. trade with Germany. By 1916, U.S. exports to the Central Powers had dropped to barely $1 million, a fall of more than ninety-nine percent in two years.

Wilson was portrayed as the peace president and, with a campaign slogan of "He kept us out of war," won reelection.

On **December 16**, Wilson intensified his quest for peace by sending a peace note to the belligerent governments, appealing to them to consider ending the conflict and to state their terms. Britain and France responded with a set of conditions too harsh for Germany ever to accept, but Wilson pressed on by secretly negotiating for peace with both sides.

1917

In early **January,** the German government embarked on a bold strategy to crush the Allies, and, sensing the imminent collapse of Russian forces on the eastern front, Germany decided to throw its full military might at France and Britain.

President Wilson outlined his plans for a possible peace before the Senate on **January 22**. In his speech, he reaffirmed his commitment to a League of Nations as an institution capable of preserving peace and listed the crucial principles of a lasting peace: freedom of the seas; disarmament; and, for all countries, the right to self-determination, democratic self-government, and security against aggression.

The U.S. learned of Germany's intention to resume unrestricted submarine warfare and on **February 1** broke off diplomatic relations. Wilson continued to hope for a negotiated settlement but, on **February 25**, the British showed him the "Zimmermann telegram," which asked Mexico to attack the United States in the event of war between Germany and America.

In **March**, news arrived that Tsar Nicholas II's autocratic regime in Russia had collapsed and he had been replaced by a liberal, democratic government under the leadership of Alexander Kerensky. The fall of the tsar and the need of Russia's fledgling government for support gave Wilson the rationale he needed to justify American intervention to Congress on **April 2**.

On **April 6**, Congress voted to declare war by a vote of 373 to 50 in the House and 82 to 6 in the Senate. The U.S. entry gave the Allies the muscle needed to defeat the Central Powers, but it almost came too late. Germany's resumption of unrestricted submarine warfare took a heavy toll. From **February** through **July**, German subs sank almost four million tons of shipments, more than one-third of Britain's entire merchant fleet.

The Selective Service Act empowered the administration to register men eighteen years and older for military service. By war's end, twenty-four million men had been registered, three million had been drafted, and another two million had volunteered for service.

Wilson became the first president to address a convention of the American Federation of Labor.

Wilson set up a new agency, the Committee on Public Information (CPI), to publicize and popularize the war. Under the chairmanship of George Creel, a Progressive muckraker, the CPI conducted an unprecedented whirlwind propaganda campaign.

The U.S. and British navies began to use sound waves (later called sonar) to pinpoint the location of underwater craft, and this new technology increased the effectiveness of destroyer attacks. By the end of **1917**, the tonnage of Allied shipping lost each month to U-boat attacks declined by two-thirds, from almost one million tons in **April** to 350,000 tons in **December**. The increased flow of supplies stiffened the resolve of exhausted British and French troops.

A second Russian revolution in **November** overthrew Kerensky's government and brought to power a revolutionary socialist government under Vladimir Lenin and his Bolshevik Party.

Congress passed the Immigration Restriction Act, over Wilson's veto, which escalated the general anti-immigrant crusade and marked the beginning of a movement in Congress that, four years later, would close the immigration door to virtually all transoceanic peoples.

1917–1918   Congress passed the Espionage, Sabotage, and Sedition Acts, giving the Wilson administration sweeping powers to silence and even to imprison dissenters. These acts made it illegal to write or utter any statement that could be construed as profaning the flag, the Constitution, or the military. These constituted the most dramatic restriction of free speech at the national level since enactment of the Alien and Sedition Acts of 1798.

1918   In **January**, President Wilson reaffirmed the American commitment to the New Diplomacy and rejected territorial expansion as a war aim in his Fourteen Points.

Vladimir Lenin pulled Russia out of the war and, in **March**, signed a treaty at Brest-Litovsk that added to Germany's territory and resources and enabled Germany to shift its eastern forces to the western front. Russia's exit from the war dealt a severe blow to the Allies.

Germany launched a huge offensive against British and French positions that reached within striking distance of Paris. At this point, a large, fresh American army arrived to reinforce the remaining French lines.

In **September**, the Allied troops staged a major offensive of their own, advancing across the Argonne forest in France. By late **October**, they had reached the German border. Faced with an invasion of their homeland and with rapidly mounting popular dissatisfaction with the war, German leaders asked for an armistice, to be followed by peace negotiations. After the Germans accepted numerous concessions, the war was ended on **November 11**.

In the regular congressional elections, the Republicans won a majority in both houses of Congress. The victorious Republicans were hostile to Wilson because the President had said that a Republican victory would embarrass the U.S. abroad.

1919

To capitalize on his fame and to maximize the chances for peace based on his Fourteen Points, Wilson broke sharply with diplomatic precedent and decided to head the American delegation to the Paris Peace Conference in **January** himself.

For a time, the military justified its discrimination against blacks with the use of crude IQ, or intelligence, tests that were administered by psychologists. This approach finally was rejected and the program was discontinued in 1919.

The Eighteenth Amendment was ratified quickly by the states, and Prohibition became the law of the land.

The Treaty of Versailles was signed by Great Britain, France, the United States, Germany, and other nations on **June 28**.

Racial tensions escalated into race riots during the summer months. The deadliest violence occurred in Chicago, where riots broke out across the city and lasted for five days.

Facing serious opposition from the Republican-controlled Senate, President Wilson undertook a whirlwind cross-country tour in **September** to speak directly to the public regarding the treaty. The trip took a fatal toll on Wilson's health. On **October 2**, he suffered a near-fatal stroke, and remained partially paralyzed until his death in 1924.

After refusing to consider Republican amendments to the treaty, Wilson ordered Senate Democrats in **November** to vote against the amended version. Immediately, the unamended version was voted down.

Four million workers went on strike. This was one-fifth of the country's manufacturing workers.

The American economy was the strongest in the world.

1919–1920

Americans feared a perceived threat of internal subversion known as the "red scare." Attorney General A. Mitchell Palmer fostered public hysteria and blamed internal problems on "revolutionary activity."

1920

Wilson's last-ditch effort for ratification of the Treaty of Versailles and his dream of a new world order died in the Senate on **March 8**, by a margin of seven votes.

Two Italian-born anarchists, Nicola Sacco and Bartolomeo Vanzetti, were arrested and charged with armed robbery and murder in Massachusetts. Both men claimed they were being punished for their political beliefs; however, the men were executed seven years later.

Raids under the direction of Attorney General A. Mitchell Palmer took place in **January**. They broke into homes and meeting places of suspected revolutionaries and arrested six thousand people.

Early 1920s	The Universal Negro Improvement Association enrolled millions of members in seven hundred branches in thirty-eight states.
1921	An Allied commission notified Germany that it was to pay the victors $33 billion, a sum well beyond what a defeated and economically ruined Germany could muster.
1924	Woodrow Wilson died.

GLOSSARY OF IMPORTANT TERMS

covenant
Binding agreement or promise, usually written; organization of the League of Nations was contained in a covenant attached to the Treaty of Versailles.

doughboys
American soldiers during World War I. The term possibly originated with the large buttons on American military uniforms of the 1860s. The buttons resembled fried bread dough.

irreconcilables
A group of fourteen midwesterners and westerners who opposed the Treaty of Versailles in the Senate. Most of them were conservative isolationists who wanted to preserve American separation from Europe.

Liberty Bonds
Thirty-year government bonds sold to individuals with an annual interest rate of three and one-half percent. They were offered in five issues between 1917 and 1920, and their purchase was equated with patriotic duty.

New Diplomacy
Wilson's vision of foreign affairs and a world order in which relations between nations would be governed by negotiation rather than war. Justice would replace power as a fundamental principle of diplomacy.

red scare
Fear of internal subversion. Many Americans assumed that there existed a radical movement determined to establish a Communist government in the United States.

total war
Every combatant or country involved in a war commits virtually all of its resources and population to the war. World War I was considered to be total war.

trench warfare
Type of warfare in which long, narrow ditches are dug by both sides to protect their soldiers. It is used most commonly as a defensive method of fighting, which was the primary focus on the western front of World War I.

universal conscription
Drafting of all men of a certain age, irrespective of their family wealth, ethnic background, or social standing. Wilson was firmly committed to this as a way of raising an American military.

Unterseeboot
Better known as the U-boat; first militarily effective submarine.

WHO? WHAT? WHERE?

WHO WERE THEY?

Complete each statement that follows (questions 1–18) by writing the letter preceding the appropriate name in the space provided. Use each answer only once.

a. A. Mitchell Palmer
b. Alexander Kerensky
c. Alvin York
d. Arthur Zimmermann
e. Bernard Baruch
f. Calvin Coolidge
g. Eugene V. Debs
h. Edward M. House
i. Henry Cabot Lodge
j. Herbert Hoover
k. Jane Addams
l. John J. Pershing
m. Marcus Garvey
n. Martin Glynn
o. Theodore Roosevelt
p. William Jennings Bryan
q. William McAdoo
r. Woodrow Wilson

_____ 1. American politicial leader who was convinced the United States should join the Allies early in the war.

_____ 2. Wilson's closest foreign-policy adviser.

_____ 3. Secretary of state under Wilson who was immune to the appeal of the English.

_____ 4. Founder of the women's Peace Party.

_____ 5. Irish-American governor of New York who nominated Wilson for a second term.

_____ 6. German foreign secretary who sent a telegram to the German minister in Mexico to ask the Mexican government to attack the United States in the event of a war between the United States and Germany.

_____ 7. Leader of the liberal, democratic government that replaced the tsar of Russia.

_____ 8. Commander of the American Expeditionary Force.

_____ 9. Head of the Food Administration.

_____ 10. Secretary of the Treasury and head of the U.S. Railroad Administration.

_____ 11. Wall Street investment banker who became chairman of the War Industries Board.

_____ 12. First American president to address a convention of the American Federation of Labor.

_____ 13. Most-decorated soldier in the American military in World War I.

_____ 14. Aging head of the Socialist Party who received a ten-year jail term for an antiwar speech.

_____ 15. Chairman of the Senate Foreign Relations committee who openly opposed Wilson and the Treaty of Versailles.

_____ 16. Governor of Massachusetts who refused to negotiate during the Boston police strike.

_____ 17. Attorney general who directed raids meant to expose revolutionary activities in the United States.

_____ 18. Leader from Jamaica who wanted to help American and Caribbean blacks achieve economic and cultural separatism and self-sufficiency.

WHAT WAS IT?

Complete each following statement (questions 1–10) by writing the letter preceding the appropriate response in the space provided. Use each answer only once.

    a. American Legion
    b. American Protective League
    c. Article X
    d. barbed wire
    e. doughboys
    f. IWW
    g. Trading with the Enemy Act
    h. Universal Negro Improvement Association
    i. War Labor Board

_____ 1. Item that made World War I more of a defensive rather than offensive war.

_____ 2. Term used to describe American soldiers during World War I.

_____ 3. Group that brought together representatives of labor, industry, and the public to resolve disputes.

_____ 4. Requirement that foreign-language publications submit war-related stories to censors for approval.

_____ 5. Labor group that the federal government persecuted severely.

_____ 6. Largest patriotic organization—functioned as an agency of surveillance during the war.

_____ 7. Part of the Covenant of the League of Nations that maintained that aggression would be subject to economic isolation and military retaliation.

_____ 8. Newly formed veterans' organization that took over the postwar role of encouraging American nationalism.

_____ 9. Group that enrolled millions in 700 local branches of the organization, published a newspaper with a circulation of 200,000, and owned a shipping company.

WHERE WAS IT?

Complete each statement below (questions 1–9) by writing the letter preceding the appropriate response in the space provided. Use each answer only once.

   a. Argonne forest
   b. Boston, Massachusetts
   c. Chicago, Illinois
   d. Gary, Indiana
   e. Italy
   f. Marne River
   g. Ottoman Empire
   h. Paris, France
   i. Pueblo, Colorado

_____ 1. One of the two empires that was in its final stage of disintegration in the Balkan area of Europe.

_____ 2. European country that dropped out of the Triple Alliance.

_____ 3. Closest the German army got to Paris before it was stopped.

_____ 4. Two-hundred-mile–wide area through which the German supply line ran. Cutting this line forced German surrender.

_____ 5. Location of the peace conference ending World War I.

_____ 6. Town where Wilson gave a speech and subsequently was ordered back to Washington by his doctor because of serious physical problems.

_____ 7. City where a major police strike helped turn public opinion against labor.

_____ 8. Location of a confrontation between steel workers and armed guards.

_____ 9. Scene of the most deadly of the postwar race riots.

CHARTS, MAPS, AND ILLUSTRATIONS

1. The trench line of the Western front in 1915 was located primarily in _____ _____ .

2. The first country to use poison gas during a war was _____ .

3. The American city with the largest number of African Americans in 1920 was _____. The U.S. city with the greatest percentage increase in African Americans between 1910 and 1920 was _____ .

4. The occupation with the largest number of women workers in 1920 was _____
   _____.

5. Based on the table of Wilson's Fourteen Points (p. 804), how many were fulfilled?
   _____

6. The steamship line _____ was planned to connect all the African peoples of the world.

MULTIPLE CHOICE

Circle the letter that best completes each statement.

1. What event in 1914 ignited an intricate series of treaties that divided Europe into two hostile camps and precipitated "the Great War"?
   a. the sinking of the *Lusitania*
   b. the British attack on the *Chesapeake*
   c. the assassination of a Serbian nationalist
   d. the assassination of the heir to the Austro-Hungarian throne

2. The Triple Alliance consisted of alliances between
   a. Britain, France, and Russia.
   b. France, Italy, and Switzerland.
   c. Germany, Austria-Hungary, and Italy.
   d. Switzerland, Britain, and Germany.

3. Which countries aligned themselves as part of the Triple Entente?
   a. Britain, France, and Russia
   b. France, Italy, and Switzerland
   c. Germany, Austria-Hungary, and Italy
   d. Switzerland, Britain, and Germany

4. The Triple Entente commonly was referred to as
   a. the Rebels.
   b. the Allies.
   c. the SS.
   d. the Resistance.

5. Many Americans, especially those with economic and political power, identified more closely with the culture of Britain than they did with the culture of Germany for all of the following reasons, except
   a. They shared a common language.
   b. They shared a common ancestry.
   c. They shared a common border.
   d. They shared a commitment to liberty.

6. U.S. officials judged Germany harshly for each of the following reasons, except
   a. They disapproved of Germany's close ties with Britain, France, and Russia.
   b. They disapproved of Germany's acceptance of monarchical rule.

    c. They disapproved of the prominence of militarists in German politics.

    d. They disapproved of the weakness of democratic traditions in Germany

7. To combat British control of the seas and to check the flow of U.S. goods to the Allies, Germany unveiled the first militarily effective submarine called the *Unterseeboot*, or the
   a. E-boat.
   b. S-boat.
   c. W-boat.
   d. U-boat.

8. The German warning in March 1916 that it might resume unrestricted submarine warfare (if the United States did not prevail upon Great Britain to permit neutral ships to pass through the naval blockade) became known as the
   a. Kellogg-Briand Pact.
   b. Roosevelt Corollary.
   c. German covenant.
   d. *Sussex* pledge.

9. Wilson sought and won congressional approval of bills to do all of the following except
   a. to increase the size of the army and navy.
   b. to tighten federal control over National Guard forces.
   c. to authorize the establishment of the Council of National Defense to advise the president of matters of war mobilization.
   d. to create a Central Intelligence Agency (CIA) for the purpose of gathering information and to handle undercover operations.

10. President Wilson appeared before the Senate on January 22, 1917, to outline his plans for a possible peace. In his speech, he reaffirmed his commitment to a League of Nations as an institution capable of preserving peace. Which of the following was not one of his crucial principles of a lasting peace?
    a. freedom of the seas
    b. disarmament
    c. protection of capitalism
    d. the right of all people to self-determination, democratic self-government, and security against aggression

11. A second Russian revolution in November 1917 overthrew the liberal, democratic government and brought to power a revolutionary, socialist government under the Bolshevik leader
    a. Mikhail Gorbachev.
    b. Nicholas II.
    c. Vladimir Lenin.
    d. Joseph Stalin.

12. In January 1918, President Wilson reaffirmed the American commitment to the New Diplomacy and rejected territorial expansion as a war aim in his
    a. Fourteen Points.

    b. Points of Light.
    c. New Frontier.
    d. New World Order.

13. The U.S. Railroad Administration was one of many agencies that performed well during the war. Which of the following was not one of its successes?
    a. adding three million miles of track
    b. shifting the rail system from private to public control
    c. coordinating dense rail traffic
    d. making capital improvements that allowed goods to move rapidly to eastern ports

14. Revenues from taxes provided the government with only about one-third of the $33 billion that it ultimately spent on the war. The rest came from the government sale of thirty-year bonds, known as
    a. doughboy bonds.
    b. U.S. savings bonds.
    c. Liberty Bonds.
    d. Allied bonds.

15. Which of the following was not included in the propaganda campaign created by the Committee on Public Information (CPI)?
    a. the distribution of 75 million pamphlets explaining U.S. war aims in several languages
    b. the training of 75,000 "four-minute men" to deliver uplifting war speeches across America
    c. the placing of advertisements in mass-circulated magazines and plastering the walls of every public institution with posters
    d. refusing to deal with members of the press; instead, preferring to release their own war-progress reports

16. By early 1918, the CPI's campaign developed a darker, more coercive side. Its hymns for national unity were accompanied by accusations of ethnic disloyalty and working-class subversion. Which of the following statements does not characterize this "dark side"?
    a. Inflammatory advertisements called on patriots to report on neighbors, co-workers, and ethnics whom they suspected of subverting the war effort.
    b. Propagandists called on all immigrants, especially those from central, southern, and eastern Europe, to repudiate all ties to their homeland, native language, and ethnic customs.
    c. No one ever was arrested for suspected subversive activities.
    d. Congress passed a Trading with the Enemy Act that required foreign-language publications to submit all war-related stories to post office censors for approval.

17. As part of extreme anti-German sentiment, American patriots sought to remove every trace of German influence from American culture. Which of the following was not included in this process?
    a. German Americans were detained in isolated, fenced camps for the duration of the war.

b. German foods that Americans enjoyed were renamed—sauerkraut became "liberty cabbage" and hamburgers became "liberty sandwiches."

c. Libraries removed works of German literature from their shelves, and schools were urged to prohibit the teaching of the German language.

d. German Americans began hiding their ethnic identity, changing their names, speaking German only in the privacy of their homes, and celebrating their holidays only with trusted friends.

18. The anti-German campaign escalated into a general anti-immigration crusade as Congress passed the Immigration Restriction Act of 1917 that resulted in all of the following, except

a. the denial of the right to immigrate to all adults who failed a reading test.

b. a ban on the immigration of laborers from India, Indochina, Afghanistan, Arabia, the East Indies, and several other countries within the "Asiatic barred zone."

c. the declaration of martial law in ethnic neighborhoods.

d. the beginning of a movement in Congress that, four years later, would close the immigration door to virtually all transoceanic peoples.

19. The manufacture and distribution of alcoholic beverages was banned by the

a. Fifteenth Amendment.

b. Sixteenth Amendment.

c. Seventeenth Amendment.

d. Eighteenth Amendment.

20. Congress made it illegal to write or utter any statement that could be construed as profaning the flag, the Constitution, or the military with the

a. Alien and Sedition Acts.

b. Espionage, Sabotage, and Sedition Acts.

c. Jones Act.

d. Wagner Act.

21. Of the original "Big Four" representatives that controlled negotiations at the Paris Peace conference in 1919, which one quit the conference after a dispute—making the Big Four the Big Three?

a. Prime Minister Vittorio Orlando of Italy

b. President Wilson of the United States

c. Premier Georges Clemenceau of France

d. Prime Minister David Lloyd-George of Great Britain

22. Which of the following statements incorrectly characterizes the League of Nations?

a. It was intended to function as an international parliament and judiciary, establishing rules of international behavior and resolving disputes between nations through rational and peaceful means.

b. It included a nine-member executive council; the United States, Britain, France, Italy, and Japan had permanent seats.

c. Four of the nine executive seats would rotate among smaller nations.

d. Wilson's dream of a League of Nations was enhanced by U.S. membership in the organization.

23. U.S. membership in the League of Nations would not have magically solved Europe's postwar problems. This was true for all of the following reasons, except
   a. The U.S. government was experienced in diplomacy and was able to avoid mistakes.
   b. The United States's freedom to negotiate solutions to international disputes would have been limited by the large number of voters who remained strongly opposed to American entanglements in European affairs.
   c. Even if opposition could have been overcome, the United States still would have confronted European countries determined to go their own way.
   d. International organizations are not infallible in their peace-keeping responsibilities.

24. A number of Republicans were more interested in humiliating Wilson than in debating the Treaty of Versailles. They disliked him for all of the following reasons, except
   a. They never liked his domestic policies.
   b. They were angry that he failed to place any distinguished Republicans on the Paris Peace delegation.
   c. They thought his role in the war was too pro-Ally.
   d. They still were bitter about the election of 1918.

25. The chairman of the Senate Foreign Relations Committee did everything possible to stop ratification of the treaty. However, he did not
   a. invite Wilson to address the committee.
   b. pack the committee with senators likely to oppose the treaty.
   c. delay action by reading aloud all three hundred pages of the document.
   d. add nearly fifty amendments to the treaty as a precondition for adoption.

26. Beginning in 1919, Americans were seized by fear concerning a perceived threat of internal subversion, known as the
   a. red scare.
   b. socialist threat.
   c. yellow peril.
   d. Palmer alarm.

27. The postwar repression of radicalism closely resembled the wartime repression of dissent in all of the following ways, except
   a. None of the states participated in passing sedition laws to punish people who advocated revolution.
   b. Public and private groups intensified Americanization campaigns designed to strip foreigners of their "subversive" ways and remake them into loyal citizens.
   c. Universities fired radical professors.
   d. Vigilante groups wrecked the offices of socialists and tortured Industrial Workers of the World (IWW) agitators.

ESSAY

Description and Explanation (one- to two-paragraph essay)

1. Describe the events and issues that led to World War I in Europe.

2. Describe the circumstances surrounding the sinking of the *Lusitania*.

3. Describe the purposes, leaders, and effectiveness of the War Industries Board.

4. Describe the improved role of labor during World War I.

5. Describe ethnic and racial differences in the American military and how they were handled.

6. Describe the two groups of Republican senators opposed to the Treaty of Versailles.

7. Describe the treatment of African Americans just after the war. Did this encourage the black separatist movement?

Discussion and Analysis (class discussion or one- to two-paragraph essay)

1. Discuss the factors encouraging American closeness to Britian.

2. Discuss the activities of the Committee on Public Information and the positive and negative results of these activities.

3. Would American participation in the League of Nations have altered the course of world history significantly?

What If (include an explanation of your position)

1. If you were a male of military age in 1917, would you support or oppose U.S. entry into World War I? Would it be different if you were of German ancestry?

2. If you were an African-American veteran in 1919, what would be your opinion of the way the American military treated the members of your unit? Would you feel welcome in your new home town of Chicago?

3. If you were President Woodrow Wilson at the end of World War I, describe your reaction to the way different groups in the Senate dealt with the Treaty of Versailles.

Crossword Puzzle: War and Society, 1914–1920

DOWN

1. New weapon of World War I (2 wds.)
2. Germany's postwar burden
3. Food administrator
4. Labor's voice on WLB
5. Workplace for Lodge
6. Liberty bond buyer
8. Constitutional first
12. Title for Francis Ferdinand
14. New nation of 1919
17. What seemed to be lacking during World War I
18. An irreconcilable
19. Wilson, Lloyd-George, Clemenceau, and Orlando were the ___ Four.
20. Stalemate

ACROSS

1. AEF commander
5. Freedom of ___ was one of Fourteen Points
7. Have an obligation
9. Part of Garvey's UNIA
10. Rower's need
11. Nicholas II was last one
13. Germany was stripped of its navy and ___ after the war (2 wds.).
15. Top gun, World War I-style
16. One of Zimmermann's "lost provinces"
18. WIB, WLB, and others
19. Police strike city
21. Chosen ones of the Selective Service
22. War profiteer's motive

ANSWER KEY

WHO? WHAT? WHERE?

Who Were They?

1. o. Theodore Roosevelt, p. 780
2. h. Edward M. House, p. 781
3. p. William Jennings Bryan, p. 781
4. k. Jane Addams, p. 783
5. n. Martin Glynn, p. 783
6. d. Arthur Zimmermann, p. 784
7. b. Alexander Kerensky, p. 784
8. l. John J. Pershing, p. 787
9. j. Herbert Hoover, p. 788
10. q. William McAdoo, p. 788
11. e. Bernard Baruch, p. 789
12. r. Woodrow Wilson, pp. 789–790
13. c. Alvin York, pp. 793–794
14. g. Eugene V. Debs, p. 797
15. i. Henry Cabot Lodge, p. 803
16. f. Calvin Coolidge, p. 805
17. a. A. Mitchell Palmer, p. 806
18. m. Marcus Garvey, p. 810

What Was It?

1. d. barbed wire, p. 780
2. e. doughboys, p. 787
3. i. War Labor Board, p. 789
4. g. Trading with the Enemy Act, p. 796
5. f. I.W.W., p. 797
6. b. American Protective League, p. 797
7. c. Article X, p. 803

8. a. American Legion, p. 806
9. h. Universal Negro Improvement Association, p. 810

Where Was It?

1. h. Ottoman Empire, p. 779
2. e. Italy, p. 778
3. f. Marne River, p. 786
4. a. Argonne Forest, p. 787
5. h. Paris, France, p. 801
6. i. Pueblo, Colorado, p. 803
7. b. Boston, Massachusetts, p. 805
8. d. Gary, Indiana, p. 805
9. c. Chicago, Illinois, p. 809

CHARTS, MAPS, AND ILLUSTRATIONS

1. France, p. 779
2. Germany, p. 880
3. New York; Detroit, p. 788
4. semiskilled operatives, p. 791
5. Big Three, p. 800
6. Black Star Line, p. 810

MULTIPLE CHOICE

1. d (p. 778)
2. c (p. 778)
3. a (p. 778)
4. b (p. 778)
5. c (p. 780)
6. a (p. 781)
7. d (p. 781)
8. d (p. 782)

9. d   (p. 782)

10. c   (p. 783)

11. c   (p. 785)

12. a   (pp. 785–786)

13. a   (p. 789)

14. c   (p. 795)

15. d   (pp. 795–796)

16. c   (p. 797)

17. a   (p. 797)

18. c   (p. 797)

19. d   (p. 798)

20. b   (pp. 798–799)

21. a   (p. 801)

22. d   (p. 802)

23. a   (p. 805)

24. c   (p. 804)

25. a   (p. 804)

26. a   (p. 807)

27. a   (p. 807)

Essay

Description and Explanation

1. pp. 778–780

2. p. 781

3. p. 789

4. pp. 790–791

5. pp. 792–793

6. pp. 803–804

7. pp. 808–810

Discussion and Analysis

1. pp. 780–781

2. pp. 795–796

3. pp. 805–806

What If

1. pp. 782, 784–785

2. pp. 792–793, 808–809

3. pp. 802–805

Crossword Puzzle

CHAPTER 24

THE 1920s

The 1920s seemed to be a decade of fun rather than reform, of good times rather than high ideals. Americans devoted more attention to sports heroes and movie stars than to presidents or reformers. The quest for personal gratification replaced the quest for public welfare. Fed by a proliferation of consumer products, the nation rushed headlong away from the past and into the future.

After a period of postwar readjustment, America's economy grew at a remarkable rate. The government helped large corporations and banks to consolidate their power, and corporate America lifted productivity and efficiency to new heights through advances in technology and management. Many Americans believed that it was business that made America great and that it was businessmen who provided the nation with its wisest, most vigorous leadership.

Some Americans deplored the trend toward modernism and tried to revive the values of traditional America with its moral code, set forth in the Bible. Their views were that women were not equal to men, and blacks and immigrants were inferior to Anglo-Saxon whites. They made their voices heard in such movements as the Ku Klux Klan, support for prohibition and immigration restrictions, and fundamentalism. Modernists and traditionalists confronted each other in party politics, in courtrooms, and in the press over such issues as prohibition and evolution. There was a general feeling that the country's economic leadership and vitality had shifted from the rural areas to the urban regions.

Not all Americans benefited from the good times of the 1920s. There were problems with an economic system that lacked adequate regulatory controls, and farmers could not make an adequate living. Skilled industrial workers enjoyed rising wages, but semiskilled and unskilled workers had to contend with seasonal layoffs and a labor surplus throughout the decade. There were attacks on European ethnic groups, especially Catholics and Jews. African Americans and Mexican Americans faced severe discrimination at times. Some white intellectuals felt uneasy in 1920s America; they began to question democracy itself and to disparage rural, small-town America.

LIBERTY, EQUALITY, POWER

In the decade of the 1920s, the period of political reform seemed to be over. Many rural white Protestants believed that the country was being overrun by racially inferior and morally suspect foreigners, European ethnics, Mexican immigrants, and African Americans. This view produced a surge of racial discrimination and religious bigotry. Immigration restrictions enacted in this period deliberately discriminated against those from other parts of the world—certainly not an act mindful of liberty or equality. Catholic ethnics and Jews in the United States, who were favorite targets

125

of the Klan and its politics of hate, responded by strengthening their own cultural institutions and groups. They developed their own political power, and there was a sharp rise in the number of immigrants who became citizens. Catholics and Jews increasingly voted, were active in the national Democratic Party, and, subsequently, grew in power.

Mexican immigrants in the Southwest were seen as a source of cheap, easily manipulated labor, not as future citizens or social equals. African Americans continued to leave rural areas for the industrial centers. They generally found only arduous, low-paying jobs and were forced into urban locations where they suffered the highest rate of residential segregation of any minority group. Despite this, African Americans developed a vigorous and productive culture through music, art, and literature. But they still could not escape white prejudice. Many jazz clubs would not admit blacks as customers, and black intellectuals often were expected to defer to wealthy, white patrons. Overall, there were a great many hardships during the 1920s—signified for many by a substantial lack of liberty, equality, or power.

OBJECTIVES

After studying this chapter, a student should be able to

1. Explain the role of prosperity in the lifestyles of the 1920s, including the role of advertising and consumer credit in this.

2. Examine the role of women in the 1920s.

3. Describe the close connection between business and government in the 1920s.

4. Compare the ideas and effects of associationalism and laissez faire on foreign affairs.

5. Describe the ways rural Americans tried to protect their way of life.

6. Examine the revival of racism and religious bigotry during the 1920s.

7. Describe the development of ethnic cultures in the cities among immigrants, African Americans, and Mexican Americans. Compare them as to political involvement, societal acceptance, economic success, and cultural developments.

CHRONOLOGY

1910s–1920s   To answer to a customer's desires, corporations turned to professional advertising designers to sell their products. Advertising firms first appeared in the 1910s and 1920s and devised advertisement campaigns to evoke the emotions and vulnerabilities of consumers.

1915   William Simmons, a white Southerner who had been inspired by the racist film *Birth of a Nation*, created a new Klan.

1919–1921   The United States experienced economic turmoil and depression for a short time after the war ended. During these years, the country struggled to redirect industry from wartime production to civilian production.

1920

With 61 percent of the popular vote, Republican Warren Harding's election to the presidency was the greatest landslide since 1820.

The Eighteenth Amendment to the Constitution, prohibiting the manufacture and sale of alcohol, went into effect in **January**.

For the first time, a slight majority of Americans lived in urban areas.

1920s

During this decade, growth rested more on the proliferation of consumer goods than on anything else. Some products, such as cars and telephones, had been available since the 1900s, but in the 1920s sales of these items reached new levels. For example, in **1920**, twelve years after Ford introduced the Model-T, there were eight million cars on the road. By **1929**, there were 27 million cars—one for every five Americans.

Middle-class Americans were drawn in by the allure of the stock market, and, by the end of the decade, as many as seven million Americans owned stocks. This widespread ownership of stocks met the need of the nation's corporations for working capital.

Young, liberated, single middle-class women who wore their hair bobbed, raised their hemlines, drank in public, and painted their lips, alarmed those who still clung to Victorian codes of morality.

Though many Americans benefited from the prosperity of this decade, overproduction brought hard times to considerable numbers of farmers after the boom period of the war years. By **1929**, the per capita income of rural America was one quarter that of the nonfarm population.

A majority of industrial workers enjoyed rising wages and a reasonably steady income over the decade. Real wages of skilled craftsmen rose by 30 to 50 percent. However, an estimated 40 percent of the working class, semiskilled and unskilled, remained in poverty.

Despite the urban race riots of **1919**, African Americans continued to leave their rural homes for the industrial centers of the South and the North. In the 1920s alone, nearly a million blacks traveled North.

Blacks enjoyed some important economic breakthroughs during the decade. For example, Henry Ford began hiring large numbers of African-American workers in his Detroit auto factories. However, their strongest gains occurred in terms of black culture. Black musicians coming north brought with them distinctive southern music styles of the blues and ragtime. These harmonies, influenced by European classical music, metamorphosed into jazz. This was also the period of a black literary and artistic awakening known as the Harlem Renaissance.

1920–1929

Federal, state, and local measures to cripple the efforts of organized trade unions, a labor movement slow to open its ranks to semiskilled and unskilled workers, and the decision by workers that they no longer needed unions all combined to induce a decrease in membership, from a high of five million in **1920** to less than three million in **1929**, a mere 10 percent of the nation's industrial workforce.

1920–1930   Thousands of Mexican laborers had built military installations in San Antonio, Texas, during the war, and, by **1920**, the forty thousand immigrants who lived there comprised the largest Mexican community in the United States. As the decade progressed, that distinction shifted to Los Angeles, where a rapidly growing Mexican population reached 100,000 by **1930**.

1921–1922   The Washington Conference on the Limitation of Armaments resulted in a Five-Power Treaty by which the United States, Britain, Japan, France, and Italy agreed to scrap more than two million tons of their warships. Never before had the world powers agreed to such a vast program of disarmament.

1921–1929   During his eight years as secretary of commerce, Republican Herbert Hoover used the department as the grand orchestrator of economic cooperation. However, his dynamic conception of government brought him into conflict with Republicans and President Coolidge, whose shared economic philosophy began and ended with laissez faire.

1922–1929   Beginning in 1922, the United States embarked on a period of remarkable growth. The gross national product grew at an annual rate of 5.5 percent, rising from $149 billion to $227 billion, and the unemployment rate never exceeded 5 percent.

1923   Three years into Harding's presidency, the corruption in his administration could no longer be concealed—even from the president. Suffering from disillusionment and depression over the shady circumstances surrounding his cabinet, Harding fell ill and died of a heart attack. It was not until after his death that the extent of the corruption finally was revealed to the American public **(summer)**.

France sent troops into the Ruhr Valley when Germany suspended its payments on war reparations. This touched off a major crisis in Europe. Secretary of State Charles Evans Hughes forced the French to back down by demanding payment on the French debt to America.

Yankee Stadium opened. Its size dwarfed every other sports amphitheater in the country.

1924   Disgruntled workers and farmers joined forces to form a national Farmer-Labor Party, which for a time threatened to disrupt the country's two-party system in the upper Midwest.

The second Ku Klux Klan expanded its ideological focus from a loathing of blacks to a hatred of Jews and Catholics and increased membership to approximately four million Americans by 1924. In Indiana, voters elected a Klansman to the office of governor.

By the early 1920s, most Americans felt that the country could no longer accommodate the one million immigrants who had been arriving each year prior to the war and more than 800,000 more who arrived in 1921. Congress responded to concerns by passing the Johnson-Reid Immigration Restriction Act of 1924, which would dominate U.S. immigration policy for the next forty years.

The growing national strength of European ethnics first became apparent at the Democratic National Convention, when urban-ethnic delegates almost won approval of planks calling for the repeal of prohibition and condemnation of the Klan.

A group of American bankers produced the Dawes Plan, which reduced annual German reparation payments sharply and called on American and foreign banks to stimulate the German economy.

Calvin Coolidge easily defeated his Democratic opponent, John W. Davis.

1925

Fundamentalists attempted to outlaw the teaching of evolution in public schools. The Scopes trial, held in Dayton, Tennessee, captured national attention when William Jennings Bryan (representing the state) and Clarence Darrow (representing Scopes) clashed in court. The controversy between the two ideologies involved in the Scopes trial proved to have far-reaching effects. Worried over sales, publishers quietly removed all references to Darwin from their science textbooks.

1926

The concept of the annual auto model change was introduced by General Motors. It was used to make a product seem more attractive than the old model or to make consumers feel embarrassed for not having the latest model. The increased sales due to this campaign made GM the world's largest car manufacturer.

President Coolidge was proud of legislation that reduced governmental control over the economy, such as the Revenue Act of 1926. This act reduced the high income and estate taxes that progressives had pushed through Congress during World War I.

Only one-half of coal that was mined was being sold to consumers. New England's textile-producing cities experienced levels of unemployment approaching 50 percent.

1927

A national-origins immigration system reduced the total annual quota of immigrants to 150,000 and reserved more than 120,000 of these slots for immigrants from northwestern Europe.

Hoover was appointed by Coolidge to organize a relief effort when the Mississippi River overflowed its banks in 1927. He successfully persuaded local public and private groups to engage in long-range plans for flood control.

In response to General Motors's precedent-setting annual model change, Henry Ford reluctantly introduced his Model-A. However, he remained skeptical that consumers would spend money on changes he regarded as trivial and irrelevant to a car's utility.

Charles A. Lindbergh became the first individual to cross the Atlantic in a solo flight.

1928   Representatives of the United States, France, and thirteen other nations met in Paris to sign the Kellogg-Briand pact, which committed its signatories to avoid war and settle all international disputes through "pacific means."

At the Democratic Party convention, European ethnics finally were successful in securing the presidential nomination for Al Smith, an Irish-American Catholic. Never before had a major political party nominated a Catholic for such a high office.

1930   Not all Americans shared in the nation's 1920s prosperity. By 1930, 75 percent of American households did not own a washing machine, 70 percent were without a vacuum cleaner, 60 percent did not even own a radio, and 50 percent did without a car.

GLOSSARY OF IMPORTANT TERMS

agrarians   Group of southern writers who argued that the agricultural character of the South offered a more hopeful path to the future than did the mass-consumption society of the North.

associationalism   Term used by historian Ellis Hawley to describe Secretary of Commerce Herbert Hoover's approach to managing the economy in which all types of economic groups formed a trade association whose members would share economic information, discuss problems of production and distribution, and seek ways of achieving greater efficiency and profit. Hoover believed that the very act of cooperation over competition, of negotiation over conflict, of public service over selfishness would achieve greater efficiency and profit.

californios   Spanish-speaking people whose families had been residents of California for many years, often generations.

consumer credit   Also known as the installment plan, consumer credit allowed Americans to purchase consumer goods and products by making a down payment and then paying the remainder in installments.

consumer durables   Term used to describe consumer goods that were meant to last, such as washing machines and radios.

corrido	Type of Mexican folk ballad that emphasized the suffering, hope, and frustration of ordinary folk.
eugenics	Pseudoscience based on the idea that nations could improve the race of their population by pruning some of its weaker racial strains.
flappers	Young, single, middle-class women who wore their hair and dresses short, rolled their stockings down, used cosmetics, and smoked in public. They were signaling their desire for independence and equality, but not through politics. The new female personality was endowed with self-reliance, outspokenness, and a new appreciation for the pleasures of life.
Liberal Protestants	Those who held the belief that religion had to be adapted to the scientific temper of the modern age. The Bible was to be mined for its ethical values rather than for its literal wording.
modern	Term that came into widespread use during the 1920s. Modernity implied that science was a better guide to life than religion, that people should be free to choose their own lifestyle, that sex should be a source of pleasure for both genders, and that women and minorities should enjoy the same rights as white males.
people's capitalism	The philosophy that everyone could own a piece of corporate America, not just a few. All could have a share of the luxuries and amenities of life.
Protestant Fundamentalism	Regarded the Bible as God's word and thus the source of all fundamental truth. Its followers believed that every event depicted in the Bible happened just as the Bible described it.
stretch-out	Term used in the textile industry to describe an increase in the number of spinning or weaving machines each worker was expected to operate. Normally these workers did not receive any higher wages for an increase in their workload.
welfare capitalism	Designed to encourage employee loyalty to the firm and to the capitalist system. Provided increasing benefits and social and recreational activities for workers. Some companies offered stock options as rewards for loyal service. The original motive was fear of unions and the memory of the strikes of 1919. As the decade continued, programs reflected the confidence that capitalism had become humane.
yellow-dog contracts	Written pledges by employees promising not to join a union while they were employed.

WHO? WHAT? WHERE?

WHO WERE THEY?

Complete each statement that follows (questions 1–20) by writing the letter preceding the appropriate name in the space provided. Use each answer only once.

- a. Aaron Douglas
- b. Al Capone
- c. Al Smith
- d. Albert Fall
- e. Aristide Briand
- f. Calvin Coolidge
- g. Charles Dawes
- h. Charles Evans Hughes
- i. Charles R. Forbes
- j. Charlotte Mason
- k. F. Scott Fitzgerald
- l. Gertrude Stein
- m. Harry M. Daugherty
- n. H. L. Mencken
- o. John Dewey
- p. Langston Hughes
- q. Sidney Hillman
- r. Sinclair Lewis
- s. Walter Lippmann
- t. William Simmons

_____ 1. Writer who developed the term "Jazz Age" for the decade of the 1920s.

_____ 2. Author of the quote "The business of America is business."

_____ 3. Leader of Amalgamated Clothing Workers who argued that unionization actually would increase corporate profits.

_____ 4. Head of the powerful Ohio Republican political machine and attorney general under President Harding.

_____ 5. Secretary of interior who persuaded Harding to transfer control of large government oil reserves.

_____ 6. Head of the Veterans Bureau who went to federal prison for swindling the government out of $200 million in hospital supplies.

_____ 7. Secretary of state who consolidated control over foreign affairs and used his office to promote laissez-faire views of foreign affairs.

_____ 8. Chicago banker and chief negotiator at the conference that reduced annual German payments to the Allies.

_____ 9. French foreign minister who helped negotiate a treaty outlawing war as a tool of national policy.

_____ 10. Richest and most-feared gangster in America.

_____ 11. White southerner who created a new Klan in 1915.

_____ 12. Baltimore journalist who was famous for his savage attacks on the alleged stupidity and prudishness of small-town Americans.

_____ 13. First Catholic nominated for president by a major party.

_____ 14. Young black poet and one of the leaders of the Harlem Renaissance.

_____ 15. Artist who fashioned a new painting style through the fusion of African and American materials.

_____ 16. New York City wealthy white matron who financially supported several leaders of the Harlem Renaissance.

_____ 17. Novelist who became famous for creating a series of books that dwelled on the stupidity and chicanery of Americans.

_____ 18. American writer in Paris whose apartment became a gathering place for American intellectuals living in the city.

_____ 19. Former progressive and radical who declared that modern society rendered democracy obsolete.

_____ 20. Columbia University philosopher who spoke of democracy more articulately than did other intellectuals.

WHAT WAS IT?

Complete each following statement (questions 1–12) by writing the letter preceding the appropriate response in the space provided. Use each answer only once.

    a. agrarians
    b. Border Patrol
    c. _corrido_
    d. flappers
    e. General Motors
    f. Harlem Renaissance
    g. K Street House
    h. people's capitalism
    i. The Spirit of St. Louis
    j. tractor
    k. Yankee Stadium
    l. yellow-dog contracts

_____ 1. Idea that everyone, not just a few, could own a piece of corporate America.

_____ 2. Company that introduced the concept of annual model changes.

_____ 3. Young, single middle-class women who were outspoken, wore their dresses short, and used cosmetics.

_____ 4. Largest sports amphitheater in the country.

_____ 5. Single engine monoplane used in a solo flight of the Atlantic.

_____ 6. Written pledges by workers that they would not join a union.

_____ 7. Headquarters of the Ohio Gang, where they drank, gambled, womanized, and got rich selling government appointments.

_____ 8. New technology that greatly increased the acreage each farmer could cultivate.

_____ 9. Agency established that made entry into the United States from Mexico more difficult.

_____ 10. Black literary and artistic awakening in the 1920s.

_____ 11. Type of Mexican folk ballad.

_____ 12. Group of southern writers who argued that the southern agricultural character offered a more hopeful path to the future than did the mass consumption of the North.

WHERE WAS IT?

Complete each following statement (questions 1–10) by writing the letter preceding the appropriate response in the space provided. Use each answer only once.

a. California
b. Dayton, Tennessee
c. Harlem
d. Indiana
e. Los Angeles, California
f. Northwestern Europe
g. Oregon
h. Ruhr Valley
i. San Antonio, Texas
j. Teapot Dome, Wyoming

_____ 1. Location of one of the largest government oil reserves.

_____ 2. Important German industrial area where the French sent troops to force Germany to resume payment of war debts.

_____ 3. State where voters elected a Klansman to the office of governor and sent several other Klan members to the statehouse.

_____ 4. Region that was allowed the largest quotas under the Immigration Restriction Acts.

_____ 5. Town where the Scopes trial was held.

_____ 6. State that passed a law ordering all children aged eight to sixteen to enroll in public schools.

_____ 7. Area in New York City that became the center of African-American urban culture while remaining a ghetto with poverty, diseases, and low life expectancy.

_____ 8. State where Mexican immigrants made up 75 percent of the state's agricultural work-force.

_____ 9. Location of the largest Mexican community in the United States in 1920.

_____ 10. Center of Mexican-American culture in the 1920s.

CHARTS, MAPS, AND ILLUSTRATIONS

1. Compare the pictures of Harding and Coolidge relaxing (pp. 824, 825). Describe two differences between the men. _____

2. The year in which the price of corn was lowest was _____.

3. The city whose regional economic influence covered the largest territorial area was _____.

4. A place where liquor was sold illegally was known as a _____.

5. The two countries with the largest immigration quotas were _____ and _____.

6. The only section of the United States that Al Smith carried in the election of 1928 was _____.

7. The leading cause of death among African Americans in New York City in 1925 was _____.

8. The Spanish-language radio station in 1920s Los Angeles was _____.

MULTIPLE CHOICE

1. Despite the strains placed on the U.S. economy after World War I, it remained strong and innovative during the 1920s for all of the following reasons, except
   a. The nation had suffered some of the loss of factories, roads, and electrical lines that Germany and France had experienced.
   b. The nation's industries had emerged intact, even strengthened, by the war.
   c. The war needs of the Allies had created an insatiable demand for American goods and capital.
   d. Manufacturers and bankers had exported so many loans to the Allies that, by war's end, the United States was the world's largest creditor union.

2. Disgruntled workers and farmers joined forces to form a national Farmer-Labor Party, which, for a time, threatened to disrupt the country's two-party system in the

upper Midwest. In 1924, they received an impressive 16 percent of the presidential vote by running

a. F. Scott Fitzgerald.
b. Robert Lynd.
c. Bruce Barton.
d. Robert LaFollette.

3. What term was coined to describe goods, unlike food or clothing, that were made to last?

a. consumption goods
b. perishables
c. consumer durables
d. marginal product

4. Social scientists Robert and Helen Lynd, in a study of Muncie, Indiana, discovered that when working-class families purchased a major appliance or consumer good they often did not have enough money left for other goods. This classic study of the economics of a small industrial city of 35,000 was entitled

a. *Middletown.*
b. *Main Street.*
c. *Babbitt.*
d. *The Waste Land.*

5. With many industrialists resisting wage increases and workers lacking the organizational strength to demand higher wages, one solution to limited consumer buying power was the introduction of

a. consumer equilibrium.
b. cash transfer.
c. consumer credit.
d. capital account.

6. Advertising firms first appeared in the 1910s and 1920s and were led by people who were well-educated, were sensitive to public taste, and understood human psychology. Examples of these leaders were

a. James Cox, Harry M. Daugherty, and Leonard Wood.
b. Albert Fall, Harry F. Sinclair, and Andrew Mellon.
c. Charles R. Forbes, Ellis Hawley, and Frank Kellogg.
d. Edward Bernays, Doris Fleischmann, and Bruce Barton.

7. All of the following were heroes of the 1920s except

a. Babe Ruth
b. Charles A. Lindbergh
c. John Wayne
d. Jack Dempsey

8. The first woman to fly the Atlantic solo was

a. Julie Nixon
b. Amelia Earhart
c. Gertrude Stein
d. Edith Gault

9. *The Man That Nobody Knows*, a satire on the extreme influence business had on society, was written by
   a. Bruce Barton.
   b. Edward Bernays.
   c. Doris Fleischmann.
   d. Charles Evans Hughes.

10. In the 1920s, the nation's two largest industries were
    a. automobiles and small appliances.
    b. steel and lumber.
    c. coal and textiles.
    d. oil and mining.

11. Which political party controlled the presidency from 1921 to 1933?
    a. Whig
    b. Democrat
    c. Republican
    d. Progressive

12. Which 1920 presidential candidate swept into office with 61 percent of the popular vote, the greatest landslide in a century?
    a. James M. Cox
    b. Eugene V. Debs
    c. Robert M. LaFollette
    d. Warren Harding

13. Which of the following men is matched incorrectly with his position in the 1921 presidential cabinet?
    a. Herbert Hoover—secretary of commerce
    b. Charles Evans Hughes—secretary of state
    c. Andrew Mellon—secretary of the treasury
    d. Harry Daugherty—secretary of the navy

14. Who was the Republican secretary of commerce who did not support Coolidge's belief that the United States could return to the simplicities of the past, because industry had become too powerful and too predatory?
    a. William C. Redfield
    b. Charles Nagel
    c. Herbert Hoover
    d. Joshua W. Alexander

15. Coolidge's secretary of commerce made the department the grand orchestrator of economic cooperation. Which of the following measures was not carried out during Hoover's term as Coolidge's secretary of commerce from 1921 to 1929?
    a. organization of over 250 conferences around such themes as unemployment or the problems of a particular industry or economic sector
    b. gathering of government officials, representatives from business, policy makers, and others who had a stake in strengthening the economy

c. persuasion of farmers to disband cooperatives, which he believed would create problems of inefficiency and overproduction

d. standardization of the size and shape of a great variety of products so as to increase their usefulness and strengthen their sales

16. Which conference in 1921–1922 on the limitation of armaments resulted in a Five-Power Treaty by which the United States, Britain, Japan, France, and Italy agreed to scrap more than two million tons of warships?
a. Paris Peace Conference
b. Washington Conference
c. Panama Conference
d. Yalta Conference

17. Which of the following is not a reason that the 1920s brought hard times to the nation's farmers after the boom period of the war years?
a. European farmers quickly resumed previous levels of production, thus reducing foreign demand for American foodstuffs.
b. A sharp rise in agricultural productivity, made possible by the tractor, flooded the market with produce.
c. Falling prices cut per capita income and forced many farmers to sell out.
d. Various farm areas of the United States were damaged by drought, flooding, and locust infestations.

18. The McNary-Haugen Bill, passed in Congress in 1926 and 1928 and vetoed by the president both times, called on government to
a. buy out bankrupt farmers and bring agriculture under government control.
b. legislate high tariffs on foreign produce and purchase surplus U.S. crops at prices that enabled farmers to cover their production costs.
c. train displaced farmers for jobs in industry and provide subsidies to farmers barely able to make a living as tenants.
d. lower tariffs on foreign produce to help U.S. farmers bring more acreage under cultivation.

19. In the 1920s, control of the second Ku Klux Klan passed to Hiram Evans, and its ideological focus expanded from a loathing of blacks to a hatred of Jews and Catholics. Evans's Klan sought to restore all of the following, except
a. Anglo-Saxon racial "purity."
b. Protestant supremacy.
c. social harmony between races and religions.
d. traditional morality to national life.

20. In 1924, Congress passed the Johnson-Reid Immigration Restriction Act, a basic quota system that resulted in all of the following except
a. It effectively locked out immigrant groups who were poorly represented in the 1890 population—Italians, Greeks, Poles, Slavs, and eastern European Jews.
b. It reaffirmed the long-standing policy of excluding Chinese immigrants and added Japanese and other Asians to the list of ethnic groups barred from entry.

c. It officially limited immigration from nations in the Western Hemisphere.

d. It accomplished Congress's underlying goals of reducing immigration from transoceanic nations by 80 percent.

21. Which of the following statements incorrectly characterizes Protestant Fundamentalists?
    a. They regarded the Bible as God's word and thus as the source of all "fundamental" truth.
    b. They believed in a literal interpretation of events depicted in the Bible.
    c. They considered God a deity whose presence is palpable, who intervenes directly in the lives of individuals, and who makes known both his pleasure and his wrath to those who acknowledge his divinity.
    d. They turned away from a quest for salvation and toward a pursuit of good deeds, social conscience, and love for one's neighbor.

22. Which of the following statements incorrectly characterizes Liberal Protestants?
    a. They believed that sin must be purged actively and salvation must be sought aggressively.
    b. They believed that religion has to be adapted to the skeptical and scientific temper of the modern age.
    c. They removed God from his active role in history and refashioned him into a distant and benign deity who watches over the world but does not intervene to punish or to redeem.
    d. They believed the Bible was to be mined for its ethical values rather than for its literal truth.

23. Though characterized by conflicting beliefs, Liberal Protestants and Fundamentalists both understood that science was the source of all challenges to Christianity. Which of the following statements did not characterize those scientific challenges?
    a. Scientists respected natural law rather than the theory of divine intervention.
    b. Scientists discarded the theory of evolution as blasphemy.
    c. Scientists believed that rational inquiry was a better guide to the past and to the future than prayer and revelation.
    d. Scientists challenged the very idea that God had created the world and had fashioned humans in his own image.

24. In the famous Scopes trial, who was the former secretary of state who represented the state in prosecuting the biology teacher and died of complications of diabetes shortly after the trial?
    a. William Jennings Bryan
    b. Clarence Darrow
    c. John T. Scopes
    d. H. L. Mencken

25. Southern and eastern Europeans everywhere were the objects of intensive Americanization campaigns meant to strip them of their foreign ways. Which of the following incidents was not associated with Americanization campaigns?
    a. States passed laws requiring public schools to instruct children in the essentials of citizenship.

b. Several states extended the required citizenship classes to private schools as well, convinced that Catholic children who attended parochial schools were spending too much time learning about their native religion, language, and country.

c. An Oregon law tried to eliminate Catholic schools altogether by ordering all children aged eight to sixteen to enroll in public schools.

d. Attending a public school represented a guarantee of acceptance into any university, including the elite universities Harvard and Columbia.

26. Who built the strong all-black union known as the Brotherhood of Sleeping Car Porters?
a. A. Philip Randolph
b. Marcus Garvey
c. Neale Huston
d. Aaron Douglas

27. The strongest breakthroughs for African Americans occurred in terms of black culture. Black musicians coming north brought with them distinctive southern music styles of the blues and ragtime. These harmonies, influenced by European classical music, metamorphosed into
a. jazz.
b. big band.
c. rock-and-roll.
d. rap.

28. Which of the following African Americans was not known for his work in the field of music?
a. Langston Hughes
b. Count Basie
c. Duke Ellington
d. Louis Armstrong

29. After enactment of the Johnson-Reid Act of 1924, the country's chief source of immigrant labor came from
a. Canada.
b. China.
c. Mexico.
d. Italy.

30. Which of the following authors is matched incorrectly with his work?
a. T. S. Elliot—*The Waste Land*
b. F. Scott Fitzgerald—*The Great Gatsby*
c. Ernest Hemingway—*A Farewell to Arms*
d. William Faulkner—*Main Street*

ESSAY

Description and Explanation (one- to two-paragraph essay)

1. Describe the effects of the automobile on the American lifestyle.

2. Describe the role of women in the 1920s. How were the new views toward marriage affected by consumer products?

3. Compare Presidents Harding and Coolidge as to personal lifestyles and their views of the economy and government's role in it.

4. Describe Herbert Hoover and associationalism at home and abroad.

5. Describe how laissez faire abroad affected the conduct of foreign affairs.

6. Describe the use of sexual exploitation and lurid tales of financial extortion used by such groups as the Ku Klux Klan.

7. Explain the use of the year 1890 as the base year for immigration quotas under the Johnson-Reid Act.

8. Describe the role of jazz in the development of black culture and what it signified.

Discussion and Analysis (class discussion or one- to two-paragraph essay)

1. Discuss the role of advertising and consumer credit in prompting growth in the economy during the 1920s.

2. Compare Protestant Fundamentalists and Liberal Protestants.

3. Discuss the development of ethnic culture and politics in the cities of the 1920s.

4. Discuss the alienation of American intellectuals in the 1920s and the reasons for it. Was it justified? Why did they question democracy?

What If (include an explanation of your position)

1. If you were President Harding, how would you regard your friends and their roles in your administration?

2. If you were an African American in Harlem in the 1920s, what would you like and dislike about the area?

3. If you were a small farmer living in Georgia in the 1920s, what would you think are the strengths and weaknesses of American society? What could you do about it?

Crossword Puzzle: The 1920s

DOWN

1. Poet of "lost generation"
2. Sinclair Lewis novel (2 wds.)
3. First career for Hoover
4. Lippmann urged shift of power to educated ___.
5. Disarmament diplomat
6. 1920 landmark event for women
11. Taxes favored by the farm bloc
13. City of artisitic awakening
14. Benefits for Germany of the Dawes plan
16. Fundamentalism was a reaction against ___ life.
17. Bruce Barton promotion
18. Winesburg's state
19. Ride the waves

ACROSS

1. Cabinet post for Hoover
7. Subject for Scopes
8. Middletown model
9. He described Americans as "a timorous, snivelling, poltroonish, ignominious mob."
10. Hillman's industry
12. Taboo of the twenties
15. Continental abbreviation
16. Targets of nativist prejudice in 1928 campaign
20. Victrola marker
21. Card for short
22. Those subsidized by McNary-Haugen
23. ___ dog contracts pledged workers not to join unions.

ANSWER KEY

WHO? WHAT? WHERE?

Who Were They?

1. k. F. Scott Fitzgerald, p. 813
2. f. Calvin Coolidge, p. 819
3. q. Sidney Hillman, p. 821
4. m. Harry M. Daugherty, p. 822
5. d. Albert Fall, p. 823
6. i. Charles R. Forbes, p. 823
7. h. Charles Evans Hughes, p. 825
8. g. Charles Dawes, p. 826
9. e. Aristide Briand, p. 826
10. b. Al Capone, p. 830
11. t. William Simmons, p. 830
12. n. H. L. Mencken, p. 834
13. c. Al Smith, p. 837
14. p. Langston Hughes, p. 839
15. a. Aaron Douglas, p. 839
16. j. Charlotte Mason, p. 841
17. r. Sinclair Lewis, p. 845
18. l. Gertrude Stein, p. 845
19. s. Walter Lippmann, p. 846
20. o. John Dewey, p. 846

What Was It?

1. h. people's capitalism, p. 815
2. e. General Motors, p. 816
3. d. flappers, p. 818
4. k. Yankee Stadium, p. 818
5. i. The Spirit of St. Louis, p. 819
6. l. yellow-dog contracts, p. 821
7. g. K Street House, p. 823
8. j. tractor, p. 827
9. b. Border Patrol, p. 832
10. f. Harlem Renaissance, p. 839
11. c. *corrido*, p. 844
12. a. Agrarians, p. 846

Where Was It?

1. j. Teapot Dome, Wyoming, p. 823
2. h. Ruhr Valley, p. 826
3. d. Indiana, p. 831
4. f. northwestern Europe, p. 832
5. b. Dayton, Tennessee, p. 834
6. g. Oregon, p. 836
7. c. Harlem, p. 838
8. a. California, p. 842
9. i. San Antonio, Texas, p. 843
10. e. Los Angeles, California, p. 844

CHARTS, MAPS, AND ILLUSTRATIONS

1. The differences in the formality of their clothing and the number of people with them, pp. 823, 824
2. 1921, p. 827
3. Chicago, p. 828
4. speakeasy, p. 829
5. Germany and Great Britain, p. 832
6. the South, p. 837
7. pneumonia, p. 838
8. KMPC, p. 845

MULTIPLE CHOICE

1. a (p. 814)

2. d   (p. 814)

3. c   (p. 815)

4. a   (p. 816)

5. c   (p. 816)

6. d   (p. 817)

7. c   (pp. 818–819)

8. b   (p. 822)

9. a   (p. 819)

10. c   (p. 820)

11. c   (p. 822)

12. d   (p. 822)

13. d   (p. 822)

14. c   (p. 824)

15. c   (p. 824)

16. b   (p. 825)

17. d   (p. 827)

18. b   (pp. 827–828)

19. c   (p. 830)

20. c   (pp. 831–832)

21. d   (p. 833)

22. a   (p. 833)

23. b   (p. 833)

24. a   (p. 834)

25. d   (p. 836)

26. a   (p. 839)

27. a   (p. 839)

28. a   (p. 839)

29. c   (p. 841)

30. d   (p. 845)

ESSAY

Description and Explanation

1. p. 815

2. p. 818

3. pp. 822–824

4. pp. 824–825

5. pp. 825–826

6. p. 831

7. pp. 831–832

8. p. 839

Discussion and Analysis

1. pp. 816–817

2. pp. 833–834

3. pp. 836–839

4. pp. 845–847

What If

1. pp. 822–823

2. pp. 838–841

3. Chapter 42 *passim*

Crossword Puzzle

CHAPTER 25

THE GREAT DEPRESSION AND THE NEW DEAL, 1929–1939

The Great Depression was one of the most traumatic events in the twentieth century. The effect on the economy was catastrophic. More than 100,000 businesses went bankrupt. The unemployment rate soared, and there were few sources of relief. A type of gloom settled over Americans, and those who lived through these years never were able to forget the scenes of misery.

The complex causes of the Depression were a mix of the stock-market crash, poor decision making by the Federal Reserve Board, an ill-advised tariff, and the maldistribution of the country's wealth. President Hoover at first tried to deal with the catastrophe with the same techniques he used as secretary of commerce, but, by 1932, he gradually was expanding the role of the government in the economy. At the same time, he was reluctant to provide public relief, believing that giving money to the poor would destroy their desire to work and undermine their sense of self-worth.

In the 1932 elections, the discredited Republicans were removed from office. The voters knew little about Franklin Roosevelt or what he would do as president. During his term in office, he unleashed the power of government to regulate capitalist enterprises, thereby helping restore the economy to health and guarantee the social welfare of Americans unable to help themselves. Roosevelt's New Deal relief programs were a striking contrast to Hoover's. The new president understood the need for compassion and wielded his personal popularity and executive power effectively. Federal governmental activities were not seen as a substitute for private enterprise, but their wide variety served to inspire the American people to believe that they could make a difference.

With labor unrest growing, radical political groups developing, and the elections of 1936 coming, Roosevelt called for new programs to aid the poor and downtrodden. As the Depression entered its sixth year, he was willing to give new social and economic ideas a try. There was growing interest in a new round of legislation directed more to the needs of ordinary Americans. American voters responded by handing Roosevelt the greatest landslide victory in the history of American politics until that time. The election also won for the Democratic Party its reputation as the party of reform and the forgotten American. The second New Deal set the foundation on which the American welfare state was constructed over the next decades.

LIBERTY, EQUALITY, POWER

The Depression and New Deal brought major shifts in the power structure of the United States. This was especially true of the tremendous growth in the power of the federal government over the economy and the lives of Americans. The government demonstrated its willingness to limit the influence of interests such as big business and to augment the power of other groups such as workers, farmers, and consumers. Politics became a struggle among interest groups to increase their influence or power in government. In their rhetoric, New Dealers favored groups who contributed to economic recovery and social justice, but they rewarded groups whose power they respected and feared.

Roosevelt believed that a strong state would enhance the pursuit of liberty and equality by all people, but not everyone benefited from the results of his commitment to this ideal. Farm laborers throughout the country remained weak, and feminism made no headway. African Americans, Mexican Americans, and Asian Americans gained little influence over public policy. On the whole, the New Deal paid little attention to the special needs of racial or ethnic minorities. Most leaders believed that the inequality of wealth and power in America outweighed problems of racial and ethnic discrimination.

Roosevelt was the first president to openly welcome Jews and Catholics into his administration. Antisemitism and anti-Catholicism were far from eliminated from American society, but millions of European ethnics saw hope, for the first time, that they would overcome the second-class status they had long endured. Roosevelt and the New Deal did not weaken democracy. Instead, it was strengthened. Millions of Americans who never before had voted were inspired to go to the polls. As a result of their involvement, the nation's political institutions became more, not less, representative of the American people.

OBJECTIVES

After studying this chapter, the student should be able to

1. Discuss the reasons for the depth and length of the Depression.

2. Compare Herbert Hoover and Franklin Roosevelt on such issues as the role of government in public relief and use of federal agencies to help with the Depression. Explain how their backgrounds affected their views of federal activities.

3. Explain the rise of opposition to Roosevelt and the New Deal and describe the effects it had.

4. Compare and contrast the philosophical views and activities of the first and second New Deal.

5. Describe how the Depression affected gender roles in the U.S. and how it changed the way women were perceived and how men viewed themselves.

6. Discuss how the New Deal dealt with minority groups and which ones benefited from it and which ones did not.

CHRONOLOGY

1920s	Business leaders successfully redefined the national culture in business terms by associating American values with the values of business.

1921	Franklin D. Roosevelt contracted polio, which rendered his legs permanently paralyzed. Due to his determination, his wife Eleanor's support, and a cloak of secrecy by those close to him, the extent of his paralysis was unknown publicly for many years.
1928–1929	Stocks on the New York Stock Exchange underwent an extraordinary increase in price. Many investors bought on margin, putting up only ten percent of their own money and borrowing the rest. On **October 29, 1929**, confidence faltered, resulting in creditors demanding repayment of loans, and the stock market crashed. In a single day, the value of stocks plummeted $14 billion, helping produce the Great Depression that engulfed the country until World War II.
1929–1932	During these years, industrial production fell by 50 percent, and more than 100,000 businesses went bankrupt. The effect on the U.S. economy was catastrophic, with widespread unemployment.
1929–1935	Over a six-year period, the U.S. government repatriated 82,000 Mexican immigrants for failure to produce appropriate documentation to prove their legal status.
1930	The Hawley-Smoot Tariff Act accelerated economic decline abroad and at home by raising tariffs on 75 agricultural goods and on 925 manufactured products, prompting governments abroad to raise their tariffs in retaliation.
1930s	Eastern and southern European immigrants organized into a formidable political force in the Democratic Party in the urban North and West. No Democratic politician with presidential aspirations could afford to ignore their power.
1932	Three years after the onset of the Great Depression, $74 billion of wealth simply had vanished. This year represented the worst year of the Depression, with no end in sight.
	Hoover pushed the Glass-Steagall Banking Act through Congress to help American banks meet the demands of European depositors who wanted to convert their dollars to gold.
	The Reconstruction Finance Corporation (RFC) was created to make $2 billion in funding available to ailing banks and to corporations willing to build low-cost housing, bridges, and other public works. Along the same lines, the Home Loan Bank was created to offer funds to savings and loans, mortgage companies, and other financial institutions that lent money for home construction.
	In the spring, a group of army veterans publicly challenged Hoover's policies by establishing a shanty town near the capitol. Known as the Bonus Army, these men and their families demanded financial assistance from the government. Public opinion deepened against Hoover following an attack

and incineration of the town by federal troops led by Douglas MacArthur and George Patton.

In the **November** elections, Franklin Roosevelt and the Democrats swept President Hoover and the Republicans out of office.

1933

After being sworn in on **March 4**, Roosevelt began his first New Deal program (1933–1935) with a whirlwind "Hundred Days." During this period in Roosevelt's administration, more legislation was passed than during any other presidential administration before or since. The Emergency Banking Act made federal loans available to private bankers **(March 9)**. The Economy Act committed the government to balancing the federal budget **(March 20)**. The Beer-Wine Revenue Act repealed prohibition **(March 22)**. The Unemployment Relief Act created the Civilian Conservation Corps (CCC), which put more than two million single young men to work planting trees and preventing erosion **(March 31)**. The Agricultural Adjustment Act was established to reduce farm production by paying farmers to keep a portion of their land out of cultivation and to reduce the size of their herds **(May 12)**. The Emergency Farm Mortgage Act provided refinancing of farm mortgages **(May 12)**. The Federal Emergency Relief Administration (FERA) was a national relief system led by Harry Hopkins. It was granted $500 million for relief to the poor and included the Civil Works Administration (CWA) that hired four million unemployed to work on small-scale government projects **(May 12)**. The Tennessee Valley Authority Act called for the government itself, rather than private corporations, to promote economic development throughout the Tennessee Valley, a vast river basin that winds through parts of Kentucky, Tennessee, Mississippi, Alabama, Georgia, and North Carolina **(May 18)**. The Securities Act regulated the purchase and sale of new securities **(May 27)**. The Gold Repeal Joint Resolution canceled the gold clause in public and private contracts **(June 5)**. The Home Owners' Loan Act helped middle-class Americans, threatened with the loss of their homes, to refinance mortgages **(June 13)**. The National Industrial Recovery Act authorized the National Recovery Administration (NRA), headed by Hugh Johnson. This national system of industrial self-government included the establishment of the Public Works Administration (PWA) to sponsor internal improvements that would strengthen the nation's infrastructure **(June 16)**. The Glass-Steagall Banking Act separated commercial banking from investment banking and created the Federal Deposit Insurance Corporation (FDIC), which assured depositors that the government would protect up to $5,000 of their savings **(June 16)**. The Farm Credit Act reorganized agricultural credit programs **(June 16)**. The Railroad Coordination Act appointed a federal coordinator of transportation **(June 16)**.

The same week Roosevelt took office, Adolph Hitler assumed control of the German government. In **November**, Roosevelt became the first president to recognize the Soviet Union and to establish diplomatic ties with its communist rulers. He initiated a "Good Neighbor Policy" toward Latin America in **December**.

1933–1940   John Collier, commissioner of the Bureau of Indian Affairs, persuaded Congress to pass the Pueblo Relief Act of 1933, which compensated Pueblos for land taken from them in the 1920s, and the Johnson-O'Malley Act of 1934, which funded states to provide for Indian health care, welfare, and education. In 1935, Collier established the Indian Arts and Crafts Board to nurture traditional Indian artists and help them find a market for their works. Collier increased the number of Indian employees of the BIA from a few hundred in 1933 to a respectable 4,600 in 1940. In 1934, the Indian Reorganization Act revoked all allotment provisions of the Dawes Act.

1934   Known as the year of strikes, workers staged approximately two thousand strikes in virtually every industry and region of the country. Only a few of the strikes escalated into armed confrontation between workers and police.

Roosevelt continued to build international trade by supporting Congress in passing the Reciprocal Trade Agreement, which allowed his administration to lower U.S. tariffs by as much as 50 percent in exchange for similar reductions by other nations. By the end of the following year, the United States had negotiated reciprocal trade agreements with fourteen countries.

1935   Roosevelt described his Second New Deal as a program to limit the power and privilege of the wealthy few and to increase the security and welfare of ordinary citizens. In **May**, the Social Security Act created the nation's first comprehensive system of social insurance. It required states to establish welfare funds from which money would be disbursed to the elderly poor, the unemployed, unmarried mothers with dependent children, and the disabled. The following month, the National Labor Relations Act fulfilled the promise of the National Recovery Administration, assuring the right of every worker to join a union and requiring employers to bargain with unions in good faith.

Congress passed the $5 billion Emergency Relief Appropriation Act, dwarfing similar legislation passed during the First New Deal. Most of the money went to the Works Progress Administration (WPA), which built or improved buildings, parks, and streets. WPA provided jobs for approximately 30 percent of the nation's jobless.

John L. Lewis of the United Mine Workers, Sidney Hillman of the Amalgamated Clothing Workers, and the leaders of six other unions that had seceded from the American Federation of Labor (AFL) organized to form the Committee on Industrial Organization (CIO).

Due to the "Dust Bowl" in the Great Plains and lack of government assistance, the rural poor—tenant farmers and sharecroppers—migrated west toward California. Nearly a million "Okies" had left the Plains by 1935, and another 2.5 million would leave after 1935.

1936	The Supreme Court ruled that Agricultural Adjustment Act–mandated limits on farm production constituted illegal restraints of trade. In response, Congress passed the Soil Conservation and Domestic Allotment Act, which justified the removal of land from cultivation for reasons of conservation rather than economics. In late 1936, United Auto Workers (UAW) took on General Motors (GM) with the use of "sit-down" strikes intended to coerce GM to recognize the UAW and to negotiate a collective-bargaining agreement. Both Roosevelt and the governor of Michigan refused to use force to end the strikes, ending the fifty-year-old practice. GM relented after a month.

Roosevelt defeated Alf Landon of Kansas in the **November** election. Only two states, Maine and Vermont, went to Landon.

1937	On **February 5**, Roosevelt asked Congress to give him the power to appoint one additional Supreme Court Justice for every member of the court who was over the age of seventy and who had served for at least ten years. Roosevelt's reputation sustained substantial damage due to his court-packing scheme.
1937–1938	A sharp economic recession that struck the United States in late 1937 and 1938 polished off what remained of Roosevelt's chances for recovering his reputation. Instead of pumping money into the starving economy, Roosevelt enacted restrictive measures that resulted in yet another economic crash. From **August** to **October**, the stock market fell by almost 40 percent, and, by **March 1938**, the unemployment rate escalated to 20 percent.
1938	Superman, the new comic-strip hero, was a working-class hero who saved workers from villainous employers, reflecting the spirit of the times.

In the off-year election, voters selected many conservatives opposed to the New Deal. This group was not strong enough to overturn the New Deal, but it was able to stop any new programs.

1939	Eleanor Roosevelt resigned from the Daughters of the American Revolution when the organization refused to allow black contralto Marian Anderson to sing in Constitution Hall, Washington, D.C. With the support of Secretary of the Interior Harold Ickes, she then pressured the federal government into granting Anderson permission to sing from the steps of the Lincoln Memorial on Easter Sunday.

GLOSSARY OF IMPORTANT TERMS

bank holiday	Term Roosevelt used shortly after taking office to describe his plan to prevent any more panic runs on the nation's banks. He ordered all the nation's banks closed for a "bank holiday."

Black Tuesday	October 29, 1929, the day the spectacular New York Stock Market crash began.
Chicano	A person of Mexican-American ancestry; also a term referring to Mexican-American culture.
court packing	Scheme by Roosevelt designed to prevent the conservative Supreme Court from dismantling his New Deal. He proposed to appoint an additional justice for each justice over the age of seventy.
cultural pluralism	Position that honored the diversity of peoples and cultures in American society and sought to protect that diversity.
deficit spending	In an effort to stimulate the economy, the government spends borrowed money rather than money raised from taxes.
fireside chats	Series of inspirational radio addresses by President Roosevelt. He spoke in a plain and friendly voice to the American people.
Hooverville	Makeshift "village," usually on the edge of a city, with "homes" constructed of cardboard, scrap metal, or whatever was cheaply available. Named for President Hoover, who was despised by the poor for his apparent refusal to help.
margin	Part of an investment purchased with credit. As used by the stock market in the 1920s, many investors bought on margin or with only a small down payment (sometimes as little 10 percent). The remainder of the investment was borrowed from stockbrokers or banks. Investors expected to resell their stocks within a few months at much higher prices, repay the loan, and make a good profit. When prices began falling, creditors began demanding that margin investors repay their loans, which forced stocks to be sold and decreased their prices.
Okies	Dispossessed migrant tenant farmers and sharecroppers who left the Great Plains for the West Coast, mainly California. Known as Okies because so many of them were driven from Oklahoma by the harsh conditions of the Dust Bowl, they numbered several million.
repatriation	Return of immigrants to the country of their origin. In the 1930s, repatriation efforts focused on Mexican immigrants in California.
technocrat	Manager or administrator with expertise in some technology.
under- consumptionism	Theory that underconsumption, or a chronic weakness in consumer demand, had caused the Depression. The path to recovery lay not in restricting the output of goods but in boosting consumer expenditures through a variety of government policies, including vast public-works programs.

WHO? WHAT? WHERE?

WHO WERE THEY?

Complete each statement below (questions 1–11) by writing the letter preceding the appropriate name in the space provided. Use each answer only once.

a. Douglas MacArthur
b. Franklin Roosevelt
c. Harry Hopkins
d. Herbert Hoover
e. Huey P. Long
f. John Collier
g. John L. Lewis
h. John Nance Garner
i. John Steinbeck
j. Marian Anderson
k. Upton Sinclair

_____ 1. Leader who represented living proof that the American dream could be realized by anyone who was willing to work for it.

_____ 2. General who led federal troops in an attack on the Bonus Army, burned their shelters, and dispersed protesters.

_____ 3. One of the spokesmen of the agrarian branch of the Democratic Party that favored government regulation of both the economy and private affairs of the people.

_____ 4. First nominee in the history of the Democratic Party to deliver his acceptance speech in person to the national convention.

_____ 5. Spellbinding orator who called for a redistribution of wealth that would guarantee each American family $5,000.

_____ 6. President of the United Mine Workers and a founder of the Committee on Industrial Organizations.

_____ 7. Socialist leader and novelist who came close to winning the governorship of California in 1934.

_____ 8. Head of several important New Deal programs and known as the New Deal minister of relief.

_____ 9. Author of the best-selling novel about a family from Oklahoma that moved to California and their many problems along the way.

_____ 10. African-American singer who was denied the right to perform in Constitution Hall in Washington, D.C., because of race.

_____ 11. Commissioner of the Bureau of Indian Affairs who promised Native Americans dramatic improvements.

WHAT WAS IT?

Complete each following statement (questions 1–17) by writing the letter preceding the appropriate name in the space provided. Use each answer only once.

    a. Agricultural Adjustment Act
    b. Black Tuesday
    c. blue eagle
    d. Civilian Conservation Corps
    e. court packing
    f. FDIC
    g. fireside chats
    h. Good Neighbor Policy
    i. Hawley-Smoot Act
    j. Hoovervilles
    k. National Labor Relations Act
    l. Pins and Needles
    m. Reconstruction Finance Corporation
    n. Social Security Act
    o. Soil Conservation Service
    p. Superman
    q. Works Progress Administration

_____ 1. Day the Stock Market Crash began.

_____ 2. Makeshift towns constructed of whatever was cheaply available.

_____ 3. Bill that included the highest tariff rate in American history and that accelerated economic decline abroad.

_____ 4. Agency that represented the most widespread federal intervention into the economy in peacetime up to that point in American history. Gave rise to the largest peacetime deficit in U.S. history.

_____ 5. Series of radio addresses launched by President Roosevelt, who spoke in a plain and friendly voice to the American people.

_____ 6. Agency that guaranteed bank deposits up to $5,000.

_____ 7. New Deal program that put more than two million young men to work improving the environment.

_____ 8. Act created to pay farmers to curtail production and keep a portion of their land out of cultivation.

_____ 9. Agency designed to teach farmers how to eliminate soil erosion.

_____ 10. Logo of the National Recovery Administration, displayed to signal a business's participation in the campaign to limit production and restore prosperity.

_____ 11. Measure that created the first comprehensive system of social insurance for Americans.

_____ 12. Known as the "Magna Carta" of labor, this set up a federal board to supervise union elections and to investigate claims of unfair labor practices.

_____ 13. Government relief agency that provided jobs for about 30 percent of the nation's jobless and funded a vast program of public art.

_____ 14. Comic-strip hero of 1938.

_____ 15. Musical about the hopes and dreams of garment workers.

_____ 16. Approach used by Roosevelt to renounce America's right to intervene in the affairs of Latin American countries.

_____ 17. Scheme developed by Roosevelt to prevent the conservative Supreme Court from dismantling his New Deal.

WHERE WAS IT?

Complete each statement below (questions 1–7) by writing the letter preceding the appropriate name in the space provided. Use each answer only once.

- a. Anacostia Flats
- b. Flint, Michigan
- c. Maine
- d. Mexico
- e. Route 66
- f. Tennessee Valley
- g. the West

_____ 1. Area southeast of the capitol where the Bonus Army set up camp.

_____ 2. Path most Okies followed to California.

_____ 3. Home of the largest producer of electricity in the United States and a federal-government experiment in regional planning.

_____ 4. Region that benefited the most from the New Deal.

_____ 5. One of the two states that voted against Roosevelt in the election of 1936.

_____ 6. Location of a major labor dispute against General Motors where the sit-down strike was used successfully to force the company to negotiate with the union.

_____ 7. Country to which large numbers of immigrants were forcibly repatriated during the Depression.

CHARTS, MAPS, AND ILLUSTRATIONS

1. More than five thousand banks failed in the United States in the year _____.

2. _____ and _____ were two Dust Bowl states.

3. The male occupation in 1930 with the highest rate of unemployment was _____
_____.

The female occupation in 1930 with the highest rate of unemployment was _____
_____.

What was the difference between the male percent unemployed and the female percent unemployed in that year? _____.

4. The year with the highest rate of unemployment in the nonfarm labor force was
_____. The year with the lowest rate of unemployment in the nonfarm
labor force was _____. What was the main cause of the dramatic reduction
in employment in nonfarm industries?_____

MULTIPLE CHOICE

Circle the letter that best completes each statement.

1. Which of the following was not a cause of the stock market crash in 1929?
   a. investors who bought on 10 percent margins
   b. investors who were unable to repay their loans
   c. the outbreak of war in Europe
   d. overconfident investors trying to get rich quickly

2. Which of the following was not a reason why the Great Depression lingered for such
   a long time?
   a. There was a lopsided concentration of wealth in the hands of the rich.
   b. An ill-advised tariff took effect soon after the Depression hit.
   c. There was poor decision making by the Federal Reserve Board.
   d. European countries were unable to agree on a common currency for international
      trade.

3. Historians have concluded that leaders could have aided economic recovery and thus
   shortened the Great Depression by implementing all of the following measures except
   a. expanding the money supply.
   b. creating additional tariffs.
   c. lowering interest rates.
   d. making credit easier to obtain.

4. To combat the Depression, President Hoover first turned to a program of his associa-
   tional principles, encouraging organizations of farmers, industrialists, and bankers to
   share information, bolster one another's spirits, and devise policies to aid economic
   recovery. Which of the following statements was not included in this program?
   a. Farmers should increase output.
   b. Industrialists should hold wages at pre-Depression levels.
   c. Bankers should help one another remain solvent.
   d. The federal government should provide farmers, industrialists, and bankers with
      information, strategies for mutual aid, occasional loans, and morale-boosting
      speeches.

5. In 1931, Hoover realized that associationalism had failed. Which of the following is not one of the policies he pursued next?
   a. He secured a one-year moratorium on loan payments that European governments owed to American banks.
   b. He gave money to poor, unemployed, or homeless Americans.
   c. He steered through Congress the Glass-Steagall Banking Act of 1932 to help American banks meet the demands of European depositors who wished to convert their dollars into gold.
   d. He expanded the role of government in managing the nation's economy to provide relief for the crisis at home.

6. "Bonus Army" refers to
   a. a group of World War I veterans who traveled to Washington to demand government financial assistance for the poor.
   b. Hoover's plan of attack on the economic Depression plaguing the country.
   c. federal troops led by MacArthur and Patton that distributed food to the homeless.
   d. an advisory committee sent to offer economic recommendations to European leaders.

7. Who was the only president to break the two-term precedent?
   a. Calvin Coolidge
   b. Herbert Hoover
   c. Franklin D. Roosevelt
   d. Harry Truman

8. What as the relationship of Theodore Roosevelt to Franklin Roosevelt?
   a. There was no relationship.
   b. Theodore was an older cousin to Franklin.
   c. Theodore was an older brother to Franklin.
   d. Theodore was an uncle to Franklin.

9. In 1921, Franklin Roosevelt permanently lost the use of his legs after
   a. contracting scarlet fever.
   b. being thrown from a horse.
   c. a car accident.
   d. being stricken by polio.

10. Roosevelt was successful in all of the following except
    a. persuading Congress to pass fifteen major pieces of legislation to help bankers, farmers, industrialists, workers, homeowners, the unemployed, and the hungry.
    b. prevailing on Congress to preserve Prohibition as the law of the land.
    c. using radio to cultivate an intimate relationship with ordinary Americans.
    d. bringing confidence, excitement, and hope to the nation in an attempt to heal people as well as the economy.

11. Roosevelt's first order of business was to save the nation's financial system. Which of the following acts is matched incorrectly to its intent?
    a. Emergency Banking Act (EBA)—refinanced farm mortgages
    b. Economy Act (EA)—committed the government to balancing the budget

    c. Glass-Steagall Act—separated commercial banking from investment banking and created the FDIC

    d. Securities Act—regulated the purchase and sale of new securities

12. Who was the reformer appointed to head the Federal Emergency Relief Administration (FERA)?
    a. Hugh Johnson
    b. Harold Ickes
    c. Harry Hopkins
    d. Newton Baker

13. What two pieces of legislation did Roosevelt regard as the most important of his first hundred days?
    a. TVA and SEA
    b. EB and FERA
    c. CCC and EBA
    d. AAA and NIRA

14. Which of the following statements is not true of the Agricultural Adjustment Act?
    a. It paid farmers to keep a portion of their land out of cultivation and to reduce the size of their herds.
    b. It was controversial because many farmers, proud of their work ethic, did not readily accept the idea that they were to be paid money for working less land and husbanding fewer livestock.
    c. It made no provision for the countless tenant farmers and farm laborers who would be thrown out of work by a reduction in acreage.
    d. Its greatest success was in helping Great Plains farmers maintain their farms.

15. The economic problems of the Great Plains farmers were compounded by ecological calamity. The land, stripped of its native grasses by decades of excessive plowing, dried up and resulted in the
    a. Great Plains floods of 1935.
    b. Dust Bowl.
    c. Great Drought.
    d. Year of the Locusts.

16. The National Recovery Administration was headed by
    a. Hugh Johnson.
    b. Harold Ickes.
    c. Harry Hopkins.
    d. Floyd Olson.

17. The Tennessee Valley Authority was created to do all the following, except
    a. control flooding on the Tennessee River and harness its water power to generate electricity.
    b. develop local industry (such as fertilizer production) and to ease poverty.
    c. develop munitions and radar for the military.
    d. improve river transportation and alleviate isolation of the area's inhabitants.

18. Who was the "radio priest" who became disillusioned with the New Deal and became more pronounced in his admiration for Adolf Hitler and Benito Mussolini?
    a. Charles Coughlin
    b. Olin T. Johnston
    c. Ernest Lundeen
    d. Francis E. Townsend

19. The California doctor that claimed the way to end the Depression was to give every senior citizen $200 a month was
    a. Upton Sinclair.
    b. Francis E. Townsend.
    c. Vito Marcantonio.
    d. Philip LaFollette.

20. Which clause of the National Industrial Recovery Act granted workers the right to join labor unions of their own choosing and stipulated that employers must recognize unions and bargain with them in good faith?
    a. Clause 2
    b. Clause 5
    c. Clause 7
    d. Clause 9

21. Radical third political parties, critical of the New Deal, made an impressive showing in state politics in 1934 and 1936, especially in the states of
    a. Wisconsin, Minnesota, and California.
    b. New Jersey, New York, and Connecticut.
    c. Nebraska, Washington, and Oregon.
    d. Missouri, Kentucky, and Tennessee.

22. Advocates of the Second New Deal thought the path to recovery lay in boosting consumer expenditures through a variety of government policies. Which of the following was not one of the government policies?
    a. government support for strong labor unions to force an increase in wages
    b. government restriction on the output of producers
    c. higher social-welfare expenditures to put more money in the hands of the poor
    d. vast public-works projects to create hundreds of thousands of new jobs

23. The fiscal policy that advocated government borrowing to stimulate the economy and put an end to the Depression became known as
    a. Brandeisism.
    b. Franklinism.
    c. Keynesianism.
    d. Frankfurterism.

24. The Works Progress Administration (WPA) did all of the following types of work except
    a. build or improve schools, playgrounds, and hospitals.
    b. clean streets and landscape cities.

   c. fund a major program of public art.

   d. help the military train young soldiers.

25. All of the following groups were members of the new Democratic coalition except
   a. sons of the old New England aristocracy.
   b. European ethnic groups in the urban areas.
   c. African Americans in the South.
   d. middle-class Americans who supported the Social Security Act.

26. The Farm Security Administration (FSA), an agency designed to improve the economic lot of tenant farmers, sharecroppers, and farm laborers, drafted and promoted the passage of laws that did all the following, except
   a. outlawed child labor.
   b. set minimum wages and maximum hours for adult workers.
   c. required employers to provide health insurance for workers.
   d. committed the federal government to building low-cost housing.

27. In an attempt to pressure General Motors into participating in collective bargaining and recognizing United Auto Workers (UAW), workers participated in
   a. fire bombings.
   b. protest marches.
   c. violent riots.
   d. sit-down strikes.

28. Which of the following was not a result of John Collier's Indian Reorganization Act of 1934?
   a. refrained from allocating funds for economic development
   b. retored land to tribes
   c. granted Indians the right to establish constitutions and bylaws for self-government
   d. provided support for new tribal corporations that would regulate the use of communal lands

ESSAY

Description and Explanation (one- to two-paragraph essay)

1. Compare the views of Herbert Hoover and Franklin Roosevelt on the role of government in public relief.

2. Describe the background and personal lifestyle of Roosevelt and how it shaped his assessment of the role of government and the common man.

3. Describe the radical labor parties and what growing support of them meant.

4. Describe the philosophical underpinnings of the Second New Deal.

5. Describe the New Deal women and their part in the Roosevelt administration.

6. Describe how the Depression created a loss of self-worth and feelings of inadequacy in many men and what the result of this was.

7. Describe the role of the Depression and the New Deal on literature, art, and other cultural activities.

8. Compare the views of Franklin and Eleanor Roosevelt on racism and racial equality.

9. Describe the work of the Bureau of Indian Affairs and the views of its leaders. Were its new policies effective?

Discussion and Analysis (class discussion or one- to two-paragraph essay)

1. Discuss the reasons for the depth and longevity of the Great Depression.

2. Discuss the effects of the Depression on the working class, how it helped to unify this group, what the hardships on the job were, and what the workers did about these conditions.

What If (include an explanation of your position)

1. If you were former President Herbert Hoover, what would be your opinion of President Roosevelt's programs and ideas?

2. If you were a skilled worker in the 1930's, would you join the growing labor movement?

3. If you were an employed woman during the 1930s, would you believe that American society and the New Deal supported your need to continue working?

Crossword Puzzle: The Great Depression and the New Deal, 1929–1939

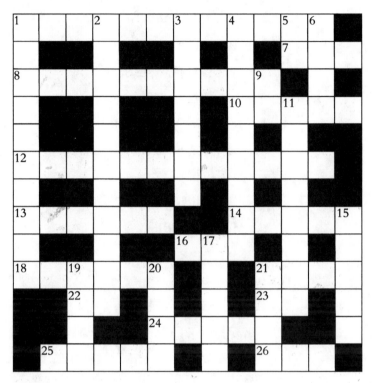

DOWN

1. NRA logo (2 wds)
2. NRA tried to set up fair ___ .
3. Upton Sinclair's vision, once considered ___ , was supported by many in 1934.
4. Author of *The Grapes of Wrath*
5. ___ shucks!
6. Ivy league school
9. Bonus Army's destination
11. TVA state
15. CCC plantings
17. Fireside chat medium
19. NRA industrial document
20. Bonneville, Boulder, etc.
21. Singles

ACROSS

1. October 29, 1929 (2 wds.)
7. New Deal rescuer
8. CWA beneficiaries
10. Harold of PWA
12. Failure of the largest ___ in 1931 started financial crisis in Europe (2 wds.).
13. A ___ combination was the name of a New Deal program
14. FDR's ___ -packing scheme was a failure.
16. Noah's ship
18. Social Security was part of the ___ New Deal.
21. Migrant in Ford film
22. Ma Joad: "…we go ___ ."
23. Short for Hyde Park's state
24. One of Landon's states
25. United Mine Workers president
26. Strikers' strategy at Flint

ANSWER KEY

WHO? WHAT? WHERE?

Who Were They?

1. d. Herbert Hoover, p. 852
2. a. Douglas MacArthur, p. 854
3. h. John Nance Garner, p. 855
4. b. Franklin Roosevelt, p. 856
5. e. Huey P. Long, p. 865
6. g. John L. Lewis, p. 866
7. k. Upton Sinclair, p. 868
8. c. Harry Hopkins, p. 872
9. i. John Steinbeck, p. 879
10. j. Marian Anderson, p. 880
11. f. John Collier, p. 882

What Was It?

1. b. Black Tuesday, p. 849
2. j. Hoovervilles, p. 849
3. i. Hawley-Smoot Act, p. 851
4. m. Reconstruction Finance Corporation, p. 853
5. g. fireside chats, p. 856
6. f. FDIC, p. 858
7. d. Civilian Conservation Corps, p. 858
8. a. Agricultural Adjustment Act, p. 859
9. o. Soil Conservation Service, pp. 859–860
10. c. blue eagle, p. 861
11. n. Social Security Act, p. 870
12. k. National Labor Relations Act, p. 870
13. q. Works Progress Administration, p. 872
14. p. Superman, pp. 877–878
15. l. Pins and Needles, p. 879
16. h. Good Neighbor Policy, p. 883
17. e. court packing, p. 884

Where Was It?

1. a. Anacostia Flats, p. 853
2. e. Route 66, p. 860
3. f. Tennessee Valley, p. 863
4. g. the West, p. 863
5. c. Maine, p. 872
6. b. Flint, Michigan, p. 878
7. d. Mexico, p. 881

CHARTS, MAPS, AND ILLUSTRATIONS

1. 1933, p. 857
2. New Mexico, Colorado, Nebraska, Kansas, Oklahoma, or Texas, p. 860
3. carpentry; stenographers and typists; 14 percent, p. 874
4. 1933; 1944; labor demands of World War II, p. 885

MULTIPLE CHOICE

1. c (p. 850)
2. d (p. 850)
3. b (p. 851)
4. a (pp. 852–853)
5. b (p. 853)
6. a (p. 853)
7. c (p. 850)
8. b (p. 854)
9. d (p. 855)

10. b (p. 856)

11. a (pp. 857–858)

12. c (p. 858)

13. d (p. 858)

14. d (p. 859)

15. b (p. 859)

16. a (p. 860)

17. c (p. 862)

18. a (p. 865)

19. b (p. 866)

20. c (p. 866)

21. a (p. 868)

22. b (p. 870)

23. c (p. 870)

24. d (p. 872)

25. a (p. 872)

26. c (p. 874)

27. d (p. 878)

28. a (p. 883)

ESSAY

Description and Explanation

1. pp. 852–853, 854–855

2. pp. 854–855

3. p. 868

4. p. 870

5. pp. 875–877

6. pp. 877–878

7. pp. 869, 878–879

8. p. 880

9. pp. 882–883

Discussion and Analysis

1. pp. 850–852

2. pp. 878–879

What If

1. pp. 878–879

2. pp. 866–867

3. pp. 875–878

Crossword Puzzle

CHAPTER 26

AMERICA DURING THE SECOND WORLD WAR

The worldwide depression of the 1930s manifested itself in international instability and a war that eventually raged across vast stretches of Europe, Asia, North Africa, and the Pacific and brought death to some 60 million people. In Japan, Italy, and Germany, economic collapse and rising unemployment nurtured political movements that promised economic recovery through military build-up and territorial expansion. Elsewhere, including the United States, governments turned inward to concentrate on domestic recovery and to avoid expensive foreign entanglements. After war was declared officially in Europe in 1939, President Roosevelt announced his intention for the United States to remain neutral, but privately he mobilized public opinion in support of the Allies. Meanwhile, tensions escalated in the Pacific. Unwilling to abandon plans for territorial conquest, Japan launched a surprise attack on American military bases at Pearl Harbor, Hawaii, and in the Philippines in an attempt to weaken the United States. The next day, the United States declared war on Japan. Japan's Axis allies, Germany and Italy, then declared war on the United States.

The most important issue in the early months of the war involved the strategy against Germany, especially the possibility of an invasion of that country. The Soviet Union suffered horrible losses to German attacks. Britain and the United States launched their first offensive attack in North Africa, followed by an invasion of Italy. Finally, the largest invasion force in history was assembled and the Allies invaded France. In the spring of 1945, Germany surrendered.

At first, Japan continued to expand in the Pacific. But, by late 1944, American planes began aerial bombings of Japan. Japan seemed determined to fight (even in the face of certain defeat) and, on the other hand, the Americans demanded unconditional surrender. In August 1945, it was decided to end the military stalemate by using the atomic bomb in an effort to end the war. At the time, most Americans sighed with relief that the devastation of much of the world was over. The United States had proved it was the richest, most powerful country on the globe.

Ultimately, the success of the United States in the war depended on mobilization at home. From 1941 to 1945, American life was transformed. The federal bureaucracy nearly quadrupled in size, and the concept of greater government regulation was accepted and survived the war. The economy expanded rapidly with a dramatic increase in government spending. Science and technology forged the links of mutual interest between business and government. The sale of war bonds, rationing of even essential items, and progressive taxation gave Americans a sense of shared sacrifice, easing the class tensions so prevalent in the 1930s. Dramatic social changes accompanied the wartime mobilization. War altered the composition of the workforce. As military service drained the supply of white male workers, women and blacks became more attractive as production workers. Jobs were plentiful and savings piled up. Great population movements from rural to urban areas of the country eroded social and geographical distinctions. The United States and its people lived through many socioeconomic changes during these few years.

LIBERTY, EQUALITY, POWER

The concept of power was certainly the focus of the war years. Military conquests by the Axis powers and the way they often ruled their new territories were visible examples of raw brutal power. In the United States, the tremendous industrial, scientific, and military expansion that had taken place would continue to affect future generations' expansion of power. The development of the atomic bomb with its tremendous destructive capability demonstrated the power of modern science.

Most Americans sincerely believed they were fighting the war not only for their own liberty but also for that of the world. This idealism was portrayed frequently in nostalgic wartime propaganda and culture. The wartime experience produced some new expectations about liberty that remained after the fighting was over. The emphasis on the fight for liberty fostered the belief that equitable participation in society was possible for most groups. At the same time, Japanese Americans were deprived of their liberty when they were relocated without due process or any apparent justification.

The nation's record on equality was mixed at best. The increase in employment opportunities for women, African Americans, Native Americans and Mexican Americans faded at the end of the war, when they were expected to relinquish their newfound economic independence to returning veterans. Women frequently were portrayed as sexual commodities, not as social equals. Violence erupted between African Americans and whites as the irony of fighting for a country that denied them equality became apparent to black veterans. Increasingly, Americans of all backgrounds realized that racial grievances had to be addressed. The war for the American way of life carried many meanings. The war years forced some to consider a new definition of liberty in the modern world.

OBJECTIVES

After studying this chapter, a student should be able to

1. Describe the outbreak of World War II in Asia and Europe and how the American government and people reacted to it.

2. Discuss the major trends and problems in the war in Europe and the Pacific. How were they different and similar?

3. Explore the role of women in the war and how they were portrayed during the war. Describe the differences between what they did and how they were portrayed.

4. Discuss the shortage of labor on the home front and how it affected business, women, African Americans, Native Americans, and Mexican Americans.

5. Examine the ways the war was portrayed on the home front. Why was it done this way?

6. Describe the postwar international settlements.

CHRONOLOGY

1931	In September Japanese military forces seized Manchuria. The international community was preoccupied with economic problems and did not counter Japan's move.
1933	Adolf Hitler's National Socialist Party, or Nazis, gained control in Germany, withdrew from the League of Nations, and began rebuilding the German military.
1934–1936	A Senate investigating committee headed by Gerald P. Nye conducted hearings that underscored claims that American bankers and munitions makers had helped maneuver the United States into World War I to preserve their profits.
1935	Benito Mussolini's Italian forces invaded the independent African kingdom of Ethiopia.
1935–1936	Congress enacted the Neutrality Acts of 1935 and 1936, which ordered an arms embargo against belligerents, forbade loans to belligerents, and reduced American travel on ships belonging to nations at war. American public-opinion polls indicated overwhelming opposition to involvement in foreign conflicts.
1936	Nazi troops violated the Versailles agreement and occupied the Rhineland. Germany, Italy, and Japan formed an alliance against the Soviet Union, and an Axis pact formalized the friendship between Germany and Italy.
1937	Roosevelt delivered his famous "Quarantine Aggressors" speech proposing modification of American neutrality legislation, but congressional leaders were determined to maintain a policy of noninvolvement.
	Japan launched a major attack on China. The *Panay*, an American gunboat, was sunk later in the year. This incident, together with Japan's brutality toward Chinese civilians, concerned Roosevelt, and he consulted with Great Britain about a possible war in Asia.
1938	Hitler annexed Austria and announced his intention to take over the Sudetenland, which was part of Czechoslovakia. In a meeting with the leaders of France and Britain in the fall in Munich, Germany, Hitler promised to stop German territorial expansion.
1939	Under a secret agreement in the Nazi-Soviet pact, the two countries agreed to divide up Poland and the Baltic states.
	Britain and France promised to defend Poland against German aggression. When Germany invaded Poland on **September 1**, Britain and France declared war two days later. World War II had begun officially in Europe.
	Congress lifted the Neutrality Act's ban on selling arms and substituted a "cash-and-carry" provision that permitted arms sales to belligerents.

Because Britain and France controlled the Atlantic sea lanes, they were the beneficiaries of this new policy.

Congressional leaders stopped the Wagner-Rogers bill, which was designed to boost immigration quotas for the entry of 20,000 Jewish children marked for Hitler's concentration camps.

1940   In **April** and **May**, German troops overran Denmark, Norway, the Netherlands, Belgium, and Luxembourg. In **June**, France surrendered. In only six weeks, the German army seized control of Europe's Atlantic coastline from the North Sea to Spain. Italy joined Germany by declaring war on the Allies.

Japan joined the Axis alliance and intensified its military campaign. Roosevelt agreed to transfer fifty World War I-era destroyers to the British navy in return for the right to build eight naval bases in British territory in the Western Hemisphere in **September**.

At Roosevelt's urging, Congress passed the Selective Training and Service Act of 1940, the first peacetime draft in U.S. history.

The United States banned the sale of aviation fuel and high-grade scrap iron to Japan. It was hoped that this would slow Japan's military advance into Southeast Asia. It only intensified Japanese militancy.

Democrats broke with tradition and nominated Roosevelt for a third term. He played to popular opposition to the war and defeated Republican Wendell Wilkie in **November**.

1940–1943   Big business benefited far more than small enterprises from federal wartime policies. The top one hundred manufacturers in America went from producing 30 percent of the nation's total output in **1940** to 70 percent by **1943**.

1940–1944   Government spending rose from $9 billion to $98 billion.

1940–1945   The economy expanded rapidly. In each year during this period, the gross national product rose by 15 percent or more.

1941   House Resolution 1776, passed in **March**, allowed the United States to lend or lease military supplies to the Allies rather than to sell them. Roosevelt assured Americans that he would keep the war away from America and its people.

A. Philip Randolph threatened to lead tens of thousands of frustrated black workers in a march on Washington to demand more defense jobs and integration of military forces. In return for cancellation of the march, Roosevelt created the Fair Employment Practices Commission to enforce the nondiscriminatory clauses in government contracts.

Hitler established death camps for the systematic elimination of Jews, Gypsies, homosexual people, and others whom Nazis deemed "unfit" for life in the Third Reich.

Roosevelt froze Japanese assets in the United States. This effectively brought under his control all commerce between the two countries. Roosevelt hoped to bring Japan to the bargaining table. Instead, Japanese leaders planned an attack on the United States.

In **August**, Roosevelt and British Prime Minister Winston Churchill met off the coast of Newfoundland and worked out the basis for what would become a formal wartime alliance.

A German submarine sank the U.S. destroyer *Reuben James*. Congress repealed the Neutrality Act, but the vote was so close and the debate so bitter that Roosevelt knew he could not yet seek a formal declaration of war.

On **December 7**, Japanese bombers attacked U.S. military bases in Hawaii and the Philippines. Much of the Pacific Fleet stationed at Pearl Harbor was destroyed by the surprise attack. The next day, Congress declared war on Japan with only one dissenting vote. On **December 11**, Japan's Axis allies, Germany and Italy, declared war on the United States.

1942

In the two months following the attack on Pearl Harbor, West Coast communities became nearly hysterical with regard to people of Japanese descent. First- and second-generation Japanese Americans were ordered to inland relocation camps.

At a conference in **January** at Rio de Janeiro, the Latin American nations (except Chile and Argentina) broke off diplomatic ties with the Axis governments. Latin American countries became important suppliers of raw materials to the United States.

The Office of War Information was devised by President Roosevelt with the purpose of centralizing and coordinating censorship and propaganda policies.

The Committee on Racial Equality was founded, composed of whites and blacks who advocated nonviolent resistance to inequality.

Japan suffered its first naval defeat at the Battle of the Coral Sea. The Battle of Midway crippled Japan's offensive capabilities. Two months later, Americans landed at Guadalcanal. They had seized the initiative.

Realizing the home front needed rapid victories, the North African operation (code name TORCH) began Anglo-American landings in Morocco and Algeria in **November**.

1943

At a meeting at Casablanca, Roosevelt and Churchill postponed the promised invasion of France. To calm Stalin's fears that his allies would sign a separate treaty with Germany, it was announced that the Allies would fight until Hitler surrendered unconditionally. Stalin still felt double-crossed.

The TORCH military campaigns prompted the surrender of approximately 200,000 Axis soldiers to the Allies in **April** and **May**.

The significant role American industry played in World War II was apparent with the passage of the Smith-Connally Act, which provided for government seizure of plants or mines if union strikes interfered with war production.

Congress abolished government-operated social programs to provide jobs and assistance to the poor, while continuing subsidies to large businesses, considered essential for victory in World War II.

The federal government stated, as a matter of policy, that it would not recognize unions as collective-bargaining agents if they refused to admit minorities.

The zoot-suit riots pitted whites against Mexican Americans, escalating into virtual warfare between the "zoot suiters" and local police.

An explosion at a naval ammunition depot at Port Chicago, California, killed three hundred stevedores, most of them black, who were loading ammunition. When the Navy assigned another group to the same duty, some of them refused. The resulting court martial of fifty African-American men was the largest mass trial in naval history. All were found guilty and were given prison terms ranging from eight to fifteen years.

The owner of the Chicago Cubs baseball team organized a women's league that eventually fielded ten teams.

Allied troops overran the island of Sicily and then moved into Italy.

During the Moscow Conference in **October**, the Allies restated their 1941 Atlantic Charter pledge to create an international organization to replace the League of Nations. At Teheran in **November**, Roosevelt informed Stalin that American voters of Polish, Latvian, Lithuanian, and Estonian descent expected their homelands to be independent after the war.

During 1943, Germany's submarine capability faded from the status of a menace to that of only a problem due to the use of radar by American and British forces.

1944

One of the largest invasion forces in history was massed in England. The long-awaited second front was launched on **June 6** on the beaches of Normandy, France. Within three weeks, over a million men had landed, and within three months Allied troops entered Paris.

At the Bretton Woods Conference in New Hampshire, Americans worked to stabilize exchange rates, provide an international lending authority and eliminate discriminatory trade practices.

The Manhattan Project, bringing together experts from science, industry, government, and the military to develop the atomic bomb, employed nearly 130,000 people. This was perhaps the most dramatic example of the new connection between science and national defense.

Women accounted for 27 percent of total union membership in America.

Roosevelt defeated Thomas E. Dewey with the smallest popular vote margin in thirty years.

By the end of the year, American bombers were within range of Japanese cities.

In *Korematsu* v. *U.S.*, the Supreme Court upheld the constitutionality of Japanese relocation during the war.

1945

A conference of the three major Allied powers was held at Yalta in the Soviet Union. They agreed to divide Germany into zones of occupation. The future of Poland was discussed. Stalin agreed to send troops to Asia as soon as Germany was defeated. The bomb fell on Hiroshima just one day before the Soviet Union was to enter the war.

Sorrow and shock enveloped the country on **April 13** as President Roosevelt died. Vice President Harry S Truman took over the government, knowing little about foreign affairs.

Military foundations for peace in Europe were completed with Germany's surrender on **May 7**. Soviet armies controlled eastern Europe, and Britain and the United States were in Italy and the other Mediterranean areas. Germany and Austria were under divided occupation.

America's growing acceptance of new international organizations was illustrated when the Senate adopted the United Nations Charter with only two dissenting votes.

The first atomic weapon was tested successfully at the Trinity site near Alamagordo, New Mexico, in **July**.

President Truman and Prime Minister Churchill agreed that it would take massive destruction to bring about Japan's unconditional surrender. On **August 6 and 9**, the Japanese cities of Hiroshima and Nagasaki were targets of atomic bombs.

Japan surrendered on **September 2**, and it was proclaimed Victory over Japan, or VJ, Day.

Germany was divided into four zones of occupation by the Allied powers. Later, as relations among victors cooled, this temporary division of Germany solidified into a Soviet-dominated communist zone in the east and three Allied zones in the west.

1946   The United States honored its long-standing pledge to grant independence to the Philippines.

During the war, women held 25 percent of all jobs in automobile factories; by mid-1946 they held only 7.5 percent of these jobs.

1947   The General Agreement on Tariffs and Trade (GATT) provided institutional structure for implementing free and fair trade agreements.

GLOSSARY OF IMPORTANT TERMS

belligerent   Country actively engaged in a war.

blitzkrieg   A "lightning war"; coordinated and unrelenting military strikes on land and in the air by the German military.

braceros   Guest-workers from Mexico, allowed into the United States because of the labor shortage.

cash and carry   American foreign policy previous to entry into World War II; required that belligerents pay cash and carry products away in their own ships. This arrangement minimized risks to American exports, loans, and shipping. Thought to help prevent the types of incidents that some felt forced the United States into World War I.

Day of Infamy   Refers to the day Japan attacked Pearl Harbor. Used as a rallying cry throughout the war for many Americans.

fascism   Type of highly centralized government that uses terror and violence to suppress opposition. Its rigid social and economic controls often incorporated strong nationalism and racism. Fascist governments were dominated by strong authority figures or dictators.

genocide   Systematic elimination of an entire racial, national, or ethnic group.

inland relocation camps   Centers where 130,000 first- and second-generation Japanese Americans were confined in flimsy barracks enclosed by barbed wire under armed guard for the duration of the war.

Luftwaffe   The German air force.

R & D   Research and development.

sitzkrieg   "Sitting war"; temporary lull between the conquest of Poland in the fall of 1939 and the resumption of military action in the spring of 1940.

Third Reich	New empire Adolph Hitler promised the German people.
VE Day	Day the war in Europe was won by the Allies; the day that Germany surrendered was May 7, 1945.
VJ Day	September 2, 1945; celebrated as Victory over Japan Day.
wolfpacks	German submarine groups that attacked enemy merchant ships or convoys.
Zionism	Movement to establish a Jewish state in ancient Palestine.
zoot suits	Flamboyant outfits that featured oversized trousers; commonly worn by young Mexican-American men. Became the symbol of rebellion for some Hispanics. The Los Angeles City Council tried to make it a crime to wear a zoot suit.

WHO? WHAT? WHERE?

WHO WERE THEY?

Complete each following statement (questions 1–14) by writing the letter preceding the appropriate name in the space provided. Use each answer only once.

a. Albert Einstein
b. Burton K. Wheeler
c. Curtis LeMay
d. Douglas MacArthur
e. Eleanor Roosevelt
f. Francisco Franco
g. Hideki Tojo
h. Jeanette Rankin
i. Joseph W. Stillwell
j. Mao Zedong
k. Frank Capra
l. Norman Rockwell
m. Paul Tibbets
n. William Allen White

_____ 1. Fascist leader who overthrew the republican government of Spain.

_____ 2. Democratic senator who distributed more than a million antiwar postcards at government expense.

_____ 3. Well-known Kansas newspaper editor who led one of the groups supporting the Allies.

_____ 4. Japanese prime minister during most of World War II.

_____ 5. Long-time peace activist who cast the only dissenting vote against war with Japan.

_____ 6. American military leader who undertook the job of trying to turn China into an effective military force.

_____ 7. Leader of the growing communist movement in China.

_____ 8. Commander of the American army in the South Pacific.

_____ 9. Leader of the incendiary raids on Japan.

_____ 10. Jewish refugee from Germany who urged Roosevelt to launch a secret program to develop an atomic bomb.

_____ 11. American who piloted the plane that dropped the atomic bomb on Hiroshima.

_____ 12. Leading illustrator who evoked small-town American life during World War II in his paintings.

_____ 13. Hollywood producer who made a series of government films entitled *Why We Fight*.

_____ 14. Outspoken advocate of civil rights in Roosevelt's administration.

WHAT WAS IT?

Complete each following statement (questions 1–15) by writing the letter preceding the appropriate name in the space provided. Use each answer only once.

a. America First Committee
b. Atlantic Charter
c. Day of Infamy
d. ENIGMA
e. ERA
f. House Resolution 1776
g. inland relocation camps
h. Kaiser Corporation
i. petroleum
j. radar
k. Security Council
l. *sitzkrieg*
m. Third Reich
n. War Labor Board
o. Zionism

_____ 1 New empire Hitler promised the German people.

_____ 2. Most formidable opposition to Roosevelt's pro-Allied policies before the United States entered the war.

_____ 3. Period between the conquest of Poland in 1939 and the resumption of military action in the spring of 1940.

_____ 4. Act passed by Congress that established that the United States would lend or lease supplies to the Allies rather than sell supplies to them.

_____ 5. Agreement worked out between Britain and the United States in 1941 that pledged the postwar creation of a new world organization.

_____ 6. Rallying cry throughout the war for many Americans.

_____ 7. Trade item Japan most wanted to obtain.

_____ 8. New technology that proved effective against submarines.

_____ 9. Complex encryption for radio messages.

_____ 10. Company that handled nearly one third of the nation's military construction during World War II.

_____ 11. This outlawed the discriminatory practice of paying different wages to whites and to nonwhites for the same jobs

_____ 12. Constitutional amendment Congress seriously considered during World War II but did not pass.

_____ 13. Places where 130,000 Japanese Americans were confined in flimsy barracks and under armed guard for the duration of the war.

_____ 14. Division of the United Nations with primary responsibility for maintaining peace.

_____ 15. Movement to establish a Jewish state in ancient Palestine.

WHERE WAS IT?

Complete each following statement (questions 1–13) by writing the letter preceding the appropriate name in the space provided. Use each answer only once.

  a. Coral Sea
  b. Ethiopia
  c. Elbe River
  d. Italy
  e. Los Angeles, California
  f. Manchuria
  g. Nagasaki, Japan
  h. Philippines
  i. Poland
  j. Solomon Islands
  k. Trinity site
  l. Port Chicago, California
  m. Yalta

_____ 1. Area in China conquered by Japan in the early 1930s and reorganized into a puppet state.

_____ 2. African kingdom attacked by Italy under Benito Mussolini.

_____ 3. Invasion of this country by Germany led to a declaration of war by Great Britain and France.

———— 4. First Axis power to be directly invaded by the Allies.

———— 5. Place where General Eisenhower halted his troops, allowing the Soviets to enter Berlin.

———— 6. Location of the first Japanese naval defeat.

———— 7. Region where Americans seized the initiative in the Pacific naval war.

———— 8. Area where the first atomic bomb was tested.

———— 9. Second city hit by an atomic bomb.

———— 10. Location of a naval ammunition depot where an explosion killed three hundred stevedores, most African Americans.

———— 11. Site of the zoot suit riots pitting whites against Mexican Americans.

———— 12. Ukrainian city where a conference was held between the United States, Britain, and the Soviet Union to settle some of the problems developing among the Allies over postwar Europe.

———— 13. American colony that was given its independence in 1946.

CHARTS, MAPS, AND ILLUSTRATIONS

1. The Soviet city on the eastern front that withstood a German attack from August 1942 to January 1943 was _____.

2. According to the map on Japanese expansion (p. 904), there were two major Allied victories in the summer of 1942. They were _____ and _____.

3. The Indian group that transmitted secret information through the use of its native language was _____.

4. Compare the photographs (p. 910) depicting the effects of total war on cities. The two cities and the methods used to damage them were _____ and _____. Was there much difference in the overall destruction of each city?

5. According to the Norman Rockwell war bond poster (pp. 916–917), the four freedoms for which Americans were fighting were _____.

MULTIPLE CHOICE

Circle the letter that best completes each statement.

1. Japan's actions on September 18, 1931, along with the subsequent creation of a puppet state, violated all of the following concordats, except the
   a. Hoover agreement.
   b. Kellogg-Briand Pact.

   c. Washington treaties.

   d. League of Nations Charter.

2. Which of the following leaders gained control of Italy in 1922 and installed a fascist government?

   a. Paolo Porcile

   b. Marcantonio Maiale

   c. Benito Mussolini

   d. Cesare Cocciuto

3. The Neutrality Acts of 1935 and 1936

   a. were designed to promote the growth of financial and emotional connections to belligerents.

   b. called for an end to the arms embargo against belligerents.

   c. provided discounts to Americans traveling on ships belonging to nations at war.

   d. were enacted to prevent a repetition of the circumstances that supposedly had drawn the United States into World War I.

4. The Japanese referred to the plan that supposedly would liberate peoples throughout Asia from Western colonialism as

   a. the Rising Sun.

   b. East Asian Co-Prosperity Sphere.

   c. North Pacific Treaty Alliance.

   d. Nissan Trading and Protection Sphere.

5. The German *blitzkrieg*, which included coordinated and unrelenting strikes on land and in the air, was commonly referred to as a

   a. tornado war.

   b. strobe war.

   c. lightning war.

   d. spear war.

6. The Selective Training and Service Act of 1940 created the first

   a. military school in U.S. history.

   b. wartime draft in U.S. history.

   c. officer-training program in U.S. history.

   d. peacetime draft in U.S. history.

7. The use of air power against civilians in the battle of Britain shocked Americans who heard the news in dramatic radio broadcasts from London. One journalist who described the city of London as it burned was

   a. Burton K. Wheeler.

   b. Charles Lindbergh.

   c. Edward R. Murrow.

   d. Robert E. Wood.

8. People who tried to keep the United States from getting entangled in the war generally were called

   a. fascists.

    b. Nazis.

    c. loyalists.

    d. isolationists.

9. Hitler's policies became deadlier after June 1941, when he established death camps for the systematic extermination of minorities whom the Nazis deemed "unfit" for life. Which of the following groups was not on Hitler's death list?

    a. Jews

    b. National Socialists

    c. Gypsies

    d. homosexual persons

10. The Atlantic Charter in 1941 between Britain and the United States resulted in all of the following, except

    a. a formal declaration of war on Germany.

    b. a disavowal of territorial expansion.

    c. an endorsement of free trade and self-determination.

    d. working out the basis of what would become a formal wartime alliance.

11. The United States's entry into the war resulted from escalated tensions with

    a. the Soviet Union.

    b. China.

    c. Germany.

    d. Japan.

12. The Axis powers in World War II were represented by

    a. Germany, Japan, and the Soviet Union.

    b. Italy, the United States, and the Soviet Union.

    c. France, Great Britain, and Italy.

    d. Germany, Italy, and Japan.

13. After 1941, the Allied Powers included

    a. Great Britain, the Soviet Union, and the United States.

    b. Germany, Italy, and Japan.

    c. France, Great Britain, and the United States.

    d. Italy, the Soviet Union, and the United States.

14. Which of the following statements does not accurately depict conditions in the United States upon entering World War II?

    a. Army morale was low.

    b. Industrial production moved at a peacetime pace.

    c. Labor-management relations were combative.

    d. The Roosevelt administration had not expected or prepared for war.

15. Roosevelt and the Joint Chiefs of Staff agreed that the primary focus for U.S. military forces would be the

    a. Pacific theater.

    b. Asian theater.

    c. European theater.

    d. African theater.

16. The brief collaboration between French Admiral Jean Darlan, a Nazi sympathizer, and General Dwight D. Eisenhower resulted in all of the following, except
    a. It outraged Americans who believed it compromised the moral purpose of the war and was not worth any short-term military advantage.
    b. It produced antagonism between Americans and the Free French movement.
    c. It offended General Charles de Gaulle's sense of national pride that Americans chose to work with Darlan rather than with de Gaulle himself.
    d. It strengthened French-American relations after the war.

17. On D-Day, June 6, 1944, Commander Eisenhower directed the largest invasion force in history, known as Operation
    a. Freedom.
    b. Overlord.
    c. Sunrise.
    d. Bulldog.

18. The country where large quantities of money, gold, and jewelry stolen by Nazi leaders were hidden from view for over fifty years was
    a. Netherlands.
    b. Switzerland.
    c. Italy.
    d. Portugal.

19. In May 1945, as Allied powers came closer to defeating Germany, Hitler allegedly
    a. escaped to Switzerland.
    b. surrendered to Soviet forces.
    c. disappeared without a trace.
    d. committed suicide.

20. Which of the following statements incorrectly characterizes the Pacific theater during World War II?
    a. By 1943, the European and Pacific theaters were receiving roughly equal resources.
    b. Americans played up racist images to their benefit.
    c. The Pacific theater, according to prewar plans, was to have highest priority in the war.
    d. American and Japanese troops were equally brutal in their torture of prisoners.

21. The Japanese group that tested bacteriological items in China was
    a. Pack 107.
    b. Unit 731.
    c. China 743.
    d. Crew 532.

22. The most secretive military research project (up to 1945), which involved developing atomic weapons, took place in New Mexico and was known as the
    a. Manhattan Project.

b. Einstein Project
c. Sand Dune Project.
d. Trinity Project.

23. The mushroom clouds over Nagasaki and Hiroshima in August of 1945 announced the dawn of the
    a. transcendental age.
    b. atomic age.
    c. enlightened age.
    d. fungal age.

24. On the American home front, World War II fostered all of the following, except
    a. an increase in personal savings.
    b. a new measure of income distribution.
    c. the dismemberment of many New Deal agencies concerned with the interests of the poor.
    d. an acceleration in the production of consumer goods.

25. In what way did World War II affect the American workforce?
    a. Women were hired for jobs previously off-limits to them.
    b. The labor market displaced black males.
    c. Per capita weekly earnings dropped by 10 percent.
    d. Union membership hit a record low.

26. As women continued to break gender stereotypes by volunteering for military duty, their number in the armed services during World War II comprised
    a. 2 percent.
    b. 4 percent.
    c. 7 percent.
    d. 9 percent.

27. Of the minority groups in the United States, which group suffered from discrimination most grievously during the war?
    a. Irish Americans
    b. Mexican Americans
    c. African Americans
    d. Japanese Americans

28. Which of the following statements incorrectly characterizes Harry S Truman?
    a. He was from the upper class, elite-educated, and worldly.
    b. He made a reputation in the Senate fighting waste in spending during World War II.
    c. He prided himself on speaking plainly and directly, but not in thinking deeply or analyzing carefully.
    d. He was poorly prepared for the job of president—Roosevelt had met with him only three times in two years.

29. Which of the following statements inaccurately depicts the new United Nations created in 1945?
    a. It embodied Wilson's vision of collective security.

   b. It reflected Wilson's concept of an international body.

   c. It included a General Assembly, in which each member nation would be represented and have one vote.

   d. It included a Security Council made up of five permanent members—the United States, Japan, France, Canada, and Germany—and ten rotating members.

30. The 1947 General Agreement on Tariffs and Trade (GATT)

   a. provided institutional structure for implementing free and fair trade agreements.

   b. created the International Monetary Fund to maintain a stable system of international exchange.

   c. created a bank to provide loans to war-battered countries.

   d. involved the Soviet Union, whose state-directed economic policies resembled western capitalism.

31. During the conference held at Yalta, the Allied powers agreed to divide Germany into zones of occupation. How many zones were eventually established?

   a. three

   b. four

   c. five

   d. seven

ESSAY

Description and Explanation (one- to two-paragraph essay)

1. Describe the divisions within groups that opposed American entrance into World War II.

2. Describe the role of antisemitism in the United States in such things as the antiwar movement, immigration, and opinions on motion pictures.

3. Describe Roosevelt's measures to aid Britain before the United States entered the war. Why did the United States refrain from entering the war earlier?

4. Describe why Eisenhower decided to move slowly along a broad front in the European war in 1945.

5. Describe the disagreement over where and how the atomic bomb should be used. Why did Truman and his top advisors decide to use it?

6. Describe the cooperation between big business and the government during World War II. How did this cooperation benefit business?

Discussion and Analysis (class discussion or one- to two-paragraph essay)

1. Discuss the Japanese attack on Pearl Harbor, including the events that took place, why it is considered to have been an act of desperation by Japan, and why the United States was not prepared for it.

2. Discuss how the labor shortage during the war affected women, African Americans, Native Americans, and Mexican immigrants.

3. Discuss the impact of the war on gender equality and on racial equality. In your opinion, were the results good or bad? Which groups benefited most, and how?

4. Discuss the problems involved in the issue of spheres of influence and the postwar political settlements among the Allies and other groups.

What If (include an explanation of your position)

1. If you were an American of Japanese descent living in California in 1941, describe your reaction to the attack on Pearl Harbor. How would it be different from that of a steel worker in Pittsburgh or a farmer in North Carolina?

2. If you were a young female living on the home front during World War II, how would you view your new opportunities?

3. If you were President Truman in 1945, decide whether or not you would use the atomic bomb and explain the reasons for your decision.

Crossword Puzzle: America during the Second World War

DOWN

1. Investment from 1942 to 1945 (2 wds.)
2. ___ and leasing was a way to get supplies to Allies.
3. OWI output
4. *Why We Fight* producer
5. The federal ___ almost quadrupled during the war.
6. Goal of America First Committee
8. Laughing sound
9. A homemaker was urged to be a ___ of fats.
11. Fifty U.S. ___ were traded for British bases in the Caribbean.
13. MacArthur's goal
18. Palestine to Zionists
20. Conference site for FDR, Stalin, Churchill
22. Hitler's promises
24. Stilwell's goal was reopening Burma ___.

ACROSS

1. Nazi menace in Atlantic (2 wds.)
7. Protest march planner of 1941
9. What *Reuben James* once stalked
10. 1940s hi-tech detection device
12. Japanese island captured in 1945
14. Night before
15. Nickname for World War II soldier
16. Milieu for King, Nimitz
17. Entrench

19. Enforcement of ___ laws was postponed during World War II.
21. Vice president who urged a "century of the common man."
23. Desire
25. Grain type
26. Business or military abbreviation
27. Operation TORCH site
28. Part of RAF

ANSWER KEY

WHO? WHAT? WHERE?

Who Were They?

1. f. Francisco Franco, p. 891
2. b. Burton K. Wheeler, p. 894
3. n. William Allen White, p. 895
4. g. Hideki Tojo, p. 897
5. h. Jeanette Rankin, p. 897
6. i. Joseph W. Stillwell, p. 905
7. j. Mao Zedong, p. 905
8. d. Douglas MacArthur, p. 906
9. c. Curtis LeMay, p. 907
10. a. Albert Einstein, p. 908
11. m. Paul Tibbets, p. 911
12. l. Norman Rockwell, p. 916
13. k. Frank Capra, p. 917
14. e. Eleanor Roosevelt, p. 919

What Was It?

1. m. Third Reich, p. 896
2. a. America First Committee, p. 894
3. l. sitzkrieg, p. 892
4. f. House Resolution 1776, p. 895
5. b. Atlantic Charter, p. 896
6. c. Day of Infamy, p. 897
7. i. petroleum, p. 896
8. j. radar, pp. 899-900
9. d. ENIGMA, p.900
10. h. Kaiser Corporation, p. 912
11. n. War Labor Board, p. 913

12. e. ERA, p. 918
13. g. inland relocation camps, p. 923
14. k. Security Council, p. 925
15. o. Zionism, p. 928

Where Was It?

1. f. Manchuria, p. 890
2. b. Ethiopia, p. 891
3. i. Poland, p. 892
4. d. Italy, p. 902
5. c. Elbe River, p. 902
6. a. Coral Sea, p. 905
7. j. Solomon Islands, p. 905
8. k. Trinity site, p. 909
9. g. Nagasaki, Japan, p. 909
10. l. Port Chicago, California, p. 921
11. e. Los Angeles, California, p. 921
12. m. Yalta, p. 927
13. h. Philippines, p. 927

CHARTS, MAPS, AND ILLUSTRATIONS

1. Stalingrad, p. 903
2. Coral Sea and Midway, p. 908
3. Navajo, p. 906
4. Dresden, Germany, had massive aerial bombing, and Hiroshima, Japan, was hit by the atomic bomb; no, p. 910
5. freedom of speech, freedom of worship, freedom from want, and freedom from fear, pp. 916-917

MULTIPLE CHOICE

1. a   (p. 890)

2. c (p. 891)

3. d (p. 891)

4. b (p. 892)

5. c (p. 892)

6. d (p. 894)

7. c (p. 894)

8. d (p. 894)

9. b (p. 895)

10. a (p. 896)

11. d (p. 896)

12. d (p. 897)

13. a (p. 897)

14. d (p. 898)

15. c (p. 900)

16. d (p. 900)

17. b (p. 902)

18. b (p. 904)

19. d (p. 904)

20. c (p. 905)

21. b (p. 905)

22. a (p. 909)

23. b (p. 911)

24. d (p. 912)

25. a (p. 913)

26. a (p. 918)

27. d (p. 923)

28. a (p. 909)

29. d (p. 925)

30. a (p. 926)

31. b (p. 927)

ESSAY

Description and Explanation

1. p. 894

2. p. 894

3. pp. 895–896

4. p. 902

5. p. 909

6. pp. 911–913

Discussion and Analysis

1. pp. 896–897

2. pp. 915, 918–921

3. pp. 918–921

4. pp. 926–927

What If

1. pp. 896–897

2. pp. 918–919

3. pp. 909–910

Crossword Puzzle

CHAPTER 27

THE AGE OF CONTAINMENT, 1946–1954

In the years after World War II, tensions strained international relations, national politics, economic markets, domestic workplaces, and lifestyles. Defeat of the Axis powers demanded that the United States and the Soviet Union cooperate, but this alliance did not last much beyond VE Day. Relations between the United States and the Soviet Union steadily eroded into a cold war of suspicion and tension. Issues of national security abroad and internal security at home increasingly dominated and narrowed the terms of a more conservative political debate. A series of crises heightened anticommunist fervor and deepened the obsession with national security, ultimately leading to the Korean War. American foreign policy focused even more narrowly on anticommunism and claimed to justify a global military offensive. The cold war was characterized by a wartime mentality, a swift military buildup, the intermingling of military and economic policies, and an emphasis on consensus and suppression of dissent.

Stresses that had lain dormant beneath the surface of American life seemed to erupt during these years. Shifts in population that disrupted established socioeconomic patterns combined with anxieties about the deepening cold war abroad to create tensions at home. Suburbia seemed a place to distance oneself from the ever-increasing change. The new suburban lifestyle epitomized the postwar spirit of confidence in the future but offered a way to cushion the impact of the social and demographic changes resulting from the new world order.

During Truman's administration, there was a growing faith that economic experts could manipulate the economy to assure constant expansion. Domestic economic growth was tied intrinsically to the global economy and thus to national security. Truman built his Fair Deal on the assumption that social reform ultimately would stem from economic growth. Postwar social policy focused on specific segments of society rather than on comprehensive programs for all. Concepts such as national health care and public housing became stigmatized as dangerous welfare schemes, but specific programs could be defended as security measures for people who were entitled to them.

When Dwight D. Eisenhower entered office in 1953, he brought moderate Republicanism with him. This meant few fundamental changes in either foreign or domestic programs, but Eisenhower helped to lower the pitch of the shrill anticommunist crusade. A new sense of calm settled over life in the United States—or so it seemed.

LIBERTY, EQUALITY, POWER

Growing concern about national security subtly altered the nation's views of liberty, equality, and power. The growing power of the executive branch of government, particularly agencies like the

CIA and the FBI, brought important changes to the nation's unwritten constitution. Older ideas about the constitutional structure of limited governmental powers gave way to the idea that broader executive authority was necessary to protect national security. Anxiety about security was used to justify limits on liberty and equality for many in the United States, such as in the accumulation of voluminous dossiers on a wide range of homosexual persons, intellectuals, and minority leaders by the FBI. Judges gave the government wide latitude in court cases, often neglecting to protect individual liberty. Extreme anticommunist fervor reached its height with McCarthyism.

Minorities and women made some headway during the postwar years. Truman issued an executive order that began desegregation of the armed forces. Major-league baseball's unofficial policy of racial segregation came to an end, but most owners discouraged further black participation in the sport. The media depicted the average American woman as a homebound wife and mother, but economic realities propelled more and more women into the job market, where opportunities remained within well-defined, sexually segregated areas. Professional opportunities for women actually narrowed. Postwar housing patterns were not simply the result of individual choice. The government actually maintained the segregationist pattern of white suburbs as the FHA made loan guarantees available only to men. In the age of anxiety, issues of liberty and equality took second place to those of national security.

OBJECTIVES

After studying this chapter, the student should be able to

1. Discuss the onset of the cold war.

2. Describe the Truman Doctrine in Europe, including the Marshall Plan and the Berlin Blockade, and the degree of success of the Truman Doctrine.

3. Describe the election of 1948.

4. Explore the Korean War as a part of American containment policy.

5. Examine how concerns about internal security affected many areas of postwar life.

6. Describe the role of economic planning and the promise of economic growth in Truman's Fair Deal programs.

7. Explore life in the suburbs and how it varied, depending on different groups.

8. Analyze the changing role of women in the postwar era.

CHRONOLOGY

1944   The Serviceman's Readjustment Act, or GI Bill, granted World War II veterans financial assistance for college, job-training programs, preferential consideration when applying for government jobs, liberal terms on home or business loans, and comprehensive medical care in veterans' hospitals.

1945   Truman, angered over growing Soviet influence in eastern Europe, suspended lend-lease assistance to the Soviet Union. Unfortunately, the strategy never worked, and lack of capital provided the Soviets with convenient excuses for tightening their grip on eastern Europe.

1945–1946   As production declined after the war, one out of every four workers lost his or her job. In the first full year after the war, there were more wildcat strikes than in any other twelve-month period in U.S. history.

1946   The Atomic Energy Commission was devised to replace the Manhattan Project in supervising development of American nuclear power.

President Truman appointed Bernard Baruch as a special representative to the United Nations. In **June**, Baruch announced his plan requiring all U.N. member nations to divulge information concerning nuclear research and materials, the forging of an international authority to guarantee compliance, and, finally, the destruction of all U.S. atomic weapons.

In **May**, Truman threatened to seize mines and railroads that had been shut down by strikes and ordered strikers back to work.

The Employment Act of 1946 called for "maximum," rather than "full" employment and expressly avowed that private enterprise, not the government, held responsibility for economic policy making.

To stimulate the economy and improve health services, the Hill-Burton Act authorized the federal government to inject billions of dollars into hospital construction.

Dr. Benjamin Spock's book on child care first appeared. It assigned virtually all child-care duties to the mothers.

In off-year elections, voters gave Republicans control of Congress for the first time since 1928.

The Supreme Court ruled that restrictive agreements were illegal and started to chip away at the "separate but equal" principle used to justify segregated schools since *Plessy* v. *Ferguson*.

1947   Harry S Truman placed his personal stamp on the presidency by concentrating on the fight against communism and orchestrating a national security state. In a speech to Congress on **March 12**, Truman declared that the fate of "free peoples" everywhere hung in the balance of American security issues. Unless the United States aided those who resisted subversion, totalitarian communism would spread worldwide and eventually would threaten the United States. This became known as the Truman Doctrine.

In **March**, the House Un-American Activities Committee (HUAC) held hearings in Hollywood to expose alleged communist infiltration in the film industry. Because they refused to testify, the "Hollywood Ten" were imprisoned for contempt of Congress. "Blacklists" were circulated with names of people who no longer could work in Hollywood because they refused to be pressured into naming friends and colleagues as communists.

Secretary of State George Marshall called on his advisers to develop a plan to strengthen the economics of western Europe. Under the Marshall Plan, western European governments coordinated their plans for postwar economic reconstruction with the help of funds provided by the United States.

George Kennan (under the pseudonym "Mr. X") coined the term *containment* in an article for *Foreign Affairs*. Containment became a catchword for global anticommunist national-security policies that took shape during the late 1940s.

With bipartisan support, Truman's request for financial assistance to Greece and Turkey was passed by Congress in the spring. This vote signaled the birth of a national-security policy that became known as containment.

Executive Order 9835, issued on **March 21** by President Truman, established a system of loyalty boards that were to be used to determine employee allegiance to the United States. The directive also empowered the attorney general's office to identify subversive organizations.

The National Security Act of 1947 initiated the transition from the antiquated War and Navy Departments to the new Department of Defense, which was established in 1949. The act established the National Security Council to plan foreign policy, created a separate but equal military branch known as the Air Force, and devised the Central Intelligence Agency (CIA) to undertake covert activities and gather information.

Adversaries of organized labor in Congress passed the Taft-Hartley Act, which rolled back some of the advances unions had made during the 1930s and forced union officials to sign affidavits denying Communist Party membership.

In **October** the new Long Island, New York, suburb of Levittown welcomed its first residents. This seemed to make the dream of affordable houses for the middle class a reality.

Organized baseball's unofficial policy of racial segregation ended when Jackie Robinson became the Brooklyn Dodgers' first-baseman.

1948

Alger Hiss, a prominent liberal Democrat with a long career in government, was accused of passing classified documents to Soviet agents in the late 1930s, thus creating a great scandal. To many Americans, this affair confirmed the domestic threat of communism.

In **June**, the United States, Great Britain, and France announced a plan, beginning with currency reform, to merge their sectors of Germany into a federal German republic. The prospect of a revitalized German state alarmed Soviet leaders. To retaliate, the Soviets cut all land transportation to West Berlin from West Germany. Air routes remained open and American and British pilots delivered supplies to the city.

In the **November** presidential election, Truman waged an energetic campaign against Republican candidate Thomas E. Dewey, States' Rights candidate Strom Thurmond, and Progressive Party nominee Henry Wallace. Truman won only 49.5 percent of the popular vote, but gained a solid majority in the electoral college.

Studies indicated that approximately 25 percent of married mothers were employed outside the home. However, employment opportunities continued to be limited to well-defined and sex-segregated areas such as nursing, teaching, and clerical professions.

1949

In his inaugural address, Truman presented the Fair Deal, calling for the extension of popular New Deal programs like Social Security and minimum-wage laws as well as new legislation regarding national health care and civil rights. The Fair Deal was based on the assumption that social reform would stem from economic growth.

Seeing that there was no alternative, Stalin abandoned the blockade in **May** and led Soviets in creating the German Democratic Republic out of their East German sector. The "two Germanys" remained a symbol of cold war tensions for the next forty years.

The United States and eleven other countries formed a military alliance by joining the North Atlantic Treaty Organization (NATO). Member nations agreed to cooperate on economic, political, and military matters and pledged that an attack against one would be an attack on all.

By 1949, Communist forces had pushed Jiang Jieshi, leader of "free China," off the mainland to the island of Formosa. Despite U.S. financial support of Jiang, Truman's administration was accused of being soft on communism.

In **September**, the West's monopoly on atomic weaponry ended as the news reached Washington that the Soviets had exploded a crude atomic device. Truman then authorized research in the area of nuclear fusion.

Paul Nitze's NSC-68, a blueprint for cold war foreign policy, included plans for covert action, economic pressure, enlarged propaganda efforts, and a massive military buildup.

1950

The dire warnings of NSC-68 seemed confirmed in **June** when communist North Korea attacked South Korea. The fighting in Korea soon escalated into an international conflict known as the Korean War.

Referring to the Fourteenth Amendment, the Supreme Court ruled racial segregation of state-financed graduate and law schools unconstitutional.

Communist Party members Julius and Ethel Rosenberg were arrested and later sentenced to death for the theft of nuclear secrets. The melodrama of the case epitomized the Cold War atmosphere.

The McCarran Internal Security Act of 1950 authorized detention of suspected subversives in special camps during times of emergency and created the Subversive Activities Control Board to investigate organizations suspected of having communist ties.

Joseph McCarthy, junior senator from Wisconsin, made wild charges that communists were at work in the State Department. After examining State Department files, the Senate Foreign Relations Committee concluded that McCarthy's charges that communists lurked in Truman's administration were untrue and were part of a propaganda campaign.

1951

In **April**, Truman relieved from command General Douglas MacArthur for ignoring orders to negotiate a truce in the Korean War at the 38th parallel.

A Japanese-American security pact granted the United States a base on Okinawa and permission for U.S. troops to be stationed in Japan. Bases were also established in the Middle East, Latin America, and the Philippines.

The Twenty-second Amendment was passed to exclude future presidents from serving more than two terms.

In Congress, Republicans and conservative Democrats condemned the Truman administration's handling of the anticommunist issue and introduced their own legislation, known as the McCarran Internal Security Act.

1952

Congress passed the McCarran-Walter Act to further restrict immigration from areas outside northern and western Europe and people suspected as possible national-security risks.

In **November**, General Dwight D. Eisenhower easily routed the Democratic presidential candidate Adlai Stevenson.

1953

On **July 27**, a truce was signed to end the Korean War; Eisenhower's presidential campaign pledge to end military involvement was realized.

1954

The legal political organization status of the Communist Party was annulled by the Communist Control Act. Communist Party candidates were barred from elections, and stricter registration requirements were sanctioned.

During the **spring**, a Senate committee conducted televised hearings to investigate McCarthy's charges that the army was tolerating subversives in its ranks. Under the glare of TV lights, McCarthy appeared as a crude, desperate bully. In **December**, the Senate voted to censure him for conduct unbecoming to a member of the Senate.

GLOSSARY OF IMPORTANT TERMS

apartheid
Legal system practiced in South Africa and based on elaborate rules of racial separation and subordination of blacks.

baby boom
Sudden increase in births in the years after World War II.

blacklist
In the postwar years, a list of people who could no longer work in the entertainment industry because of alleged contacts with communists.

cold war
War or rivalry conducted by all means available except open military action. Diplomatic relations are not commonly broken.

containment
Policy adopted by the United States to stop the expansion of communism. It became the catchphrase of the global anticommunist national-security policies that took shape during the late 1940s.

McCarthyism
Public accusations of disloyalty made with little or no regard to actual evidence; named after Joseph McCarthy, these accusations and the scandal and harm they caused came to symbolize the most virulent form of anti-communism.

POW
Prisoner of war.

RAND
An acronym for Research and Development.

separate spheres
The idea that there were two spheres in life: a public sphere of work and politics dominated by men and a private sphere of housework and child care reserved for women.

service jobs
Occupations such as secretarial work, teaching, and nursing that provide service for the public. Frequently held by women who were paid poorly.

subversive
Systematic, deliberate attempt to overthrow or undermine a government or society by people working secretly within the country.

think tank
Group or agency organized to conduct intensive research or engage in problem solving. Especially active in developing new technology, military strategy, or social planning.

totalitarian movements
Movements in which the individual is subordinated to the state. All areas of life are subjected to centralized, total control, sometimes by force.

WHO? WHAT? WHERE?

WHO WERE THEY?

Complete each following statement (questions 1–17) by writing the letter preceding the appropriate name in the space provided. Use each answer only once.

a. Alger Hiss
b. Benjamin Spock
c. Bernard Baruch
d. Douglas MacArthur
e. Dwight D. Eisenhower
f. George Kennan
g. George Marshall
h. Harry S Truman
i. Hugh Hefner
j. Jackie Robinson
k. Joseph McCarthy
l. Julius Rosenberg
m. Millard Tydings
n. Paul Nitze
o. Ronald Reagan
p. Strom Thurmond
q. Syngman Rhee

_____ 1. Prominent financier appointed by Truman as a special representative to the United Nations who offered a plan for international control of atomic power.

_____ 2. Foreign service officer who specialized in Soviet Affairs and first used the term *containment* in an article in *Foreign Affairs*.

_____ 3. Secretary of state who called on his advisers to devise a strategy that would strengthen the economies of western Europe.

_____ 4. Candidate of the States' Rights, or Dixiecrat, ticket in the presidential election of 1948.

_____ 5. Author of a famous top-secret policy paper that provided the blueprint for both the rhetoric and strategy for cold war foreign policy.

_____ 6. Head of the autocratic government of South Korea who was educated in America.

_____ 7. American military leader who challenged Truman's decision to negotiate a truce in Korea.

_____ 8. Leader of the Screen Actors Guild and a secret informer for the FBI.

_____ 9. Prominent liberal Democrat charged with passing classified documents to Soviet agents.

_____ 10. Member of the Communist Party who was executed for passing secrets to the Soviets.

_____ 11. Junior senator from Wisconsin who became the Truman administration's prime accuser.

_____ 12. Maryland senator who was defeated for reelection in part because of a fabricated photo that linked him to an alleged communist.

_____ 13. President who pressed more than any previous president to end racial discrimination.

_____ 14. First African American to play major-league baseball in the twentieth century.

_____ 15. Author of the popular book that assigned virtually all child-care duties to women.

_____ 16. Magazine publisher who preached that men who neglected their own happiness and labored constantly to support a wife and children were not saints but suckers.

_____ 17. Candidate for president in 1952 who promised to go to Korea if elected.

WHAT WAS IT?

Complete each following statement (questions 1–12) by writing the letter preceding the appropriate name in the space provided. Use each answer only once.

a. Atomic Energy Commission
b. Brooklyn Dodgers
c. Executive Order 9835
d. Fair Deal
e. Federal Housing Administration
f. GNP
g. House Un-American Activities Committee
h. National Security Council
i. 38th parallel
j. Truman Doctrine
k. uranium
l. Verona Files

_____ 1. The sweeping vision of national security under which the United States would go to the aid of those who resist communism and its spread.

_____ 2. Policy that advocated halting the spread of communism and called for a system of loyalty boards.

_____ 3. New arm of the executive branch with broad authority over the planning of foreign affairs.

_____ 4. Documents made public in 1995 containing intercepted messages between the Soviet Union and agents in the United States.

_____ 5. Dividing line between North and South Korea.

_____ 6. Agency created in 1946 to succeed the Manhattan Project.

_____ 7. Important raw material that the United States obtained from South Africa.

_____ 8. Group that conducted hearings to expose alleged communist infiltration of the film industry.

_____ 9. Name Truman gave to his domestic program.

_____ 10. Total dollar value of all the goods and services produced in a year.

_____ 11. One of the federal programs to help buyers purchase their first home.

_____ 12. First major-league baseball team to end the policy of racial segregation.

WHERE WAS IT?

Complete each statement below (questions 1–6) by writing the letter preceding the appropriate name in the space provided. Use each answer only once.

    a. Berlin
    b. Formosa
    c. Greece
    d. Hollywood
    e. Inchon
    f. Levittown, New York

_____ 1. Country where a communist-led group tried to topple a corrupt but prowestern government that Truman decided to defend.

_____ 2. City the Soviets tried to blockade by cutting most transportation routes.

_____ 3. Island to which Jiang Jieshi was forced by the communist Chinese.

_____ 4. Korean city where American marines successfully landed and pushed on to Seoul within eleven days.

_____ 5. Location of the hearings conducted by the House Un-American Activities Committee to expose alleged communist infiltration of the film industry.

_____ 6. Mass-produced town that offered suburban living at relatively affordable prices.

CHARTS, MAPS, AND ILLUSTRATIONS

1. The name of the lurid comic book distributed by some church groups out of fear of communist subversion was _____.

2. The northernmost country in the NATO alliance was _____.

3. One state carried by the States' Rights Party in the presidential election of 1948 was

   _____.

4. One of the most feared diseases during the cold war period was _____.

   The doctor who developed the first vaccination against it was _____.

5. The peak year of the baby boom was _____.

6. The film star who became a symbol of youthful alienation during the 1950s and early 1960s was _____.

MULTIPLE CHOICE

Circle the letter that best completes each statement.

1. The atomic bomb provided a crucial element of friction in the cold war. Which world leader remarked, "We have a new weapon of unusual destructive force," at the Potsdam Conference?
   a. Harry Truman
   b. Joseph Stalin
   c. Winston Churchill
   d. Jiang Jieshi

2. In 1946 Truman appointed Bernard Baruch, a prominent financier, as special representative to the United Nations. Baruch proposed a plan for international control of atomic power. His plan included
   a. a condemnation of Soviet expansion.
   b. an agreement not to use nuclear weapons on U.N. member nations.
   c. full disclosure by all U.N. member nations of nuclear research and materials.
   d. the creation of a "think tank" (RAND) to develop surface-to-surface missiles.

3. In a speech to Congress outlining what came to be known as the Truman Doctrine, the president attempted to justify U.S. aid to Greece and Turkey by announcing that U.S. security interests were
   a. isolated.
   b. in the Southern Hemishere only.
   c. in the Eastern Hemisphere only.
   d. worldwide.

4. What became the catchphrase for the global anticommunist national-security policies that took shape during the late 1940s?
   a. Kennanism
   b. containment
   c. expressionism
   d. allotment

5. Nine days after proclaiming the Truman Doctrine, the president issued Executive Order 9835, which brought the policy of containing communists to the home front. Which of the following was not part of Executive Order 9835?
   a. a system of loyalty boards
   b. implementation of an internal U.S. policy meant to contain communists
   c. identification of subversive organizations by the attorney general's office
   d. an educational campaign meant to reconcile ideological differences between the United States and communist countries

6. Which of the following statements inaccurately depicts the Central Intelligence Agency (CIA)?
   a. It was despised by Truman, who limited and cautiously controlled the agency's security mandate.

b. It was created to gather information and to undertake covert activities in support of the nation's security interests.

c. It was the most flexible tool of the national security bureaucracy.

d. It was shielded from public scrutiny and could use its funds to finance and encourage anticommunist resistance.

7. Secretary of State George Marshall called on his advisers to devise a strategy that would strengthen the economies of western Europe. The Marshall Plan

a. was viewed by Truman as a disaster.

b. closed markets and cut investment opportunities for American businesses in western Europe.

c. provided for western European governments to coordinate plans for postwar economic reconstruction.

d. was supported by Stalin, whose major goal was rebuilding capitalism in Europe.

8. The German Democratic Republic (East Germany) was created by the

a. British.

b. Americans.

c. French.

d. Soviets.

9. In 1949, the United States and eleven other nations formed NATO, pledged that an attack against one would be considered an attack against all, and agreed to cooperate on economic, political, and military matters. The acronym NATO stands for

a. Nations Align to Oppress.

b. Nuclear Alliance Trent Organization.

c. North Atlantic Treaty Organization.

d. National Allies for Trees and Oceans.

10. Between 1945 and 1948, the United States extended to Jiang Jieshi's government a billion dollars in military aid and another billion in economic assistance. But Jiang steadily lost ground to the communist forces of

a. Ngo Dinh Diem.

b. Ho Chi Minh.

c. Gamal Abdel Nasser.

d. Mao Zedong.

11. The doctrine of containment became even more wedded to the creation of a deadly technology after the Soviets tested an atomic device, and the United States responded by escalating the weapons race with the building of

a. a hydrogen bomb.

b. an armored tank.

c. a SCUD missile.

d. a satellite defense system.

12. The dire warnings of NSC-68 seemed confirmed by the Korean War, which began in June 1950 when South Korea was attacked by the communist country of

a. China.

    b. North Korea.

    c. Vietnam.

    d. Czechoslovakia.

13. Which of the following was not a repercussion of the Korean War?

    a. American policy focused more narrowly on anticommunism.

    b. The United States announced a plan to rearm West Germany.

    c. NATO's military forces were increased.

    d. North Korea adopted a democratic government and broke ties with the Soviet Union.

14. Which of the following changes did not accompany the cold war?

    a. Military and economic policies intermingled.

    b. A peacetime mentality came to the United States.

    c. The military was built up swiftly.

    d. Consensus was emphasized and dissent was suppressed.

15. In 1947, opponents of organized labor passed the Taft-Hartley Act, which

    a. compelled employers to accept closed shops in which only union members could be hired.

    b. allowed a union to conduct boycotts.

    c. allowed union officials to belong to the Communist Party.

    d. was endorsed by Truman, but not by Congress.

16. Republicans and conservative Democrats condemned the administration's handling of the anticommunist issue and introduced their own legislation, the McCarran Internal Security Act of 1950. Which of the following statements incorrectly characterizes the McCarran Act?

    a. It was intended for national emergencies.

    b. It authorized detention of alleged subversives in special camps.

    c. It created a board to investigate organizations suspected of communist activities.

    d. It was supported by Truman.

17. Who was responsible for putting Truman's administration in a defensive posture and spreading accusations that communists were at work in the State Department?

    a. Joseph McCarthy

    b. Dwight Eisenhower

    c. George Marshall

    d. Alger Hiss

18. Growing concern over the nation's security prompted changes in the constitutional structure of the United States, such as the Twenty-second Amendment in 1951, which

    a. barred future presidents from serving more than two terms.

    b. gave citizens eighteen years of age or older the right to vote.

    c. allowed the District of Columbia to participate in presidential elections.

    d. prohibited the manufacture and sale of alcoholic beverages.

19. The Employment Act, passed by Congress in 1946,
    a. rejected the liberal position that any ongoing economic involvement by Washington was proper.
    b. dissolved the Council of Economic Advisers.
    c. called for "maximum" (rather than full) employment and specifically acknowledged that private enterprise, not the government, bore the primary responsibility of economic policy making.
    d. stated that its main goal was to achieve social justice through full employment.

20. Truman began his second presidential term determined to break new ground in the arena of domestic issues; in his inaugural address of 1949 Truman presented a program called the
    a. New Deal.
    b. Return to Normalcy.
    c. New Freedom.
    d. Fair Deal.

21. Convinced that constant economic growth was possible, Truman unveiled, in his inaugural address of January 1949, the social agenda about which he already had hinted during his 1949 campaign. Which of the following was not called for in Truman's new agenda?
    a. Social Security
    b. nuclear weapons research
    c. minimum wage laws
    d. national health care

22. The GI Bill, officially known as the Serviceman's Readjustment Act of 1944, did not include
    a. comprehensive medical care in veterans' hospitals.
    b. financial assistance for college.
    c. free government housing for five years after service.
    d. job-training programs.

23. Veterans' benefits and Social Security highlighted the approach to social policy in postwar America. Specifically, the Social Security program, an expansion of Roosevelt's New Deal,
    a. was defended as economic security for people who had earned government assistance.
    b. was the most unpopular part of Roosevelt's New Deal because it called for uniform entitlements for all citizens.
    c. did not include support for the elderly, disabled, and blind.
    d. was referred to by supporters as another type of social welfare.

24. In the late 1940s, Truman sent a message to Congress that endorsed ideas advanced by the civil rights committee. The committee's report, entitled "To Secure These Rights," included all of the following proposals, except
    a. federal legislation against lynching.
    b. continued segregation in the military.

    c. a civil-rights division within the Department of Justice.

    d. antidiscrimination initiatives in employment, housing, and public facilities.

25. Suburbia was a place where the search for change and the yearning to contain its effects easily coexisted. Which of the following was not a characteristic of postwar suburbia?
    a. Women who sought careers outside the home were labeled negatively.
    b. Women spent less time doing housework and providing child care.
    c. The lack of an automobile made it difficult to make a trip to the supermarket.
    d. Women's colleges offered instruction that was supposed to lead to marriage, not work or careers.

26. One way everyday lives of Americans were changing in the postwar era was
    a. increased racial segregation.
    b. a decline in home ownership.
    c. development of new child-rearing practices.
    d. increased professional opportunities for women.

27. The Truman presidency was followed by an administration that symbolized tranquillity, and a new sense of calm settled over life in the United States with the election of
    a. Dwight Eisenhower.
    b. John Kennedy.
    c. Lyndon Johnson.
    d. Gerald Ford.

ESSAY

Description and Explanation (one- to two-paragraph essay)

1. Describe what the term *containment* meant originally and what it became.

2. Describe the Marshall Plan. What was its purpose? What were the results?

3. Explain the repercussions of the Korean War.

4. Describe Truman's loyalty program, including the controversial assumptions upon which it rested. What new agencies were created? What roles did they play?

5. Describe the integration of baseball as an interplay between the celebration and containment of changes.

6. Describe President Eisenhower as a "middle-of-the-road," or moderate, Republican. Did this political stance benefit the United States? How?

7. Describe the downfall of Joseph McCarthy and the loss of his power.

Discussion and Analysis (class discussion or one- to two-paragraph essay)

1. Discuss the origins of the cold war. How did the political views of the Soviet Union, President Truman's actions, the atomic bomb, questions of loans, and Soviet spheres of influence contribute to it?

2. Discuss why Truman won the election of 1948.

3. Discuss the rise of the suburbs and the lifestyle of those who inhabited them. How were they financed? What was the advantage of living there? What was the effect of the suburbs on the roles of women?

What If (include an explanation of your position.)

1. If you were General Douglas McArthur and had just been removed from your command in Korea, how would you react?

2. If you were one of the Hollywood 10, would you be willing to go to prison for these principles?

3. What if you were a young housewife living in suburbia in the postwar years, what would you like and dislike about it? Would it make a difference if you were professionally trained or nonwhite?

Crossword Puzzle: The Age of Containment, 1946–1954

DOWN

1. Author of plan for European economic recovery
2. NATO, for one
3. Guardian
4. Pronoun
5. High-water mark for MacArthur
6. Americans fought in Korea under ___ auspices.
8. Truman's secretary of state
9. Taft's cosponsor of antiunion law
12. Too
14. What an internationalist didn't want United States to be again.
16. GOP candidate in 1948
19. Stalin's city
20. Eisenhower's vice president
21. Benjamin Spock's readers, mostly

ACROSS

1. Redbaiting senator
7. FBI's secret agent T-10
10. Perennial Democratic stronghold (2 wds.)
11. One of the Germanys
13. Former FDR aide accused of espionage
15. Civil rights committee urged laws to stop African Americans from being ___ .
17. The sun personified
18. Area of interest for Keynes and his disciples
22. Deducting mortgage interest from ___ was middle-class welfare (2 wds.).
23. FBI director
24. NATO-type pact for Southeast Asia

ANSWER KEY

WHO? WHAT? WHERE?

Who Were They?

1. c. Bernard Baruch, pp. 932-933
2. f. George Kennan, p. 934
3. g. George Marshall, pp. 935-936
4. p. Strom Thurmond, p. 937
5. n. Paul Nitze, p. 941
6. q. Syngman Rhee, p. 941
7. d. Douglas MacArthur, p. 943
8. o. Ronald Reagan, p. 947
9. a. Alger Hiss, p. 948
10. l. Julius Rosenberg, p. 949
11. k. Joseph McCarthy, p. 950
12. m. Millard Tydings, p. 951
13. h. Harry S Truman, p. 955
14. j. Jackie Robinson, p. 956
15. b. Benjamin Spock, p. 959
16. i. Hugh Hefner, p. 961
17. e. Dwight D. Eisenhower, p. 962

What Was It?

1. j. Truman Doctrine, p. 933
2. c. Executive Order 9835, p. 934
3. h. National Security Council, p. 935
4. l. Vernona Files, p. 935
5. i. 38th parallel, p. 941
6. a. Atomic Energy Commission, p. 944
7. k. uranium, p. 946
8. g. House Un-American Activities Committee, p. 947
9. d. Fair Deal, p. 953
10. f. GNP, p. 953
11. e. Federal Housing Administration, p. 954
12. b. Brooklyn Dodgers, p. 956

Where Was It?

1. c. Greece, p. 933
2. a. Berlin, p. 936
3. b. Formosa, p. 939
4. e. Inchon, p. 942
5. d. Hollywood, p. 947
6. f. Levittown, New York, p. 957

CHARTS, MAPS, AND ILLUSTRATIONS

1. Is This Tomorrow? p. 934
2. Norway, p. 939
3. Louisiana, Mississippi, Alablama, and South Carolina, p. 937
4. polio; Dr. Jonas Salk, p. 954
5. 1947, p. 959
6. James Dean, p. 961

MULTIPLE CHOICE

1. a (p. 932)
2. c (p. 933)
3. d (p. 933)
4. b (p. 934)
5. d (p. 934)
6. a (p. 935)
7. c (p. 936)
8. d (p. 937)
9. c (p. 938)

10. d   (p. 938)

11. a   (p. 940)

12. b   (p. 941)

13. d   (p. 943)

14. b   (p. 945)

15. b   (p. 947)

16. d   (p. 950)

17. a   (p. 950)

18. a   (p. 951)

19. c   (p. 952)

20. d   (p. 953)

21. b   (p. 953)

22. c   (p. 953)

23. a   (pp. 953–954)

24. b   (p. 955)

25. b   (pp. 959–961)

26. b   (p. 962)

27. a   (p. 963)

ESSAY

Description and Explanation

1. p. 934

2. pp. 935–937

3. pp. 943–944

4. pp. 934–935

5. p. 956

6. pp. 963–964

7. pp. 951–952

Discussion and Analysis

1. pp. 931–933

2. pp. 937–938

3. pp. 957–961

What If

1. pp. 942–943

2. p. 947

3. pp. 958–961

Crossword Puzzle

CHAPTER 28

AFFLUENCE AND ITS DISCONTENTS, 1954–1963

In the mid-1950s, many of the tensions of the cold war started to abate. Instead of confrontations between the United States and the Soviet Union over Europe, there was greater reliance on nuclear deterrence and power plays in the Third World. The United States began to emphasize covert action and economic leverage over military confrontation, which had the advantages of being less expensive and provoking less public controversy at home. These methods of fighting the cold war also created more economic opportunities for Americans abroad. At the same time, covert actions provoked serious reactions from the peoples in the Third World and Europe.

Americans had become a people of plenty with their automobiles, rapid economic growth, and expanding marketplace. "Made in America" was a symbol of abundance and high-quality production. The fierce labor-capital conflicts that marked previous decades ceased. Most workers made significant economic gains in the late 1950s and early 1960s. This age of affluence spawned a youth culture with its comic books and rock music as well as new developments such as television. Social critics asserted that the new social and cultural problems appeared to stem from the youth culture and the age of affluence. The 1950s also marked the emergence of a culture dominated by national corporate institutions.

Eisenhower took few steps to enlarge governmental power. His popularity rested more on his personality rather than the specifics of his policies, many of which were assailed from both right and left. Critics accused him of doing too much or too little. Later, the Kennedy administration riveted media attention and brought prominent intellectuals into the White House. These driven young men and women promised to launch exciting new crusades. Momentum and change, however, lay more often in rhetoric and style than in action.

Rising dissatisfaction over the slow pace of the campaign against racial discrimination forced the Kennedy administration to consider new initiatives. There was growing grass-roots activism; and violence, played out on nightly television, shocked the American people. During the last part of the Kennedy presidency, civil rights issues dominated domestic politics. By the fall of 1963, it seemed that the administration might be ready to support significant social changes. Then on November 22, 1963, Kennedy was killed in Dallas. Years later, there still are conflicting theories about his assassination. Meanwhile, Vice President Lyndon B. Johnson inherited both domestic and global foreign-policy problems.

LIBERTY, EQUALITY, POWER

The age of affluence failed to address many of the larger issues of liberty, equality, and power. The Eisenhower administration lacked coherent policies on civil rights for African Americans and did not have an Indian policy that was workable. Many Mexican immigrants were rounded up and deported to Mexico, causing a stigmatism to develop for people of Mexican descent and to justify discriminatory treatment of them. None of these groups were given the liberty or power to control their lives or futures. Equality for these groups was not something that was valued by many white Americans.

The role of power in American politics was demonstrated clearly by American maneuvers around the globe. Increasingly, American officials intervened in Third World politics, often without consulting the peoples of these areas. Eventually, the United States found itself supporting military dictatorships overseas that thrived on power and afforded little or no liberty or equality to their people. In some cases, the CIA or American marines overthrew elected governments and participated in the assassinations of key officials of other countries, justifying their actions on the grounds of protecting the American national interest.

A classic example of the struggle for liberty, equality, and power is the rise of the civil rights movement in the South. White southerners had power over African Americans in their society and were determined to keep it. Rampant discrimination, even over acts as small as denying blacks the right to eat at a lunch counter in a small town, deprived blacks of much of their simple dignity and control over their lives. Blacks began to organize and demonstrate, finding strength in numbers. The demands of minority groups for liberty, equality, and power would not go away. The possible use of government power to advance equality was increasingly an issue.

OBJECTIVES

After studying this chapter, a student should be able to

1. Describe the role of the Eisenhower administration in foreign affairs in the 1950s, including the growing role of the CIA.

2. Describe the role of religion in the age of affluence and anticommunism.

3. Describe the effects of affluence on American life.

4. Examine youth culture and mass culture and their critics.

5. Discuss the election of 1960.

6. Describe the Kennedy administration's activities in foreign affairs and how they were similar and different from those of the Eisenhower administration.

7. Compare civil rights concerns during the Eisenhower and Kennedy administrations.

CHRONOLOGY

1950	For the next five years, the U.S. government deported alleged illegal Mexican immigrants. The well-published operation created a stigma for people

of Mexican descent and resulted in discrimination by both government and private employers.

1951

Under the relocation program, which began in 1951, Indians were encouraged to leave their reservations and take jobs in urban areas. This program, like the termination policy, encouraged American Indians to migrate to urban areas and to assimilate into the social mainstream.

1953

Following Joseph Stalin's death, Nikita Khrushchev became the new Soviet leader, speaking of "peaceful coexistence." Khrushchev eventually denounced Stalin's tactics and reduced Soviet armed forces to free up re-sources to produce more consumer goods.

The Central Intelligence Agency gradually broadened its scope by bringing about the election of anticommunist Philippine President Ramón Magsaysay. The CIA participated in a coup to overthrow Mohammed Mossadegh's constitutional government in Iran, restoring to power Shah Reza Pahlevi.

In **December**, Admiral Arthur Radford, chair of the Joint Chiefs of Staff, called for a reduction of the military budget and a revision of defense strategy. This reflected Eisenhower's belief that massive expenditures would hinder economic growth.

1954

The anticommunist rhetoric that accompanied McCarthyism and the Korean War began to dwindle. Foreign policy refocused on deterrence and gave way to power plays in Third World countries.

The Southeast Asia Treaty Organization (SEATO) was created as a collective defense agreement between Australia, France, Great Britain, New Zealand, Pakistan, the Philippines, Thailand, and the United States.

After overthrowing a corrupt monarchy, Gamal Abdel Nasser took power in Egypt and pledged to set Arab nations free from imperialist domination and direct them toward "positive neutralism." Nasser strengthened Egypt's economic and military power by exploiting anti-Israel sentiment and accepted aid from both the United States and Soviet Union.

The CIA, working closely with the United Fruit Company, helped to topple President Jacobo Arbenz's elected government in Guatemala.

Colonel Edward Lansdale, who had directed CIA efforts against a leftist insurgency in the Philippines from 1950 to 1953, arrived in Saigon, the capital of South Vietnam, to engineer the construction of a government under anticommunist leader Ngo Dinh Diem.

Rock-and-roll singer Elvis Presley leaped into the national spotlight.

Chief Justice Earl Warren wrote the Supreme Court's unanimous opinion in *Brown* v. *Board of Education*. Although it technically applied only to educational facilities, the decision implied that the segregation of all public facilities was open to legal challenge.

Six bills to abolish reservations, liquidate assets of tribes, and terminate federal services to American Indians were enacted.

A survey indicated that more than 95 percent of the American people identified with one of the three major faiths.

1955   An agreement was reached in **May** between superpowers to end postwar occupation of Austria, transforming the country into a neutral state. Two months later, a summit was held in Geneva, Switzerland, producing few concrete results on the issues. However, it eased cold war tension.

Eisenhower suggested verifying disarmaments with the use of reconnaissance flights. Apprehensive about opening their country to inspection, the Soviets refused the "open skies" proposal. Some progress, however, was made in negotiations to limit atomic tests.

Rosa Parks was arrested for refusing to obey a state law that required black passengers to give up their seats to whites and to sit at the back of a bus. Following Parks's lead, many African-American women spearheaded the Montgomery bus boycott. This resulted in the desegregation of city buses and demonstrated to other black communities in the South how to mobilize against acts of overt discrimination.

The *National Review* was established and represented an important venue of expression for the political right.

Automakers boosted their 1955 sales to almost eight million cars. This was about one third of the total of the automobiles owned by Americans on the eve of World War II.

The AFL and the CIO merged, a sign of declining militancy by the labor movement.

Military expenditures accounted for about 10 percent of the GNP, an indication of the important role of national security in the economy.

1956   Nasser, unsatisfied with the economic and military strength he had attained in Egypt, obtained advanced weapons from communist Czechoslovakia. The United States then canceled building loans for the Aswan Dam. The Soviet Union strengthened its ties with Nasser by agreeing to finance the project. The Egyptian leader then nationalized the British-owned Suez Canal.

Eisenhower endorsed several costly new domestic programs, such as the Highway Act of 1956. Described as the largest public-works project ever, it included a national system of limited-access expressways.

Defiance of segregation laws grew as a hundred members of the House and Senate signed a "Southern Manifesto," which promised to support any state that intended "to resist forced integration by any lawful means."

U-2 flights over the Soviet Union began.

Armed rebellion spread throughout Hungary. Secretary of State John Foster Dulles talked of supporting liberation from communism. Hungarian revolutionaries appealed to the United States to come to their aid, to no avail. Soviet armies crushed the uprising and killed thousands of Hungarians. Liberation made good political rhetoric at home, but it led to tragedy abroad.

President Eisenhower won a second term over Adlai Stevenson. Ike's personal popularity continued, but did not extend to his political party. Republicans failed to win back control of Congress from the Democrats.

1957

In the spring, the president received congressional endorsement of the "Eisenhower Doctrine," a pledge to defend Middle Eastern countries in imminent danger from armed communist aggression.

The Civil Rights Act of 1957 represented the first congressional civil rights legislation in more than eighty years. It set procedures for expediting lawsuits by African Americans who asserted their voting rights had been restricted. Included, also, was the creation of a permanent Commission on Civil Rights that would serve as an advisory body to study civil rights violations and make recommendations.

U. S. marines set up an anti-Nasser government in Beirut, Lebanon. This was part of Eisenhower's policy to support friendly, conservative governments in the Middle East.

The governor of Arkansas ordered the National Guard to block enforcement of a federal court order mandating integration of a high school. In response, President Eisenhower ordered the guard be put under federal control. Black students were escorted into Little Rock Central High School by military forces.

The Southern Christian Leadership Conference was formed by the Reverend Martin Luther King, Jr., and other black ministers. It pressed for desegregation of public facilities and launched an effort to register black voters throughout the South.

The Gaither Report, prepared by prominent figures with close ties to defense industries, warned that the Soviet Union's GNP was growing more quickly than that of the United States and that much of the expansion was in the military sector. The report urged greater spending on U.S. defense to compensate for the widening gap.

A committee of prominent scientists implored the Defense Department to provide funding for basic scientific research. Arguments for greater defense spending fell on deaf ears until the Soviets launched the world's first artificial satellite, *Sputnik*, in **October**.

1958

After the Soviet success of *Sputnik*, arguments for greater spending on education resulted in the National Defense Education Act. This legislation would allocate federal money for programs in science, engineering, and foreign languages.

In *The Affluent Society*, author John Kenneth Galbraith directed attention away from deep-rooted inequalities that persisted in American society.

1959

The United States indicated disapproval of Castro's overthrow of Batista in Cuba by imposing an economic boycott on the island. Castro responded by declaring himself a communist, siding with the Soviet Union, and pledging to support leftist insurgencies throughout Latin America.

1960

The "sit-in movement" began in North Carolina when young African-American students defied state segregation laws by sitting at a lunch counter and asking to be served with white customers.

The presidential election resulted in a victory for John F. Kennedy, the first president to be born in the twentieth century. Together with his wife, Kennedy projected an image of youth, glamour, and vigor that added to the Kennedy mystique.

A summit scheduled in Paris was canceled after the Soviets shot down an American U-2 spy plane over their territory.

Taking advantage of cheaper airfares between North America and the Caribbean, Puerto Ricans began moving to the mainland in unprecedented numbers. New York City's Puerto Rican community was nearly one hundred times greater than it had been before World War II.

A second civil rights act was passed that promised federal support for blacks who were being prevented from voting in the South.

1961

The secret CIA invasion at the Bay of Pigs on **April 17**, meant to overthrow Cuban leader Fidel Castro, ended in disaster. President Kennedy refused to provide expected air support to the invaders and at first attempted to deny any U.S. involvement.

On **August 13**, the German communist regime first began to erect a barbed-wire fence and then a concrete wall, dividing East from West Berlin. The Berlin Wall served as a symbol of the cold war and communist repression.

Alliance for Progress was proposed as a way to prevent the spread of anti-Americanism and communist insurgencies.

The new grass-roots civil rights crusade forced the Kennedy administration to send federal marshals into the South to protect freedom riders. These young activists were determined that a series of federal court rulings declaring segregation on buses and in waiting rooms to be unconstitutional would not be ignored by southern officials.

1962
Superpower confrontation escalated to its most dangerous level during the Cuban missile crisis. As the result of Soviet advanced weapons stationed in Cuba, Kennedy ordered the Navy to "quarantine" the island and the Strategic Air Command was put on a full alert.

In **October**, Khrushchev ordered the missiles on Cuba dismantled and the Soviet supply ships brought home. Kennedy promised not to invade Cuba. After the missile crisis, both superpowers seemed to recognize the perils of direct conflict.

Kennedy issued an executive order banning racial discrimination in housing financed by the national government.

1963
In the **spring**, white police officers in Birmingham, Alabama, used dogs and water hoses on African-American children who were demonstrating against segregation. Later, four children were killed when a black church was bombed. After thousands of blacks took to the city's streets in protest, the Kennedy administration took more action.

Civil rights leader Reverend Martin Luther King, Jr.'s famous "I Have a Dream" speech was delivered on **August 28** at the march on Washington.

The Equal Pay Act made it a federal crime for employers to pay lower wages to women who were doing the same work as men.

Betty Friedan published *The Feminine Mystique*, which expressed the dissatisfaction of many middle-class women with the narrow confines of domestic life.

On **November 22**, the years of "Camelot" ended as President Kennedy was assassinated during a presidential motorcade in Dallas, Texas. The nation fell silent in mourning the death of Kennedy and, for the next thirty years, questions concerning a conspiracy plagued Americans.

GLOSSARY OF IMPORTANT TERMS

affluence
Abundance of material goods or wealth.

flexible response
Kennedy approach to the cold war. The aim was to provide a wide variety of methods to combat the growth of communist movements.

freedom riders
Members of interracial groups who rode around the South on buses. They were determined that a series of federal court decisions, declaring segregation

	on buses and in waiting rooms to be unconstitutional, would not be ignored by white officials.
ICBMs	Intercontinental ballistic missiles.
life-adjustment skills	Skills such as getting along with others and accommodating social change. Many complained that schools emphasized these types of skills instead of teaching the traditional academic subjects. As a result, critics claimed, American schools were falling behind those in other countries.
massive retaliation	Eisenhower administration's assertion that the threat of U.S. atomic weaponry would hold communist powers in check.
open skies	Eisenhower's proposal that U.S. and Soviet disarmament be verified by reconnaissance flights over each other's territory.
passive civil disobedience	Nonviolent refusal to obey a law in an attempt to call attention to government policy that is considered unfair.
the projects	Self-contained urban ghettos inhabited by people with low incomes and little prospect for economic advancement.
redlining	The refusal by banks and loan associations to grant loans for home buying and business expansion in neighborhoods that contained aging buildings, dense populations, and growing numbers of nonwhites.
sit-in movement	Activity by groups of young persons challenging legal segregation by demanding that blacks have the same access to public facilities as white citizens. They staged nonviolent demonstrations at restaurants, bus and train stations, and other public places.
Third World	Less economically developed areas of the world, primarily the Middle East, Asia, Latin America, and Africa.
wetbacks	Derogatory term for illegal Mexican immigrants because they supposedly swam across the Rio Grande to reach the United States.
white flight	Movement of large numbers of white, middle-class families from older sections of cities to new, mostly white suburbs.
Yankeephobia	Strong or unreasonable dislike of Americans, referred to as Yankees; fairly widespread in Latin America at one time.

WHO? WHAT? WHERE?

WHO WERE THEY?

Complete each following statement (questions 1–19) by writing the letter preceding the appropriate name in the space provided. Use each answer only once.

a. Allen Dulles
b. Barry Goldwater
c. Chuck Berry
d. Earl Warren
e. Fannie Lou Hamer
f. Fidel Castro
g. Fulgencio Batista
h. Gamal Abdel Nasser
i. John Kenneth Galbraith
j. Lyndon B. Johnson
k. Martin Luther King, Jr.
l. Michael Harrington
m. Nikita Khrushchev
n. Ngo Dinh Diem
o. Norman Vincent Peale
p. Phyllis Schlafly
q. Reza Pahlavi
r. Robert Moses
s. Rosa Parks

_____ 1. Soviet leader who took over after the death of Joseph Stalin in 1953.

_____ 2. Iranian leader who was restored to power by the CIA and who remained a firm ally of the United States.

_____ 3. Long-time director of the CIA who oversaw its expansion in power and influence.

_____ 4. Cuban dictator publicly supported by the United States and toasted by Vice President Richard Nixon as "Cuba's Abraham Lincoln."

_____ 5. Leader of Egypt who nationalized the British-controlled Suez Canal.

_____ 6. Cuban leader targeted for assassination by the CIA.

_____ 7. American-educated and American-backed leader of South Vietnam.

_____ 8. Economist who wrote *The Affluent Society*, which topped the best-seller list for six months.

_____ 9. Protestant minister who emphasized the relationship between religious faith and "peace of mind."

_____ 10. African-American singer who merged southern country music with the blues.

_____ 11. African-American woman who refused to obey a state law requiring blacks to sit in the back of a city bus.

_____ 12. New York City housing czar who routinely covered up massive dislocations caused by urban renewal.

_____ 13. Hero of the Republican Party's right wing and author of *Conscience of a Conservative*.

_____ 14. Kennedy's vice-presidential running mate whose appeal to southern whites helped the Democrats carry the Deep South.

_____ 15. Socialist activist who tried to focus attention on the needs of citizens with low incomes.

_____ 16. Author of the famous "I Have a Dream" speech made in Washington, D.C.

_____ 17. African-American activist who helped organize an integrated Mississippi Freedom Democratic Party.

_____ 18. Leading conservative activist and author of *A Choice, Not an Echo*; one of the women active in the Republican Party's right wing.

_____ 19. Supreme Court justice who headed a special commission that investigated the Kennedy assassination.

WHAT WAS IT?

Complete each following statement (questions 1–15) by writing the letter preceding the appropriate name in the space provided. Use each answer only once.

  a. *Blackboard Jungle*
  b. Buddhist
  c. comic books
  d. Eisenhower Doctrine
  e. Green Berets
  f. military-industrial complex
  g. National Labor Relations Board
  h. *National Review*
  i. New Frontier
  j. passive civil disobedience
  k. Peace Corps
  l. Radio Free Europe
  m. relocation
  n. *Sputnik*
  o. *Tootle the Engine*

_____ 1. Established by the American government in 1951, this supported the CIA in its activities in eastern Europe through broadcasts.

_____ 2. Pledge to defend Middle Eastern countries against overt armed aggression from any nation controlled by communism.

_____ 3. Predominant religion of South Vietnam.

_____ 4. Greatest source of danger to the United States, according to Eisenhower in his farewell address.

_____ 5. Agency sought by both labor and management as an impartial umpire in disputes.

_____ 6. Phenomenon many criminologists linked to an alleged rise in juvenile delinquency.

_____ 7. Popular film in which a racially mixed gang of high-school students terrorized teachers.

_____ 8. Leading children's book that encouraged young people to obey rules mindlessly.

_____ 9. Nonviolent technique used by the civil rights leaders to persuade people of the evils of segregation and racial discrimination.

_____ 10. Federal program under which Indians were encouraged to leave reservations and take jobs in urban areas.

_____ 11. Magazine established partly by William F. Buckley, Jr., and identified as a "conservative journal of opinion."

_____ 12. World's first artificial satellite, launched by the Soviets in 1957.

_____ 13. What Kennedy called his policies during the campaign of 1960.

_____ 14. Program begun during the Kennedy administration that sent young Americans around the world to work on development projects.

_____ 15. Special group of elite U.S. troops trained in counterinsurgency and used in Vietnam.

WHERE WAS IT?

Complete each following statement (questions 1–12) by writing the letter preceding the appropriate name in the space provided. Use each answer only once.

a. Bay of Pigs
b. Berlin, Germany
c. Birmingham, Alabama
d. Dallas, Texas
e. France
f. Geneva, Switzerland
g. Greensboro, North Carolina
h. Hungary
i. Lebanon
j. Memphis, Tennessee
k. Montgomery, Alabama
l. New York City

_____ 1. City where a summit meeting was held that led to a more conciliatory period in the cold war.

_____ 2. Eastern European country where members of an uprising against Soviet control asked for American help, received none, and were crushed by Soviet armies.

_____ 3. Middle Eastern country where marines waded ashore and set up an anti-Nasser government.

_____ 4. European country that once controlled Indochina as part of its colonial empire.

_____ 5. Home town of a young singer named Elvis Presley.

_____ 6. City where a boycott of the city bus system by African-American women forced desegregation of the buses.

_____ 7. Leading city where new Puerto Rican immigrants settled.

_____ 8. Area on the southern coast of Cuba where U.S.-backed forces landed in an attempt to overthrow Castro.

_____ 9. City divided by a concrete wall that became the symbol of the cold war and of communist repression.

_____ 10. Town where a group of black college students sat down at a dime-store lunch counter and asked to be served in the same manner as white patrons.

_____ 11. Southern city where white police officers used dogs and water hoses on black children.

_____ 12. City where President Kennedy was assassinated.

CHARTS, MAPS, AND ILLUSTRATIONS

1. According to the chart on automobile sales (p. 975), 1940–1970, the year that had the highest number sold was _____. Why were none sold in the early 1940s?
_____

2. Elvis Presley's early occupation was _____.

3. The two states with the greatest increase in African-American population between 1940 and 1960 were _____ and _____.

4. Where did Rosa Parks ride on the first day of desegregated bus travel? _____
_____

5. An important organizing tool during the civil rights crusade was _____
_____.

MULTIPLE CHOICE

Circle the letter that best completes each statement.

1. As the superpowers began discussing arms limitation, Eisenhower announced his 1955 "open skies" proposal that
   a. promoted massive increases in arms production.
   b. was welcomed by Soviet leaders.
   c. was introduced by Khrushchev.
   d. included inspections to verify disarmaments.

2. During its first years, the Central Intelligence Agency (CIA) sought to fan the flames of resistance to the Soviet Union by encouraging dissidents, supporting broadcasts over Radio Free Europe, and concentrating its attention on
   a. eastern Europe.
   b. western Europe.
   c. Canada.
   d. Asia.

3. Which of the following economic strategies was not employed by Eisenhower to fight communism and win converts in the Third World?
   a. the creation of opportunities for American enterprises overseas
   b. encouraging expansion of trade
   c. encouraging state-directed economic systems abroad
   d. offering financial aid to friendly nations

4. Military aid rose sharply in the 1950s to complement the government's economic programs. The buildup of military forces in friendly Third World nations strengthened anticommunist forces, but it also contributed to the development of
   a. multiparty governments.
   b. popularly supported governments.
   c. free elections.
   d. military dictatorships.

5. After Fidel Castro tried to reduce Cuba's dependence on the United States, the Eisenhower administration imposed an economic boycott on the island. Castro responded by declaring himself a communist, pledging to support leftist insurgencies throughout Latin America, and turning for support to
   a. the Soviet Union.
   b. Great Britain.
   c. Australia.
   d. Mexico.

6. Nasser exploited anti-Israel sentiment, accepted aid from both the United States and the Soviet Union, strengthened Egypt's economic and military power, and extended diplomatic recognition to communist China. When the United States responded by canceling loans to Egypt, the Soviet Union took over financing of the
   a. Aswan Dam.
   b. Suez Canal.
   c. Hungarian revolt.
   d. Jordanian and Lebanese governments.

7. The Eisenhower administration took the position that "the loss of any of the countries of southeast Asia to communist aggression would have critical psychological, political, and economic consequences" that would ultimately "endanger the stability and security of Europe" and Japan. This formulation became known as the
   a. null theory.
   b. scramble theory.
   c. domino theory.
   d. monopoly theory.

8. Domestic opposition to the U.S.-supported anticommunist leader of South Vietnam coalesced in the National Liberation Front (NLF). Formed in December 1960, the NLF included all of the following groups except
   a. domestic supporters of Diem.
   b. nationalists who resented Diem's dependence on the United States.
   c. communists who demanded more extensive land reform.
   d. politicians who decreed Diem's corruption and cronyism.

9. The 1950s marked the midpoint in a period of steady economic growth that began during World War II and continued until the early 1970s. Which of the following statements was not characteristic of the "fabulous fifties"?
   a. Corporations turned out vast quantities of products and enjoyed steadily rising rates of profits.
   b. Investments and business ventures overseas boosted corporate profits at home.
   c. The label "Made in America" symbolized both high-quality products and the economic power of the entire nation.
   d. Limited supplies of expensive oil and natural gas increased production costs.

10. The fact that national security had become big business was dramatized in 1955 as military expenditures accounted for about
    a. 5 percent of the GNP.
    b. 10 percent of the GNP.
    c. 15 percent of the GNP.
    d. 20 percent of the GNP.

11. Eisenhower justified several costly new domestic programs by citing national-security concerns. He viewed the Highway Act of 1956 as essential to efficient movement of troops and supplies. In actuality, the Highway Act
    a. was the first centrally planned transportation system in U.S. history.
    b. provided 100 percent of the necessary construction funds.
    c. was opposed by the auto, oil, concrete, and tire industries.
    d. devastated the trucking business.

12. The Eisenhower administration and members of Congress also invoked national security to justify costly river-diversion projects in the Far West. These water projects, which included dams, irrigation canals, and reservoirs, resulted in all of the following consequences, except
    a. Ordinary people lost power to domineering government agencies and private entrepreneurs.
    b. Large corporate-style operations pushed out smaller farmers and ranchers.
    c. Large portions of American Indian lands were flooded.
    d. There were serious ecological problems.

13. The idea that public policy making proceeds from wide participation in public debate by a broad range of different groups and that no power elite dominates the political process is known as
    a. pluralism.
    b. pacifism.

    c. Marxism.

    d. socialism.

14. As part of a crusade against "atheistic communism," Congress did all of the following except

    a. construct a prayer room in the Capitol.

    b. add the phrase "under God" to the Pledge of Allegiance.

    c. adopt Protestantism as the official religion of the Senate.

    d. declare the phrase "In God We Trust" the national motto.

15. Psychologist Frederick Wertham, in *The Seduction of the Innocent* (1954), blamed rebellion in youth culture on

    a. parents.

    b. teachers.

    c. comic books.

    d. television.

16. Rock stars crossed cultural and racial barriers to create new musical forms. Which of the following older music forms was not incorporated by these musicians?

    a. African-American rhythm

    b. blues

    c. rap.

    d. country.

17. Evolving out of network radio, television was dominated by three major corporations. They were

    a. NBC, PBS, and CBS.

    b. NBC, CBS, and ABC.

    c. CBS, ABC, and FOX.

    d. PBS, FOX, and TNT.

18. Supreme Court Chief Justice Earl Warren wrote the unanimous opinion in the 1954 case of *Brown* v. *Board of Education*, which dealt with

    a. school prayer.

    b. segregation in public schools.

    c. faculty salaries.

    d. public funding.

19. The 1950s marked the beginning of a time in which the South was becoming more like the rest of the country. Which of the following was not evidence of this transformation?

    a. New cultural forces, like television, were linking the South more closely with a nationally based culture.

    b. Machines were replacing the region's predominantly black field workers.

    c. Desegregation was fully supported in housing, educational facilities, job opportunities, and the political arena.

    d. The presence of favorable tax laws was attracting national chain stores, business franchises, and northern-based industries to the South.

20. Following Rosa Parks's lead, many African-American women spearheaded the Montgomery bus boycott of 1955–1956 that resulted in
    a. higher wages for bus drivers.
    b. improved safety measures on buses.
    c. extended transportation hours.
    d. desegregation of city buses.

21. Events in Montgomery, Alabama, vaulted the Reverend Martin Luther King, Jr., into national politics. Which of the following statements does not characterize King?
    a. He was born, raised, and educated in the North.
    b. He had a broad vision of social change.
    c. He believed in integration that would be forced on society by passive civil disobedience.
    d. He persuaded people, through words and deeds, of the moral evil of segregation and radical discrimination.

22. In 1957, members of Congress passed the Civil Rights Act, which
    a. was the first civil rights legislation to be passed in the last ten years.
    b. was antidiscrimination legislation.
    c. did not address lawsuits by African Americans, who claimed their right to equal educational facilities had been abridged.
    d. dissolved the powerful Commission on Civil Rights.

23. Ethnic issues often merged with a growing sense that the United States was stumbling toward an "urban crisis." Which of the following statements does not apply to the Housing Act of 1949?
    a. People with low incomes never were evicted.
    b. It was an "urban renewal" program.
    c. It often amounted to "urban removal."
    d. Developers generally ignored replacement housing for people they displaced.

24. Prepared by prominent figures with close ties to defense industries, the 1957 Gaither Report
    a. urged an immediate decrease of about 60 percent in the Pentagon's budget.
    b. discouraged programs for building fallout shelters.
    c. warned that the Soviet Union's GNP was growing more quickly than that of the United States and much of the expansion was in the military sector.
    d. discontinued development of intercontinental ballistic missiles and reduced conventional military forces.

25. Using the magical phrase "national security," school administrators and university researchers sought and won increased monetary support from the federal treasury. The National Defense Education Act of 1958, which provided federal aid for education, funneled money to all of the following programs except
    a. science.
    b. engineering.
    c. foreign languages.
    d. home economics.

26. John Fitzgerald Kennedy, during his 1960 presidential bid, faced opposition from critics who attempted to exploit the issue of
   a. space-program funding.
   b. religion.
   c. communism.
   d. single parenting.

27. During the 1960 campaign, Kennedy stressed four issues, closely associated with critics of the Eisenhower administration, that collectively made up his "New Frontier" program. Which of the following issues was not addressed by the program?
   a. civil rights
   b. social programs
   c. stimulating economic growth
   d. ending the cold war

28. Superpower confrontation escalated to its most dangerous level during the Cuban missile crisis of 1962. In the aftermath of the crisis,
   a. a direct phone line between Moscow and Washington was established to ensure adequate communication in the event of a nuclear confrontation or accident.
   b. a nuclear war resulted.
   c. nations readily sought direct confrontation.
   d. the United States successfully invaded Cuba.

ESSAY

Description and Explanation (one- to two-paragraph essay)

1. Explain why the United States would support conservative dictators as a part of the anticommunist activities in Latin America and explain the role of the CIA in this.

2. Describe the purpose, economic growth, and consequences of the river-diversion program in the Far West.

3. Describe the role of religion in the age of affluence.

4. Explain affluence as an image and why it fitted the 1950s.

5. List the beliefs involved in pluralism.

6. What was the prevailing criticism of the youth culture, especially as it dealt with comic books and rock music?

7. Describe the flawed programs of the Eisenhower administration toward the American Indians.

8. List the Kennedy administration's activities against Cuba under Castro. Did any of them work?

Discussion and Analysis (class discussion or one- to two-paragraph essay)

1. Discuss American cold war activities in the Third World areas of the Middle East and Asia during the Eisenhower administration.

2. What was the role of mass culture in the 1950s? What were the major criticisms of it?

3. How did President Eisenhower view advocates of a more active government? What did they want? What issues concerned them?

4. Discuss John F. Kennedy and the election of 1960, including the candidates and how they handled themselves, the major issues, and why Kennedy won the presidency.

5. Discuss the Kennedy administration and the civil rights movement. How active was the administration in the movement? Did the administration initiate progress or only react to the initiative of others?

What If (include an explanation of your position)

1. If you were a teenager during the 1950s, which area of mass culture would you most enjoy?

2. If you were a young attorney, would you join the Kennedy administration?

3. If you were a middle-aged black farmer in rural Mississippi in the 1960s, would you support openly the civil rights movement?

Crossword Puzzle: Affluence and Its Discontents, 1954–1963

DOWN

1. High-level conferences
2. Group affected by termination policy (2 wds.)
3. Source of wealth for Shah of Iran
5. Critics feared that bad ___ was driving out good art.
6. Freedom riders' organization
7. *Why Johnny Can't* ___ by Rudolf Flesch
9. Democratic candidate in 1956
11. Word with fore or line
12. Attention of the ___ was focused on JFK and Mrs. Kennedy.
13. Waterway nationalized by Nasser (2 wds.)
16. Resident of Southeast Asia
21. A great lake
23. Make a fallout shelter
24. Eisenhower's nickname
25. Tax on ___ financed superhighways

ACROSS

1. Diem's capital
4. Rosa Parks's organization
8. Eisenhower doctrine pledged to defend ___ nations against communism (2 wds.).
10. August 28, 1963, speech (4 wds.)
14. Hamilton's note
15. *Sputnik*, for one
17. Indigo is one
18. Title for Martin Luther King, Jr.
19. Sukarno's nation
20. Spider's creation
22. Policy that denied housing funds to older urban areas
26. CENTO's continent
27. National Defense Education Act sought to produce more ___.

ANSWER KEY

WHO? WHAT? WHERE?

Who Were They?

1. m. Nikita Khrushchev, p. 968
2. q. Reza Pahlavi, p. 968
3. a. Allen Dulles, p. 969
4. g. Fulgencio Batista, p. 970
5. h. Gamal Abdel Nasser, p. 970
6. f. Fidel Castro, p. 972
7. n. Ngo Dinh Diem, p. 973
8. i. John Kenneth Galbraith, p. 977
9. o. Norman Vincent Peale, pp. 978-979
10. c. Chuck Berry, p. 980
11. s. Rosa Parks, p. 985
12. r. Robert Moses, p. 988
13. b. Barry Goldwater, p. 989
14. j. Lyndon B. Johnson, p. 993
15. l. Michael Harrington, p. 991
16. k. Martin Luther King, Jr., p. 998
17. e. Fannie Lou Hamer, p. 999
18. p. Phyllis Schlafly, p. 999
19. d. Earl Warren, p. 1000

What Was It?

1. l. Radio Free Europe, p. 968
2. d. Eisenhower Doctrine, p. 971
3. b. Buddhist, p. 973
4. f. military-industrial complex, p. 973
5. g. National Labor Relations Board, p. 977
6. c. comic books, p. 980
7. a. *Blackboard Jungle*, p. 980
8. o. *Tootle the Engine*, p. 979
9. j. passive civil disobedience, p. 985
10. m. relocation, p. 986
11. h. *National Review*, p. 989
12. n. *Sputnik*, p. 990
13. i. New Frontier, p. 992
14. k. Peace Corps, p. 993
15. e. Green Berets, p. 995

Where Was It?

1. f. Geneva, Switzerland, p. 968
2. h. Hungary, p. 969
3. i. Lebanon, p. 972
4. e. France, p. 972
5. j. Memphis, Tennessee, p. 980
6. k. Montgomery, Alabama, p. 985
7. l. New York City, p. 987
8. a. Bay of Pigs, p. 993
9. b. Berlin, Germany, p. 994
10. g. Greensboro, North Carolina, p. 996
11. c. Birmingham, Alabama, p. 997
12. d. Dallas, Texas, p. 1000

CHARTS, MAPS, AND ILLUSTRATIONS

1. 1965; World War II stopped production, p. 975
2. truck driver, p. 980
3. Alaska and Nevada, p. 984
4. on the front seat, p. 985
5. freedom songs, p. 996

MULTIPLE CHOICE

1. d (p. 969)
2. a (p. 968)
3. c (p. 969)
4. d (p. 970)
5. a (p. 970)
6. a (p. 971)
7. c (p. 973)
8. a (p. 973)
9. d (p. 974)
10. b (p. 974)
11. a (p. 975)
12. a (p. 976)
13. a (p. 978)
14. c (p. 978)
15. c (p. 980)
16. c (p. 980)
17. b (p. 981)
18. b (p. 983)

19. c (p. 983)
20. d (p. 985)
21. a (p. 985)
22. b (p. 986)
23. a (p. 988)
24. c (p. 990)
25. d (pp. 990–991)
26. b (p. 992)
27. d (p. 992)
28. a (p. 993)

ESSAY

Description and Explanation

1. pp. 969–973
2. p. 976
3. pp. 978–979
4. pp. 977–978
5. p. 978
6. p. 981
7. pp. 986–987
8. pp. 993–995

Discussion and Analysis

1. pp. 970–973
2. pp. 980–983
3. pp. 989–991
4. pp. 991–993
5. pp. 995–998

What If

1. pp. 980–983
2. pp. 992–993
3. pp. 995–998

Crossword Puzzle

CHAPTER 29

AMERICA DURING ITS LONGEST WAR, 1963–1974

President Lyndon B. Johnson promised to finish what John F. Kennedy had begun, but his troubled presidency bore little resemblance to Kennedy's. Johnson undertook an ambitious legislative program he called the Great Society, declaring unconditional war on poverty in America through a variety of programs. Controversial from the start, Johnson's Great Society never achieved its objectives. It represented, however, the first significant new outlay of federal dollars on social programs in thirty years. Johnson had little experience in foreign affairs, and the escalation of the war in Vietnam demanded more and more of the administration's energy and resources. The administration's policies in Vietnam eventually alienated many in America, especially the young. Millions opposed the war in Southeast Asia and the Great Society programs at home. People began to worry about the political and social stability of the nation amidst assassinations and growing violence.

Soon after Richard Nixon took office, he embraced policies that proved as divisive as those of his predecessor. His term in office coincided with a series of economic problems, but he was preoccupied with foreign policy. Working with Henry Kissinger, first as his national security advisor and later as secretary of state, Nixon improved relations with the Soviets and opened diplomatic contacts with communist China. His major attention was concentrated on the war in Vietnam. The Nixon Doctrine pledged that the United States would provide military assistance to anticommunist governments in Asia, but they would have to provide their own military forces. In theory, this would allow the United States to extract itself from the war, called Vietnamization. Actually the war accelerated both on the ground and in the air. Subsequently, Cambodia, an ostensibly neutral country, was invaded. In 1973, North Vietnam and the United States signed a peace accord. The South Vietnamese government grew increasingly demoralized and disorganized, and, in the spring of 1975, it collapsed. What most Americans wanted now was never to repeat what had occurred in Vietnam.

Nixon's downfall ultimately resulted from his decisions made in his own office. When a surveillance team with ties to the White House was caught in the Democratic headquarters at the Watergate, Nixon and his closest aides immediately launched an illegal cover-up. Eventually, Nixon was linked to an elaborate Watergate cover-up and other illegal activities. The constitutional system closed in on the president. The Supreme Court ruled that his claim of executive privilege could not be used to justify his refusal to release evidence needed in the criminal investigation. The House Judiciary Committee moved toward a vote on impeachment. Abandoned by almost everyone, Nixon caved in. He announced that he would resign. At the time, most people believed that Watergate was one of the greatest crises in the history of the republic and that the Nixon administration had posed a serious threat to constitutional government. The incident was a part of a much broader pattern of political, social, economic, and cultural tensions that clashed during America's longest war. The divisions of the Vietnam era would continue to strain American life during the rest of the twentieth century.

LIBERTY, EQUALITY, POWER

Liberty and equality continued to be important issues during America's longest war, but power, the love of it, the expansion of it by various groups, and the abuse of it by government officials were paramount issues during this period. President Johnson was hungry for power and loved to wield the power of his office. He hoped to use his powers to improve life for many Americans; however, his Great Society failed to challenge the prevailing distribution of political and economic power. The black power movement sought a radical redistribution of power that would free African Americans to create new institutions of their own. Native Americans sought the power to practice their traditional tribal customs. Feminist groups sought the power for women to control their own bodies, as in the fight for abortion rights. Richard Nixon was obsessed with power. This was demonstrated by the manner in which he tried to expand his powers as president and the techniques he used for dealing with any opposition. His serious abuses of power would lead to a constitutional crisis for the country and the downfall of his presidency.

During this period, the Supreme Court spearheaded a rights revolution. Political dissenters, religious and racial minorities, and those accused of crimes benefited from this new way of looking at constitutional issues. Such fundamental liberties as the right to dissent and the constitutional guarantee of legal counsel were expanded. At times, the Court was attacked for making law rather than simply applying it, but it continued to use its power to advocate the growth of liberty for many groups. The Court drew a sharp distinction between the government's responsibility to respect individual liberties of all citizens (such as the right to vote) and the government's ability to make policy in the administration of socioeconomic programs. In other words, welfare was not a national right. During all of these deliberations and decisions, the power of the Supreme Court to influence the direction of liberty and equality had grown by leaps and bounds.

OBJECTIVES

After studying this chapter, a student should be able to

1. Evaluate President Johnson's Great Society.

2. Describe the counterculture and its effects on the American people.

3. Describe 1968 as a year of violence abroad and at home.

4. Explain the economic problems of the Nixon era.

5. Evaluate the role of the Supreme Court in defining constitutional rights.

6. Describe Nixon's role in the Vietnam War and compare it with President Johnson's.

7. Discuss Nixon's downfall.

CHRONOLOGY

1962   Gradually, Students for a Democratic Society, a newly formed political organization that endorsed liberal causes and confronted the dominant culture, gave rise to the "New Left." This new radical political initiative sought to create an alternative social vision.

1963   Following Kennedy's death, Lyndon Johnson assumed the presidency and promised to finish what his predecessor had begun. Kennedy's death provided Johnson with the opportunity to realize his dream of transforming the entire nation.

1964   Johnson pushed an expanded version of Kennedy's civil rights bill through Congress. The Civil Rights Act, administered by a new Equal Employment Opportunity Commission, created federal remedies for fighting job discrimination. It barred discrimination based on gender and prohibited discrimination by hotels and restaurants.

Freedom Summer represented the efforts of volunteers assisting anti-discrimination efforts by traveling into Mississippi to help register voters.

Congress created the Office of Economic Opportunity (OEO) to coordinate an attack on poverty.

In **August**, after unverified reports of an "attack" against U.S. battleships, Johnson stated that U.S. forces had been the target of "unprovoked aggression." Congress overwhelmingly passed the Gulf of Tonkin Resolution, which authorized "all necessary measures to repel armed attack" and which Johnson cited as legal authorization for all subsequent military action in Vietnam.

The Berkeley Free Speech movement began in 1964 and continued until 1965. During this time, students and faculty protested Berkeley's restrictions on political activity. This protest set off nearly a decade of turmoil at many colleges and universities.

President Johnson led the Democrats to a crushing victory over Barry Goldwater and the Republicans in **November**. This would be the last election Democrats would win with the old New Deal–Fair Deal strategy.

1965   Johnson announced his Great Society legislative program, which included nationally funded medical coverage for elderly and low-income citizens. He believed that new governmental initiatives would "enrich and elevate our national life" by building a society that was wealthy "in mind and spirit."

In **January**, the regime that succeeded Diem fell, and factionalism prevented any stable government from emerging in South Vietnam. This turn of events resulted in an increased U.S. military role. As Johnson attempted to break the enemy's will, the war intensified in 1965, and a strategy to escalate the number of enemy casualties was devised and implemented.

The United States used North Vietnam's rejection of an unrealistic peace plan as an excuse to increase levels of military spending and action.

Johnson brought his anticommunist crusade closer to home in **April** by sending U.S. troops to the Dominican Republic, which violated the long-standing good-neighbor pledge not to intervene militarily in the Western Hemisphere.

Congress approved $400 million for military expenditures in **May**. By mid-summer Johnson intensified bombing efforts and sent 50,000 additional troops to Vietnam. He privately agreed to send an additional 50,000 and left open the possibility to sending even more.

Ralph Nader's exposé about auto safety, *Unsafe at Any Speed*, started an ardent consumer-rights movement and attracted political support.

Black civil rights leader Malcolm X was assassinated by old political enemies. He remained a powerful symbol of the link between militant politics and renewed pride in African-American culture.

The Voting Rights Act mandated federal oversight of elections in the South.

A devastating race riot took place in the Watts area of Los Angeles.

1966   *Miranda* v. *Arizona* required police officers to advise people arrested for a felony offense of their constitutional right to remain silent and to consult an attorney before making a statement.

The National Organization for Women (NOW) was founded.

The war in Vietnam dominated the agenda of student protesters.

1967   The United States was spending over $2 billion a month on the war and was subjecting the Vietnamese countryside to widespread devastation.

Racial violence in Detroit was put down by federal troops, but the incident ruined many African-American neighborhoods.

1968   In **January,** the North Vietnamese and National Liberation Front troops violated a truce and staged a series of attacks on South Vietnam. The Tet Offensive was a strategic and psychological defeat for the United States because it implied military claims of success that could not be trusted.

Faced with dwindling support and a revolt within his own party, Johnson pledged in **March** not to run for reelection.

The Civil Rights Act was passed in the **spring** but was weakly enforced.

Continuing his struggle for social reconstruction, Martin Luther King, Jr., traveled to Memphis, Tennessee, where he was assassinated on **April 4**. The death of the civil rights leader sparked violent protests. Then, on **June 5**, minutes after claiming victory in California's Democratic presidential primary, Robert Kennedy was assassinated.

The violence of 1968 continued at the national political conventions. At the Republican convention in Miami, racial violence led to the death of four people. In Chicago, Mayor Richard Daley ordered police to crush demonstrators outside the Democratic convention hall. Later studies maintain that police provoked the violence, but at the time, it was seen as part of the violent drift of radical politics.

Richard Nixon, in **November**, defeated candidate Democratic Hubert Humphrey and third-party candidate George Wallace.

1969

To ease tensions with the Soviet Union and to promote an agreement on arms control, the two superpowers opened the Strategic Arms Limitation Talks (SALT). The impact of SALT was negligible, but it did signal a dramatic shift away from cold war distrust.

Nixon and Henry Kissinger, national security adviser, decided to begin to withdraw U.S. ground forces while stepping up the air war and intensifying diplomatic efforts to attain a settlement in Vietnam. In **July**, the Nixon Doctrine pledged U.S. military assistance to anticommunist governments in Asia, but not military troops.

1970

The House of Representatives passed a modified version of the 1969 Family Assistance Plan to replace post-New Deal welfare. However, caught up in the problems of Vietnam, the program was dropped.

President Nixon and Secretary of State Henry Kissinger approved a military incursion into Cambodia, a neutral country. This action set off a new wave of protests at home with violence on several university campuses. It was clear that the Vietnam War had broadened into an Indochinese war.

Over 40 percent of federal spending was on social welfare programs. This spending had risen more than 10 percent a year since Johnson had taken office. Half of all persons in families headed by women were receiving Aid to Families with Dependent Children.

In *Dandridge* v. *Williams* the Supreme Court refused to hold, as a matter of constitutional law, that welfare is a national right.

1971

Unemployment rose to 6 percent, and for the first time in the twentieth century, the United States began importing more than it exported.

During the summer months, the Pentagon Papers, a top-secret study of U.S. involvement in Vietnam, was leaked to the press. Nixon responded by having his secret intelligence unit, "the plumbers," stop leaks to the press. Thus began a series of dirty tricks and illegal schemes that would culminate in the Watergate incident.

1972

The newly energized women's movement, represented by the National Organization for Women (NOW), pushed for an equal rights amendment to the Constitution. Passed by Congress in 1972, the ERA emerged as one of the most controversial issues of the mid-1970s.

President Nixon visited China as an early step to normalization of relations between the United States and the communist country. The following year, the two countries exchanged informal diplomatic missions.

Social Security benefits were indexed to rise with the rate of inflation. Between 1970 and 1980, the federal government's spending on welfare rose from 40.1 percent of total government outlays to slightly over 53 percent.

In **June**, members of a surveillance team with ties to Nixon were arrested in Washington, D.C., for breaking and entering. They were attempting to adjust eavesdropping equipment in the Watergate office complex that served as headquarters to the Democratic Party.

The **November** election resulted in a Nixon win by one of the largest margins in U.S. history. This was the first presidential election after the voting age had been lowered to eighteen.

In **December**, the heaviest bombardment in history took place when B-52 bombers pounded North Vietnamese military and civilian targets around the clock.

1973

In **January** the United States and North Vietnam signed peace agreements in Paris that provided for the withdrawal of U.S. troops. However, peace was slow in coming, and all U.S. troops were not removed until nearly two years later.

In **January**, Judge John Sirica refused to accept claims that the Watergate burglars acted independently and had no connection to the White House. While he pushed for more information, a special Senate Watergate Committee, headed by Senator Sam Ervin, convened to look into dirty tricks during the 1972 campaign.

The Nixon administration devalued the dollar, cheapening the price of American goods in foreign markets in order to make them more competitive. This action did little to improve the deterioration of American trade balances. Over the next decade, U.S. exports more than tripled in value, but imports more than quadrupled in value.

In *Roe* v. *Wade*, the Supreme Court ruled that a state law that made abortion a criminal offense violated a woman's right to privacy. The case touched off more than three decades of angry protest and debate between the right-to-life movement and the pro-choice movement.

In **October**, Vice President Spiro Agnew resigned after pleading no contest to income-tax evasion. Under the Twenty-fifth Amendment, ratified in 1967, Nixon appointed, and both houses of Congress confirmed, Representative Gerald Ford of Michigan as the new vice president.

1974	By the end of **July**, only a few loyal supporters stood behind Nixon. In *United States* v. *Nixon*, the Supreme Court ruled that executive privilege could not justify the president's refusal to release evidence needed in a criminal investigation. After nearly a full week of televised deliberations, a majority of the House Judiciary Committee voted three formal articles of impeachment against the president. Under threat of impeachment, Nixon announced his resignation on **August 8**, and the following day Gerald Ford became president, the first to assume office without having won a national election. A month later, Ford granted Nixon an unconditional presidential pardon.
1975	Two years after the peace agreements, North Vietnamese armies entered Saigon, and U.S. helicopters lifted the last remaining officials out of the besieged U.S. embassy. America's longest war had ended.

GLOSSARY OF IMPORTANT TERMS

black power
Movement that developed in the mid-1960s calling for renewed pride in, and new emphasis on, racial pride in African-American heritage. Followers of this group believed that to seek full integration into the existing (white) order would be to capitulate to the institutions of racism.

block grants
Part of Nixon's new economic plan in which a percentage of federal tax dollars is returned to state and local governments to spend the funds as they see fit, within certain limits.

counterculture
Anti-establishment movement that symbolized the youthful social upheaval of the 1960s. Even though only a relatively small percentage of young people fully embraced the counterculture, they set the tone in mass-media discussions. Ridiculing traditional attitudes on such matters as clothing, hair styles, and sexuality, devotees of the counterculture urged a more open and less repressive approach to daily life.

dirty tricks
Actions designed to destroy the reputation or credibility of political opponents.

doves
Traditional term for those opposed to military action. In the late twentieth century, doves were people who wanted to end U.S. involvement in Southeast Asia.

establishment
The de facto social order; the group controlling the most power and influence in a society.

Freedom Summer
Summer of 1964, when about a thousand volunteers went to Mississippi to aid in voter registration.

free-fire zones
Designated areas in which anything could be shot at in the southern part of Vietnam.

hawks	Those who favored intensified military efforts in the Vietnam War.
hippies	People who rejected customary standards of society. In the 1960s counter-culture, they were depicted as dabbling with mind-altering drugs, communal living arrangements, and new forms of music.
in loco parentis	"In the place of a parent." Universities were considered to have the responsibility of parent over students while they were enrolled.
living-room war	Television coverage brought the Vietnam War into the living rooms of Americans. Media coverage eventually made many Americans question the war.
napalm	Chemical that burned both foliage and humans and allowed the Air Force to bomb new targets in North Vietnam.
plumbers	Nixon's secret intelligence unit. He used this group to stop the leak of information to the media.
saturation bombing	Intensive bombing to destroy a target totally.
stagflation	Period of economic stagnation and price inflation; an unprecedented period when both unemployment and prices rise.
student deferment	All young men at the time were required by law to register for possible military service. Local draft boards usually granted men who were attending college a deferment, but that expired upon their graduation and could be revoked or denied.
Vietnamization	Policy whereby the South Vietnamese were to assume more of the military burdens of the war. It was expected that this transfer of responsibility eventually would allow the United States to withdraw.

WHO? WHAT? WHERE?

WHO WERE THEY?

Complete each following statement (questions 1–16) by writing the letter preceding the appropriate name in the space provided. Use each answer only once.

    a. Abbie Hoffman
    b. Barry Goldwater
    c. Bob Dylan
    d. George McGovern
    e. George Wallace
    f. Gerald Ford
    g. John Sirica
    h. Martin Luther King, Jr.
    i. McGeorge Bundy
    j. Ralph Nader

k. Richard Daley
l. Ronald Reagan
m. Stokely Carmichael
n. Warren Burger
o. William J. Fulbright
p. William Westmoreland

_____ 1. Republican candidate for president in the election of 1964 and the hero of the right wing.

_____ 2. Alabama's governor who ran strongly against President Johnson in several northern states during the primaries of 1965.

_____ 3. Actor who so impressed conservative Republicans with a TV speech for Goldwater that they decided to groom him for a political career.

_____ 4. Johnson's national security adviser who predicted inevitable defeat unless the United States escalated its military role in the Vietnam War.

_____ 5. American commander in Vietnam who recommended moving U.S. forces out of their enclaves and sending them on search-and-destroy missions against the enemy.

_____ 6. Chair of the Senate Foreign Relations Committee who warned of the dangers of the Vietnam War.

_____ 7. Singer the media cast as the musical prophet for an entire generation.

_____ 8. Self-proclaimed leader of the fictitious Youth International Party.

_____ 9. Head of the Student Non-Violent Coordinating Committee in 1966.

_____ 10. Civil rights leader who denounced the war in Vietnam because it drained resources needed for social reconstruction at home.

_____ 11. Mayor of Chicago who ordered the police to crush demonstrators protesting the 1968 Democratic National Convention.

_____ 12. Moderately conservative Republican whom Nixon appointed as Chief Justice of the Supreme Court.

_____ 13. Leader of a vigorous consumer-rights movement.

_____ 14. Outspoken antiwar liberal senator from South Dakota who won the Democratic nomination in 1972.

_____ 15. Presiding judge in the trial of the Watergate burglars.

_____ 16. First president to assume the office without having won a national election.

WHAT WAS IT?

Complete each following statement (questions 1–14) by writing the letter preceding the appropriate name in the space provided. Use each answer only once.

    a. body count
    b. CREEP
    c. Gulf of Tonkin Resolution
    d. Khmer Rouge
    e. Medicare
    f. *Miranda* v. *Arizona*
    g. Pentagon Papers
    h. Ping-Pong
    i. RANCHHAND
    j. Students for a Democratic Society
    k. Tet Offensive
    l. Title VII
    m. Twenty-sixth Amendment
    n. *Washington Post*

_____ 1. Provision added to the Civil Rights Act of 1964 barring discrimination based on gender.

_____ 2. Program that provided nationally funded medical coverage for the elderly.

_____ 3. Statement passed by Congress that Johnson regarded as tantamount to a congressional declaration of war and cited as legal authorization for subsequent military action in Vietnam.

_____ 4. Military operation in South Vietnam that scorched croplands and defoliated half its forests in an effort to eliminate the natural cover used to hide enemy troop movements.

_____ 5. Test by which the Johnson administration gauged its progress in the war.

_____ 6. New political organization that gave rise to a radical political initiative known as the New Left.

_____ 7. Series of attacks on targets throughout South Vietnam in January 1968.

_____ 8. Supreme Court case that required police officers to advise people arrested for a felony of their constitutional right to remain silent and to consult an attorney before making a statement.

_____ 9. Sport that preceded a diplomatic visit to communist China by President Nixon.

_____ 10. Communist guerrilla force in Cambodia that grew into a well-disciplined army.

_____ 11. Top-secret study of U.S. involvement in the Vietnam War leaked to the press by a member of the national security bureaucracy.

_____ 12. Acronym for the Committee to Re-Elect the President. This organization raised millions, much of it from illegal contributions.

_____ 13. This lowered the voting age from twenty-one to eighteen.

_____ 14. Newspaper whose reporters took the lead in pursuing the Watergate scandal.

WHERE WAS IT?

Complete each statement below (questions 1–9) by writing the letter preceding the appropriate name in the space provided. Use each answer only once.

   a. Cambodia
   b. Chicago, Illinois
   c. Dominican Republic
   d. Kent State
   e. Memphis, Tennessee
   f. Mississippi
   g. Paris, France
   h. Saigon
   i. Watts

_____ 1. State targeted by about a thousand volunteers during Freedom Summer.

_____ 2. Capital of South Vietnam.

_____ 3. Small country where President Johnson ordered the military to install a government favorable to American economic interests.

_____ 4. Largely African-American community in Los Angeles where serious urban violence left thirty-four people dead.

_____ 5. City where Martin Luther King, Jr., supported a sanitation workers' strike. While there, he was killed.

_____ 6. Location of the 1968 Democratic National Convention, where thousands of demonstrators were crushed by police.

_____ 7. Allegedly neutral country in Southeast Asia attacked by the American military in 1970.

_____ 8. Place where National Guard troops fired on demonstrators and killed four students.

_____ 9. City where peace accords between North Vietnam and the United States were signed in 1973.

CHARTS, MAPS, AND ILLUSTRATIONS

   1. The capital of North Vietnam at the time of the war was _____.

   The body of water adjacent to the coast of North Vietnam is _____.

   2. The only Pacific Coast state carried by Humphrey in the presidential election of 1968 was _____.

3. The historically black college where police gunfire killed two students and wounded fifteen others was _____.

4. The only state carried by George McGovern in the 1972 presidential election was

_____.

MULTIPLE CHOICE

Circle the letter that best completes each statement.

1. After the 1963 assassination of President Kennedy, who promised to finish what JFK had begun?
   a. Ronald Reagan
   b. Richard Nixon
   c. Gerald Ford
   d. Lyndon Johnson

2. Pushed through Congress by Lyndon Johnson as a memorial to Kennedy, the Civil Rights Act of 1964 stood as a testament to the political and moral power of civil rights workers, especially those who still were organizing in the South during the summer of 1964. The 1964 legislation
   a. prohibited discrimination in public accommodations connected with interstate commerce.
   b. was administered by the Supreme Court.
   c. ignored discrimination based on gender.
   d. did not deal with job discrimination.

3. Freedom Summer refers to
   a. women involved in the Republican National Convention.
   b. volunteers traveling to Mississippi to help with voter registration.
   c. America's youth congregating at a rock concert in Woodstock, New York.
   d. the climax of drug use among college students.

4. Johnson prepared for the 1964 presidential campaign with great care. Overseeing almost every detail of the Democratic convention held in Atlantic City, he chose as his running mate, a prominent liberal,
   a. Hubert Humphrey
   b. Barry Goldwater
   c. George Wallace
   d. Ronald Reagan

5. Johnson believed he could build a nation that was wealthy "in mind and spirit" with his
   a. New Frontier.
   b. Great Society.
   c. New Deal.
   d. Return to Normalcy.

6. Johnson, using a military metaphor, declared an unconditional war and promised to eliminate
   a. poverty.
   b. socialism.
   c. discrimination.
   d. drugs.

7. One Johnson program was created to assist preschool children from low-income families to climb the education ladder and was known as
   a. Young Learners.
   b. New Beginnings.
   c. Prodigy.
   d. Head Start.

8. Johnson feared the political hazards of a defeat by communists in Vietnam. To those who argued that Vietnam had little strategic importance to the United States, Johnson countered that a communist victory anywhere in the world would set off a
   a. "tornado effect."
   b. "monopoly effect."
   c. "domino effect."
   d. "stagnation effect."

9. Fighting in Vietnam intensified in 1965 as Johnson tried to break the will of the enemy. Accordingly, the administration authorized the use of napalm,
   a. a South Pacific island nation necessary to maintain strategic domination.
   b. a chemical that burned both foliage and humans.
   c. a poisonous type of vegetation.
   d. military maneuvers that allowed for quickly relocating troops.

10. Congress was empowered to impose strict controls on what journalists could report to the public. However, Johnson had to resort to other ways of managing information because the Vietnam War was
    a. declared.
    b. undeclared.
    c. not in the Western Hemisphere.
    d. not in Europe.

11. During the Berkelely free speech movement of 1964–1965, dissident students and sympathetic faculty protested the university administration's restrictions of
    a. faculty-student organizations on campus.
    b. alcohol use on campus.
    c. drug use on campus.
    d. political activity on campus.

12. Accompanying the spread of New Left politics was the rise of the counterculture. This counterculture
    a. was characterized by "hippies," since members experimented with communal living, mind-altering drugs, and new forms of folk-rock music.
    b. was embraced by a large percentage of America's youth.
    c. expressed middle-class attitudes regarding clothing, hair styles, and sexuality.
    d. was extremely close-minded and repressive in its approach to daily living.

13. In the mid-1960s, social activists argued that sporadic violence stemmed from frustration and despair over all of the following except
    a. a complex mix of racism.
    b. a lack of educational and employment opportunities.
    c. inadequate government response to social problems.
    d. mass media.

14. Although assassinated in 1965 by old political enemies within the Muslim community, which leader remained a powerful symbol of the link between politics and renewed pride in African-American culture?
    a. Martin Luther King, Jr.
    b. Malcolm X
    c. Stokely Carmichael
    d. James Brown

15. To describe the puzzling and unprecedented convergence of economic stagnation and price inflation, economists invented the term
    a. Phillips curve.
    b. stagflation.
    c. deficit spending.
    d. recession.

16. In August 1971, Nixon announced a "new economic policy" calling for
    a. a ninety-day freeze on wages and prices.
    b. a 188-day freeze on inflation.
    c. government monitoring of savings and loan institutions.
    d. government monitoring of federal spending.

17. Which of the following statements does not apply to Nixon's proposed Family Assistance Plan (FAP)?
    a. It suggested replacement of most welfare programs, including the controversial Aid to Families with Dependents plan.
    b. It was a complex reform package.
    c. It guaranteed an annual income for all families.
    d. It attracted significant support in Congress.

18. Which of the following judges was not a Nixon appointee?
    a. Sandra Day O'Connor
    b. Harry Blackmun
    c. William Rehnquist
    d. Lewis Powell

19. In what case did the Supreme Court rule that a state law that made abortion a criminal offense violated a woman's right to privacy?
    a. *Dandrige* v. *Williams*
    b. *Roe* v. *Wade*
    c. *Engel* v. *Vitale*
    d. *Miranda* v. *Arizona*

20. During the Nixon administration, the National Security Council emerged as the most powerful maker of foreign policy within the government. The Nixon appointee as national security adviser was
    a. Spiro Agnew.
    b. Gerald Ford.
    c. J. Edgar Hoover.
    d. Henry Kissinger.

21. To ease tensions with the Soviet Union and to promote arms control, the two super-powers opened the Strategic Arms Limitation Talks (SALT I) in 1969. The SALT agreement was significant because it
    a. limited further development of both antiballistic missiles and offensive interconti-nental ballistic missiles.
    b. signaled a shift toward increased cold war hostilities.
    c. limited the number of warheads each missile could carry.
    d. outlawed nuclear-weapons research.

22. In July 1969, the United States pledged to provide military assistance to anticommu-nist governments in Asia but left it to them to provide their own military forces. This policy was announced as the
    a. Nixon Doctrine.
    b. Monroe Corollary.
    c. Watergate.
    d. SALT.

23. The goal of Vietnamization was to
    a. propagandize the war and gain public support.
    b. stop media coverage of the war.
    c. withdraw U.S. ground troops without accepting compromise or defeat.
    d. get more countries involved in the war.

24. In the wake of the scandal, only a few loyal supporters stood behind Nixon by the end of July 1974. After nearly a full week of deliberations, a majority of the House Judi-ciary Committee voted three formal articles of impeachment against the president. Which of the following was not a basis for impeachment?
    a. Obstruction of justice in the cover-up of the Watergate break-in.
    b. Nixon's violation of constitutional liberties.
    c. Nixon's knowledge that weapons were being sold to Contra rebels.
    d. Nixon's refusal to produce evidence requested during the impeachment proceedings.

ESSAY

Description and Explanation (one- to two-paragraph essay)

1. Explain why President Johnson did not give the American public full information about the war in Vietnam.

2. Describe the internal divisions within the civil rights movement. Were these differences of opinion good or bad for the movement?

3. Compare the background, political behavior, and ideology of Presidents Lyndon Johnson and Richard Nixon.

4. Describe the causes of the economic problems in the early 1970s.

5. Discuss the invasion of Cambodia and how Americans reacted to it.

6. Describe the elections of 1972, including the candidates and why Nixon won so easily.

7. Explain why Watergate faded as an issue in American history.

Discussion and Analysis (class discussion or one- to two-paragraph essay)

1. Discuss the election of 1964, including why Johnson won and whether his winning was a harbinger of political change.

2. Why was the Great Society subjected to so much criticism? Overall, was the Great Society a success or failure?

3. Discuss the role of the media and the different ways they covered such issues as the counterculture, the Vietnam War, and the civil rights movement. How did media coverage affect the American people?

4. Discuss 1968 as a critical year in American history, considering the Vietnam War and domestic violence.

5. Discuss the rights revolution of the Supreme Court, including important cases, and why the Warren Court became the focus of controversy.

What If (include an explanation of your position)

1. If you were a middle-class taxpayer in the 1960s, would you support or oppose Johnson's Great Society?

2. If you were a teenage girl in the mid-1960s, would you think the counterculture was Important? Would you participate in it?

3. If you were a male of military age in 1969, would you be willing to serve in Vietnam?

Crossword Puzzle: America during Its Longest War, 1963–1974

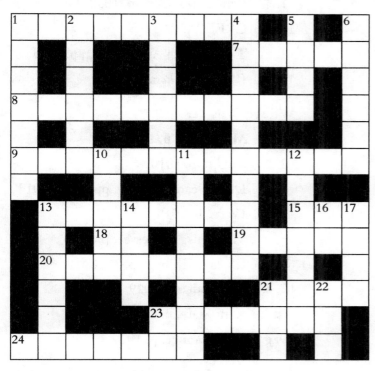

DOWN

1. Prosegregationist presidential candidate
2. Status of ___ put U.S. relations with China in difficult straits.
3. Title VII of Civil Rights Act barred ___ discrimination.
4. Agnew pled "no contest" that he did ___ (2 wds.).
5. Flag feature
6. What Nixon froze in 1971
10. Site of racist violence
11. U.S. dollar was less ___ compared with foreign currencies in 1973.
12. Tonkin Gulf nation
13. Contender for Democratic nomination in 1972
14. Lincoln profile site
16. Common prefix
17. Part of SALT
21. War on poverty acronym
22. Memphis assassin
23. Word with last or least

ACROSS

1. "Third-rate burglary"
7. The Twenty-sixth Amendment changed who could be a ___ .
8. What Nixon promised to restore (3 wds.)
9. Goldwater supporters
13. He rejected legalism, non-violence of Martin Luther King, Jr. (2 wds.).
15. Goal for NOW
18. Short for home state of 13 down

19. Decision for U.S. troops to ___ Cambodia was protested on college campuses.
20. 1 across and 4 down
21. Topic for Nader exposés
23. Voting Rights Act of 1965 grew out of TV coverage in this state.
24. Nixon's easing of tensions with the Soviet Union

246   CHAPTER 29

ANSWER KEY

WHO? WHAT? WHERE?

Who Were They?

1. b.   Barry Goldwater, p. 1006
2. e.   George Wallace, p. 1006
3. l.   Ronald Reagan, p. 1006
4. i.   McGeorge Bundy, p. 1011
5. p.   William Westmoreland, p. 1012
6. o.   William J. Fulbright, p. 1013
7. c.   Bob Dylan, p. 1015
8. a.   Abbie Hoffman, p. 1016
9. m.   Stokely Carmichael, p. 1019
10. h.   Martin Luther King, Jr., p. 1020
11. k.   Richard Daley, p. 1020
12. n.   Warren Burger, p. 1026
13. j.   Ralph Nader, p. 1026
14. d.   George McGovern, p. 1032
15. g.   John Sirica, p. 1033
16. f.   Gerald Ford, p. 1034

What Was It?

1. l.   Title VII, p. 1005
2. e.   Medicare, p. 1007
3. c.   Gulf of Tonkin Resolution, p. 1009
4. i.   RANCHHAND, p. 1012
5. a.   body count, p. 1012
6. j.   Students for Democratic Society, p. 1013
7. k.   Tet Offensive, p. 1019
8. f.   *Miranda* v. *Arizona*, p. 1026
9. h.   Ping-Pong, p. 1028
10. d.   Khmer Rouge, p. 1029
11. g.   Pentagon Papers, p. 1032
12. b.   CREEP, p. 1032
13. m.   Twenty-sixth Amendment, p. 1033
14. n.   *Washington Post*, p. 1033

Where Was It?

1. f.   Mississippi, p. 1006
2. h.   Saigon, p. 1010
3. c.   Dominican Republic, pp. 1011–1012
4. i.   Watts, p. 1018
5. e.   Memphis, Tennessee, p. 1020
6. b.   Chicago, Illinois, p. 1020
7. a.   Cambodia, p. 1029
8. d.   Kent State, p. 1029
9. g.   Paris, France, p. 1029

CHARTS, MAPS, AND ILLUSTRATIONS

1. Hanoi; Gulf of Tonkin, p. 1010
2. Washington, p. 1022
3. Jackson State University, p. 1029
4. Massachusetts, p. 1033

MULTIPLE CHOICE

1. d   (p. 1004)
2. a   (p. 1005)
3. b   (p. 1006)
4. a   (p. 1006)
5. b   (p. 1007)
6. a   (p. 1008)
7. d   (p. 1008)

8. c (p. 1011)

9. b (p. 1011)

10. b (p. 1013)

11. d (p. 1014)

12. a (p. 1015)

13. d (p. 1018)

14. b (p. 1019)

15. b (p. 1023)

16. a (p. 1023)

17. d (p. 1024)

18. a (p. 1026)

19. b (pp. 1026–1027)

20. d (p. 1027)

21. a (p. 1028)

22. a (p. 1028)

23. c (p. 1028)

24. c (p. 1034)

ESSAY

Description and Explanation

1. pp. 1012–1013

2. pp. 1017–1019

3. pp. 1004, 1022–1023

4. p. 1023

5. p. 1029

6. pp. 1032–1033

7. pp. 1034–1035

Discussion and Analysis

1. pp. 1005–1007

2. pp. 1008–1009

3. pp. 1013, 1016–1017, 1018–1019

4. pp. 1019–1021

5. pp. 1025–1027

What If

1. pp. 1007–1009

2. pp. 1015–1017

3. Chapter 9 *passim*

Crossword Puzzle

CHAPTER 30

ECONOMICS AND SOCIAL CHANGE IN THE LATE 20TH CENTURY

The decade of the 1960s, with its political assassinations, foreign war, and domestic dissent, seemed a period unique in its upheavals. In fact, though, the decades that followed brought even more far-reaching changes to the nation's population, economic structure, culture, and social fabric.

After 1970, the population became older, more urban, and ethnically and racially more diverse. The center of power shifted from the Northeast and toward the South and West. Birth rates sank to the lowest levels in U.S. history, save for those of the Depression of the 1930s. There was a dramatic rise in immigration to America, but the point of origin and place of entry shifted from Europe and the Northeast to Asia and Latin America and the Southwest and South. By 2000, one out of ten Americans were foreign born. These changes in demographics had substantial consequences for economic trends and domestic politics.

The pace of the technological change brought an astonishing transformation in the availability of consumer products, in production processes, in the labor force, and in the structure of the economy itself. This was especially true in biotechnology, computing, and information communications. Revolutionary changes in technology and the economy profoundly affected American lives. As mass-produced electronically based technology spread, the nature of cultural activities became increasingly fragmented. Mass commercial culture continued to be a topic of lively controversy and was studied by serious scholars.

The post-Vietnam decades saw an intensification rather than a diminution of social activism. As the United States became home to fragmented and highly political cultures, people debated the complex meanings of multiculturalism and tolerance. Racial identity became increasingly important, and ethnic groups embraced the politics of group solidarity. Government efforts to promote racial equality moved beyond eliminating discriminatory barriers and strove to increase individual opportunities for minorities and women. Social justice, according to the new credo, required government to focus on affirmative action so that groups that historically had faced discrimination now would receive an equitable share of the nation's jobs, public spending, and education programs.

LIBERTY, EQUALITY, POWER

The social and political activists of the post-Vietnam years debated the subjects of liberty, equality, and power, and, unlike activists of previous decades, increasingly acknowledged multiculturalism and ethnicity in their discussions. It was not enough that individuals of minority background be permitted to compete for jobs and opportunities, the government also needed to make certain that a representative sample of minorities actually secured employment or were admitted into educational programs. Some found the new emphasis on ethnicity a dangerous form of racism. Reverse discrimination became a concern, as minority and female job applicants were given priority over white males in the search for qualified employees. The struggle to create an atmosphere of liberty, equality, and power for all individuals or groups ensued in the latter portion of the 20th century.

As different cultural or ethnic groups became involved in social concerns, the more complex these issues became. Women's groups, for example, increasingly became concerned that the maldistribution of power in the United States could not be separated from the very personal power relationships that shaped their own lives. Environmental groups were concerned not only about the future of their world but also about the power to control the environment, its use, and even its destruction. The ethnic mix of 20th-century America shaped the issues facing its government more than ever before.

OBJECTIVES

After studying this chapter, a student should be able to

1. Describe the rise of the Sunbelt.

2. Describe immigration in the late 20th century.

3. Evaluate the technological revolution and its effects on American society.

4. Describe the growing environmental movement and its issues and demands.

5. Discuss the revolution in media culture, especially the role of television.

6. Describe the New Women's Movement and its issues.

7. Compare social activism among African Americans, Indians, Spanish-speaking groups, and Asian Americans.

8. Analyze the development and issues of the New Right.

CHRONOLOGY

1961	President Kennedy announced the Apollo program, under the recently formed National Aeronautics and Space Administration (NASA), with the goal of sending a man to the moon by 1970.
1962	Congressional action designated Cubans who were fleeing Castro's regime as refugees eligible for admittance. Over the next thirty years, 800,000 Cubans fled to America—chiefly in south Florida.
	Rachel Carson published *Silent Spring*, which warned of the dangers of agricultural pesticides.

1965   President Lyndon Johnson's Immigration Act of 1965, one of the most important pieces of Great Society legislation, ended immigration quotas and laid the basis for a substantial shift in region of origin.

1968   With funding from the Ford Foundation, the Mexican-American Legal Defense and Educational Fund (MALDEF) emerged as the most visible national group ready to lobby or litigate on behalf of the interests (as MALDEF saw them) of Mexican Americans.

The Civil Rights Act contained sections that became known as the "Indian Bill of Rights." Most of the Bill of Rights was finally extended to Indians still living on the reservations.

1969   Twelve years after the Soviet Union's launch of its *Sputnik* satellite, U.S. astronauts Neil Armstrong and Edwin "Buzz" Aldrin took the first steps on the moon.

A new spirit of rebellion and self-assurance for sexual minorities emerged after police in New York City raided a gay club. The "Stonewall incident" marked a turning point in homosexual politics and a goal of political leverage.

1970–1990   Birth rates sank to their lowest levels in U.S. history. During these decades, 90 percent of the country's population growth came in the South and the West. By 1990, more than one in ten Americans lived in California.

1970s   Under pressure from international competition and declining profits, more than a dozen steel plants closed. The auto industry laid off thousands of workers.

Under the leadership of Ernesto Cortes, Jr., Communities Organized for Public Service (COPS) concentrated efforts on achieving visible changes that touched everyday lives of average people.

A social philosophy called Afrocentrism had begun attracting a number of African-American intellectuals and professionals.

The availability of microchips boosted the capability and reduced the size and cost of computer hardware.

This was the last decade in which the three giant television networks commanded the daily attention of a nation of loyal viewers.

During the 1970s, environmental hazards emerged as a major concern of public policy. In response, Earth Day was organized, largely by college students, with the goal of raising the nation's consciousness about environmental degradation and the science of ecology. Legislation was passed to establish the Environmental Protection Agency (EPA), the Resources Recovery Act (dealing with waste management), and the Clean Air Act. Over the next three years, legislators, prompted by concerned citizens, passed the Water Pollution Act (1972), the Pesticides Control Act (1972), and the Endangered Species Act (1973).

1970   During the pinnacle of student protests and youth culture, the median age of Americans was twenty-eight.

1972   The Apollo space flights concluded as NASA turned to the development of a space station for conducting experiments and research.

1973   Created by a group of young activists in 1968, the American Indian Movement (AIM) adopted a confrontational strategy to achieve its goals. The ensuing violence eventually led to clashes with federal officials and conservative Indian leaders, such as in 1973 at the Pine Ridge Reservation in South Dakota.

1975   The Federal Communications Commission ordered networks to dedicate the first sixty minutes of prime time each day to family programming. A federal court ruled that the order violated the First Amendment's guarantee of free speech.

1976   The Asian Pacific Planning Council (APPCON) united into a single pan-American movement that worked to obtain government funding for projects that benefited Asian-American communities.

1977   President Jimmy Carter created the Department of Energy and supported the development of renewable resources and conservation as part of his promise to decrease American dependence on imported fossil fuel.

1979   Expansion of the nuclear power industry was halted after Pennsylvania's Three Mile Island incident. The malfunction created public alarm concerning the safety of nuclear sites.

1980s   Advances in space technology allowed NASA to begin launching a series of manned space shuttles. These shuttles, which served as space laboratories, continued to bring the United States closer to the goal of establishing a permanent space station.

Over the next decade, steel and automotive industries stabilized. Other large corporations began to downsize and laid off large numbers of workers.

Acquired immune deficiency syndrome (AIDS), a fatal condition attacking the immune system, made news headlines. At first, the disease was mistakenly associated only with homosexual men, but it eventually was declared a public-health issue, affecting a majority of Americans.

1980   In response to the growing number of people who sought admittance to the United States as "refugees," Congress passed the Refugee Act of 1980, which sanctioned the admittance of political refugees but denied entry to refugees seeking only economic improvement.

Microsoft licensed a computer operating system software called MS-DOS for use in personal computers.

1981 Music Television (MTV), with its twenty-four-hour supply of rock-music videos, was launched.

1986 Activists pushed government organizations and private employers to ban behavior, whether verbal or physical, that demeaned women. Guided by public opinion, the Supreme Court ruled that under the Civil Rights Act of 1964, sexual harassment constituted a form of discrimination.

As illegal immigration became a prominent political issue, Congress devised the Immigration Reform and Control Act of 1986. It imposed penalties on businesses employing illegal aliens and granted residency to workers who could prove that they had been living in the United States since 1982.

1988 In the wake of Love Canal and similar revelations of environmental hazards across the country, Congress created a clean-up "Superfund" to be financed by taxes imposed on polluting industries. The U.S. government itself turned out to be one of the country's most flagrant polluters. It was disclosed that the price tag for cleaning up U.S. nuclear facilities would exceed a billion dollars.

Congress issued a formal apology and voted reparation payments for Japanese Americans that the U.S. government had placed in internment camps during World War II.

The Supreme Court ruled that states could not prohibit gambling operations, such as bingo, on Indian tribal lands. Congress followed by passing the Indian Gaming Regulatory Act, which permitted casino operations.

1990 Nearly eight out of every ten Americans were living in metropolitan areas.

Well over 50 percent of the sticker price on most American model automobiles went to foreign businesses and workers. This was a sign of the increasing global nature of American business.

1991 Thirty thousand Korean Americans staged a march for peace. Despite the fact that this was the largest demonstration ever conducted by Asian Americans, it received almost no attention—even from local media.

The issue of sexual harassment attracted national attention when Clarence Thomas, an African-American nominee for the Supreme Court, was accused of harassing Anita Hill, an African-American law professor, when both had worked for the Office of Economic Opportunity.

1992 The 1992 Earth Summit, held in Brazil, took up global population issues.

In **April,** outrage erupted into violence after police officers were acquitted in the beating of an African-American man, which had been videotaped by a passing motorist. Angry mobs stormed south-central Los Angeles, looting businesses and beating civilians.

1993   The Department of Energy released records relating to radiation testing and experimentation. Americans located downwind of nuclear test sites in the 1940s and 1950s experienced an abnormally high incidence of cancer and leukemia. For decades, government officials had warned site workers inadequately about the dangers of radiation and refused to provide information to the public.

1995   More than one third of the population used a computer in their daily work, and more than half of all schoolchildren used one in the classroom.

Bill Gates, founder of the Microsoft company, became the richest person in the world.

In October the "Million Man March" in Washington, D.C., sought to mobilize African-American men behind social improvements in the black communities.

1996   The trial of O. J. Simpson raised a debate about the place of African Americans in American life. It also indicated a significant division among Americans along racial lines.

California voters passed Proposition 209. This attempted to abolish racial or gender preferences in state hiring, contracts, and college admissions.

1997   The Conservation Reserve Program stipulated payments to farmers to restore wetlands on their land. This new approach promoted change through incentives rather than penalties.

The National Asian Pacific American Network Council began to lobby on immigration and education issues. This was the first civil rights group founded by Asian Americans.

1999   *Africana: The Encyclopedia of the African and African American Experience* was published. This offered the latest scholarly perspective on thousands of issues and individuals.

Thousands of people representing worker rights and environmental causes tried to disrupt an international meeting of the World Trade Organization in Seattle.

2000   Virtually every home had at least one TV, and more than sixty-five percent were wired for CATV. The percentage watching programs on the networks had fallen from 90 to 60 percent.

Eighty percent of American homes had a personal computer.

Scientist announced that they had successfully mapped the entire human genetic code.

The median age of the American population was 34.

One out of every ten Americans were foreign born.

2001   In Los Angeles, fewer than half of the schoolchildren were proficient in English.

GLOSSARY OF IMPORTANT TERMS

affirmative action   Program or policy that attempts to rectify past injustice or discrimination. This policy was meant to ensure equal employment and education opportunities.

bilingual education   Education conducted in two languages.

chicanismo   Populistic pride in the Mexican-American heritage that emerged in the late 1960s. Chicano, once a term of derision, became the rallying cry for social and cultural crusades.

consciousness-raising   Technique used to create awareness of social issues, especially those involving injustices or racial and gender discrimination.

de-skill   In the post-Vietnam years, a great number of jobs were downgraded from skilled to semiskilled or unskilled. A growing number of Americans became unemployed because the jobs for which they were trained no longer existed.

ecology   Branch of biology that studies the interrelationships between living organisms and their physical environments.

e-commerce   Buying over the Internet. This was the newest ripple in the consumer culture.

edge cities   Former suburban areas that came to rival their adjacent cities as centers of business and population.

evangelicals   Religious groups that generally place more emphasis on converting non-Christians and less on defending the literal word of the Bible.

fossil fuels   Fuels such as coal, natural gas, and petroleum that were formed from plant or animal remains from a previous geological period.

fundamentalists   Religious groups that preach the necessity of fidelity to a strict moral code, individual commitment to Christ, and faith in the literal truth of the Bible.

Hmong   An ethnically distinct people who inhabited lands extending across the borders of the Indochinese countries of Vietnam, Cambodia, and Laos.

homophobia   Strong dislike or aversion to homosexual people or to their lifestyles.

microchips   Technological improvement that boosted the capability and reduced the size and cost of computer hardware.

neoconservatives	Prestigious group of intellectuals, many of whom had been anticommunist liberals during the 1950s and 1960s. Many of them renounced their liberal heritage on social issues. They offered intellectual subsistence to a new generation of conservationists.
OPEC	Organization of Petroleum Exporting Countries, a group dominated by the oil-rich nations of the Middle East. Members raised the price of oil that precipitated the acute shortages in the industrialized world in the 1970s.
paramilitary	Civilian groups organized as military units.
peyote	Variety of cactus that produces a narcotic drug used by some Native Americans in their traditional religious ceremonies.
preservationist agenda	Political agenda that was concerned primarily with the aesthetics of nature and the protection and enjoyment of the natural environment.
sagebrush rebellion	Movement in which western interests protested what they viewed as restrictive policies on the use of public lands.
sanctuary movement	Church-based movement that opposed U.S. policies in Central America and that helped illegal aliens in the United States.
space shuttle	Manned rocket that served as a space laboratory and could be flown back to the earth for reuse.
space station	Earth-orbiting platform from which to conduct experiments and research.
Sunbelt	Southern part of the United States, from Florida to California.
UHF independents	Ultrahigh-frequency channels between 14 and 81 on the standard TV dial.
urban corridors	Metropolitan strips of population running between older cities.
zapping	Process in which viewers rapidly switch from TV program to TV program with a remote control. Also called channel surfing.

WHO? WHAT? WHERE?

WHO WERE THEY?

Complete each following statement (questions 1–14) by writing the letter preceding the appropriate name in the space provided. Use each answer only once.

    a. Anita Hill
    b. Bill Gates
    c. Hazel O'Leary
    d. Henry Cisneros

  e. Jerry Falwell
  f. Madonna
  g. Malcolm X
  h. Pat Robertson
  i. Phyllis Schlafly
  j. Queen Latifah
  k. Rachel Carson
  l. Ted Turner
  m. Tipper Gore
  n. William Bennett

_____ 1. Young engineer who headed the Microsoft company, which licensed the computer software that became the standard operating system for personal computers.

_____ 2. Author of *Silent Spring*, a book that warned of the dangers of the pesticide DDT for the bird population.

_____ 3. Energy secretary who released records relating to radiation testing and experimentation.

_____ 4. One of the first to recognize the possibilities of cable television.

_____ 5. Singer who launched a career on MTV and was noted for an innovative mix of image and sound.

_____ 6. Secretary of education who used his office to denounce multicultural education.

_____ 7. Spouse of a prominent politician who disassociated herself from a campaign to censor rock lyrics.

_____ 8. African-American law professor who publicly accused a Supreme Court nominee of sexual harassment.

_____ 9. Heroic figure from the recent past in whom many Afrocentric blacks were encouraged to take pride.

_____ 10. One of the first female rappers to incorporate feminist themes in her music.

_____ 11. Mexican-American mayor of San Antonio, Texas, who joined President Clinton's cabinet in 1993.

_____ 12. One of the leaders of the New Right who assumed a prominent role in mobilizing opposition to ratification of the Equal Rights Amendment.

_____ 13. One of the founders of the Moral Majority, established in the 1970s.

_____ 14. Builder of a multimedia empire that included the Christian Broadcasting Network and host of the *700 Club*.

WHAT WAS IT?

Complete each following statement (questions 1–15) by writing the letter preceding the appropriate name in the space provided. Use each answer only once.

    a. Apollo program
    b. Apple
    c. Bank of America
    d. *chicanismo*
    e. Earth Day
    f. Filipino Americans
    g. gambling
    h. Love Canal
    i. McDonald's
    j. microchips
    k. OPEC
    l. "sagebrush rebellion"
    m. Smithsonian Institution
    n. Superfund
    o. zapping

_____ 1. Program launched in 1961 by President Kennedy with the goal of sending a manned mission to the moon.

_____ 2. Fledgling company that led the way in early sales of home computers.

_____ 3. New technology that boosted the capability and reduced the size and cost of computer hardware.

_____ 4. Financial giant that introduced the VISA credit card.

_____ 5. Company that pioneered nationwide standards in fast-food franchises.

_____ 6. Event largely organized by college students, meant to raise the nation's consciousness about the environment.

_____ 7. Housing development in New York where the soil under the homes was contaminated by chemical wastes.

_____ 8. Created by Congress, this was to be financed by taxes imposed on polluting industries.

_____ 9. Movement in which western interests protested restrictive policies on the use of public land.

_____ 10. Group dominated by the oil-rich nations of the Middle East that raised the price of oil.

_____ 11. Technique whereby TV viewers rapidly switch from program to program with a remote-control device.

_____ 12. Most lucrative entertainment business in the mid-1990s and one of which Native Americans had become a major part.

_____ 13. Storehouse of the remains of more than eighteen thousand Indians.

_____ 14. Populist pride amongst Mexican Americans.

_____ 15. Second-largest Asian-American group in the United States in 1990.

WHERE WAS IT?

Complete each statement below (questions 1–8) by writing the letter preceding the appropriate name in the space provided. Use each answer only once.

a. Brazil
b. Ellis Island, New York
c. Greenwich Village, New York City
d. Mexico
e. Miami, Florida
f. Pea Ridge, South Dakota
g. Silicon Valley, California
h. Three Mile Island, Pennsylvania

_____ 1. Area near San Francisco with tremendous growth based on the computer industry.

_____ 2. Country from which the largest number of non-European immigrants arrived in the late 20th century.

_____ 3. City where Cubans comprised one third of the population in 1990.

_____ 4. Location of a museum celebrating America's immigrant origins.

_____ 5. Country where the Earth Summit was held in 1992.

_____ 6. Location of a nuclear reactor that malfunctioned.

_____ 7. Location of a gay club where a confrontation took place between homosexual patrons and police that marked a turning point in homosexual politics.

_____ 8. Scene of a violent confrontation between Indian leaders and federal officials.

CHARTS, MAPS, AND ILLUSTRATIONS

1. In 1990, the center of population in the United States was located in _____. In what state was it located in 1790? _____.

2. The point of origin for the largest number of immigrants from 1970 to 1990 was _____.

3. The three states with the lowest percentage of urban population in 1990 were _____.

4. The two states with only one EPA-designated Superfund site were _____ and _____.

5. The group that represented homosexual militants and protested inattention to the issue of AIDS was _____.

MULTIPLE CHOICE

Circle the letter that best completes each statement.

1. Twenty-eight was the median age of Americans during the height of student protests and youth culture in 1970. By the 1990s the median age became
   a. 25.
   b. 34.
   c. 43.
   d. 51.

2. The census of 1980 revealed that, for the first time, more Americans were living in the South and the West than in the North and the East. Which of the following was not a reason for this demographic shift?
   a. the availability of affordable air conditioners for both homes and offices
   b. the rise of tourism and the proliferation of retirement communities in Nevada, California, Arizona, and Florida
   c. higher labor costs and the presence of strong unions prompted manufacturers to build new plants and relocate in the South and West
   d. the growth of high-tech industries

3. After the Soviet Union's launch of its satellite *Sputnik* in 1957, the United States stepped up its own space program under the newly formed
   a. National Aviation and Space Association (NASA).
   b. National Aeronautics and Space Administration (NASA).
   c. New Association of Space Advancement (NASA).
   d. Network of Advancement in Space and Air (NASA).

4. In July 1969, the first astronauts stepped from their spacecraft onto the moon. The men were
   a. John H. Glenn, Jr., and L. Gordon Cooper.
   b. Roger B. Chaffee and David R. Scott.
   c. Virgil Grissom and Walter M. Schirra, Jr.
   d. Neil Armstrong and Edwin Aldrin, Jr.

5. President Johnson's Immigration Act of 1965
   a. accorded no priority to those with special skills.
   b. provided no preference for those with ties to the United States.
   c. laid the basis for a smaller volume of immigration.
   d. ended quotas for immigration based on national origin.

6. In response to the growing number of refugees, Congress passed the Refugee Act of 1980. The act specified that
   a. fines would be imposed on businesses employing illegal aliens.
   b. workers living in the United States for the past five years would be granted residency.
   c. political refugees—those fleeing overt persecution—would be admitted.
   d. those seeking to improve their economic lot would be admitted.

7. As the problem of illegal immigration grew, Congress passed the Immigration Reform and Control Act of 1986, which
   a. increased immigration quotas.
   b. lowered immigration quotas.
   c. granted residency to political refugees.
   d. imposed penalties on businesses employing illegal aliens and granted residency to workers who could prove that they had been living in the United States since 1982.

8. By the early 1990s, the federal government was allocating approximately $4 billion a year to research in biotechnology, which included all of the following, except
   a. biochemical weapons.
   b. new techniques for gene transfer.
   c. embryo manipulation.
   d. tissue regeneration.

9. When did the computer revolution begin?
   a. after World War I
   b. after World War II
   c. after the Korean War
   d. after the Vietnam War

10. The computer revolution, enhanced by new communication technologies, such as fiber-optic networks and satellite transmission, fueled
    a. an environmental revolution.
    b. a back-to-paper revolution.
    c. a software revolution.
    d. an information revolution.

11. New technologies and the trend toward internationalization brought structural changes to American businesses and the workforce. These changes included
    a. an increase in traditional manufacturing and extractive jobs.
    b. a decrease in service, management, and information/entertainment sector jobs.
    c. many companies doubling their workforces and management staffs.
    d. pressure from international competition and declining profits that encouraged downsizing and layoffs.

12. Who was the charismatic leader who organized agricultural workers in the United Farm Workers (UFW)?
    a. Bill Gates
    b. Cesar Chavez
    c. Martin Luther King, Jr.
    d. Kevin Phillips

13. Early environmental organizations, such as the Sierra Club, Audubon Society, and Wilderness Society, focused on
    a. urban housing.
    b. opening public lands for private development.
    c. development of natural resources.
    d. a preservationist agenda.

14. During the 1970s, environmental hazards and balances emerged as major concerns. However, some requiring higher smokestacks to eliminate smog helped to clear city skies, but elevating pollutants produced chemical changes in the atmosphere that resulted in
    a. asbestos formation.
    b. DDT.
    c. acid rain.
    d. Agent Orange.

15. Increasingly, public attention during the 1980s focused on international hazards. Those hazards, which threatened life on a global scale, included all of the following, except
    a. global warming and holes in the ozone layer caused by chlorofluorocarbons.
    b. the rapid decline of biological diversity among other plant and animal species.
    c. nuclear-reactor accidents and the resulting radioactive contamination.
    d. massive deforestation and desertification with accompanying climatic changes.

16. During the 1980s, television networks suffered a slow, yet steady, loss of viewers. Which of the following was not a reason for this loss of viewership?
    a. Sophisticated market research made it increasingly easier to create successful prime-time programs.
    b. Independent stations captured small but lucrative markets.
    c. Remote-control devices and VCRs provided viewers with greater control over what they watched.
    d. The growth of cable television further fragmented TV viewership.

17. The National Endowment for the Humanities and the National Endowment for the Arts
    a. provided financial backing for projects that focused on multiculturalism and on politically sensitive reinterpretations of traditional works.
    b. was supported by Secretary of Education William Bennett.
    c. championed traditional education programs.
    d. refused to support controversial artistic projects.

18. A conservative movement, initially created in response to the Supreme Court decisions of the 1960s banning prayer and Bible-reading in public schools, staged an attack on educational practices in public schools by
    a. embracing proponents of multicultural education and the new cultural studies.
    b. rejecting claims that multicultural education and the new cultural studies should be seen as part of a progressive movement.
    c. supporting an antireligious philosophy they called "secular humanism."
    d. protesting corporal punishment.

19. Social activism continued into the early 1980s, with activist groups such as the Clamshell Alliance protesting
    a. nuclear weapons and reactors.
    b. unlicensed hunting and fishing.
    c. offshore oil drilling.
    d. child neglect and abuse.

20. Women's groups staged annual "Take Back the Night" marches in major cities to protest the rising tide of
    a. drunk driving.
    b. divorces.
    c. sexual assaults.
    d. high-school dropouts.

21. Throughout the 1970s, women came together in "consciousness-raising" sessions. They prompted a discussion of a wide range of personal questions involving all of the following, except
    a. housework.
    b. child rearing.
    c. nuclear weapons storage.
    d. economic independence.

22. Feminism grew into a highly diverse movement. During the 1970s and 1980s, American society was transformed by an explosion of women-oriented organizations, which included all of the following, except
    a. battered women's shelters, rape crisis centers, and clinics specializing in women's medicine.
    b. a retro-movement toward traditional women's roles and stereotypes.
    c. union-organizing efforts and women's studies programs in colleges and universities.
    d. organizations of women in specific businesses or professions and journals devoted to historical and contemporary research on women.

23. Sports star prosecuted for two murders whose trial demonstrated the divisions among Americans along racial lines was
    a. Michael Jordan.
    b. O. J. Simpson.
    c. Babe Ruth.
    d. Dennis Rodman.

24. "Affirmative action" sparked fierce controversy for all of the following reasons, except
    a. Many who had supported previous policies against discrimination found the new emphasis on group identity a dangerous form of racial thought.
    b. Groups that had historically faced discrimination now would receive an equitable share of the nation's jobs, public spending, and educational programs.
    c. Since there always would be more applicants than job openings, some viewed affirmative action on behalf of minority groups and women as reverse discrimination.
    d. Some beneficiaries of affirmative-action programs began to feel that their own accomplishments were stigmatized, no matter what their individual talents, by the affirmative-action label.

25. American Indians pursued a variety of different strategies for social change during the 1970s and 1980s and, like other ethnic groups, they
    a. stressed bilingualism to forestall the disappearance of their languages.
    b. resisted rediscovery of their traditional ethnic practices.
    c. refrained from drawing international attention to problems they faced.
    d. endorsed the use of stereotypical names by sports teams.

26. Following the suggestion of American-Indian lawyers and tapping the expertise of the Native American Rights Fund (NARF), many tribes used the courts aggressively in all of the following ways except
    a. pressuring Congress to pass laws that provided for the repatriation of sacred religious artifacts.
    b. working to prohibit gambling operations on tribal land.
    c. suing to protect tribal water, fishing, and agricultural rights and traditional religious ceremonies.
    d. suing to secure repatriation of Native American skeletal remains that were displayed and stored in museums.

27. In the 1970s, Ernesto Cortes, Jr., took the lead in founding a group that focused on achieving concrete, tangible changes that touched the everyday lives of ordinary citizens. This grass-roots organization was known as
    a. NEH (National Endowment for the Humanities).
    b. NOW (National Organization for Women).
    c. APPCON (Asian Pacific Planning Council).
    d. COPS (Communities Organized for Public Service).

28. The measure passed in California that aimed at eliminating racial or gender preferences was
    a. Amendment 214.
    b. Proposition 209.
    c. Title 43.
    d. Code 193.

29. The New Right of the 1970s attracted massive grass-roots support from Protestants who belonged to fundamentalist and evangelical churches. Fundamentalists and evangelicals generally espouse the same doctrinal tenets except that evangelicals place more emphasis on
    a. converting non-Christians.
    b. defending the literal truth of the Bible.
    c. the necessity of fidelity to a strict moral code.
    d. an individual commitment to Christ.

30. By the late 1990s the unemployment rate was low, but the type of jobs held by Americans that were expanding the most were
    a. computer high-tech jobs
    b. professional such as teachers and attorneys
    c. service sector such as clerks and cleaners
    d. heavily unionized and based on overseas trade

ESSAY

Description and Explanation (one- to two-paragraph essay)

1. Compare the three groups of Spanish-speaking immigrants arriving in the United States during the last three decades of the 20th century as to place of origin and point of settlement.

2. Describe how computerized communication helped transform economic production through franchising and globalized industries.

3. Describe how new technologies brought changes to the American workforce. Were they for better or worse?

4. Describe how the new generation of writers and reviewers studies mass culture.

5. Describe the social philosophy called Afrocentrism and its encouragement of black pride.

6. Explain the dilemmas of ethnic identity in the late 20th century.

7. Describe the change to a political culture in which group identity was becoming increasingly important. How did this produce controversy?

8. Describe the beliefs and politics of the New Religious Right.

Discussion and Analysis (class discussion or one- to two-paragraph essay)

1. Discuss the reasons for the demographic shift to the Sunbelt.

2. Compare the three immigration laws passed in the late 20th century. How did they reflect the changes in immigration during these years?

3. Discuss changes in TV programming since 1970 and describe why the changes took place. Did technology affect these changes?

4. Discuss feminism as a diverse movement and the role of power, personal and political, in the movement.

5. Compare ethnicity and social activism among Asian Americans, Spanish-speaking groups, and American Indians. What issues were the same or different among them? How were the techniques they used the same or different?

What If (include an explanation of your position)

1. If you were responsible for selecting the most important technological change in the last thirty years, what would you select?

2. If you were a member of a minority group in 2000, what would you consider the most significant changes in the status of your group in recent years? Would it be different from one group to another?

Crossword Puzzle: Economic and Social Change in the Late 20th Century

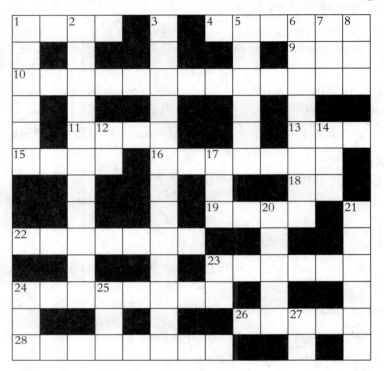

ACROSS

1. Computers or hamburgers
4. Twentieth-century president
9. Love Canal agency
10. California high-tech community (2 wds.)
11. Speech that's a censor's dilemma
13. Stock market indicator
15. Apollo's goal
16. Stump speaker of MTV
18. Constitution starter
19. Where Armstrong and Aldron "rocked"
22. Neoconservative writer Irving
23. Controversial Justice of 1991
24. Four winning women in 1992
26. Cola combatant
28. Some rap to feminists

DOWN

1. Ellis Island now
2. One of ten Americans is one
3. Genetic engineering field
5. He urged easier business access to public land
6. Three Mile Island threat in 1979
7. Imitate
8. Opposite of aye
12. Nurse
14. Number of La Raza Unida
17. Apple's rival
20. Layer of greenhouse effect
21. Fuels such as petroleum
23. Certain shirts or squares
24. Everybody's uncle
25. A long time ___
27. Double-duty abbreviation

ANSWER KEY

WHO? WHAT? WHERE?

Who Were They?

1. b. Bill Gates, p. 1050
2. k. Rachel Carson, p. 1050
3. c. Hazel O'Leary, p. 1053
4. l. Ted Turner, p. 1057
5. f. Madonna, p. 1058
6. n. William Bennett, p. 1076
7. a. Anita Hill, p. 1061
8. g. *Malcolm X*, p. 1063
9. j. Queen Latifah, p. 1064
10. d. Henry Cisneros, p. 1068
11. i. Phyllis Schlafly, p. 1073
12. e. Jerry Falwell, p. 1075
13. h. Pat Robertson, p. 1076

What Was It?

1. a. Apollo program, p. 1039
2. b. Apple, p. 1047
3. j. microchips, p. 1047
4. c. Bank of America, p. 1047
5. i. McDonald's, p. 1047
6. e. Earth Day, pp. 1050-1051
7. h. Love Canal, p. 1051
8. n. Superfund, p. 1052
9. l. sagebrush rebellion, p. 1052
10. k. OPEC, p. 1053
11. o. zapping, p. 1056
12. g. gambling, p. 1066

13. m. Smithsonian Institution, p. 1066
14. d. *chicanismo*, p. 1067
15. f. Filipino Americans, p. 1069

Where Was It?

1. g. Silicon Valley, p. 1039
2. d. Mexico, p. 1040
3. e. Miami, Florida, p. 1042
4. b. Ellis Island, New York, p. 1044
5. a. Brazil, p.1053
6. h. Three Mile Island, Pennsylvania, p. 1054
7. c. Greenwich Village, New York City, p. 1061
8. f. Pea Ridge, South Dakota, p. 1065

CHARTS, MAPS, AND ILLUSTRATIONS

1. Missouri; Maryland, p. 1040
2. Asia, p. 1043
3. Kentucky, West Virginia, and Vermont, p. 1045
4. Nevada; Hawaii, p. 1052
5. Act Up, p. 1062

MULTIPLE CHOICE

1. b (p. 1038)
2. c (p. 1038)
3. b (p. 1039)
4. d (p. 1039)
5. d (p. 1042)
6. c (p. 1042)
7. d (p. 1043)

8. a   (p. 1047)

9. b   (p. 1047)

10. d   (p. 1047)

11. d   (pp. 1048–1049)

12. b   (p. 1049)

13. d   (p. 1050)

14. c   (p. 1051)

15. c   (p.1053)

16. a   (p. 1056)

17. a   (p. 1076)

18. b   (pp. 1075–1076)

19. a   (p. 1059)

20. c   (p. 1060)

21. a   (p. 1060)

22. c   (p. 1061)

23. b   (p. 1064)

24. b   (p. 1071)

25. b   (p. 1067)

26. b   (pp. 1065–1066)

27. d   (p. 1068)

28. b   (p. 1071)

29. a   (p. 1074)

30. c   (p. 1049)

ESSAY

Description and Explanation

1. pp. 1040–1042

2. pp. 1047–1048

3. pp. 1047–1049

4. pp. 1058–1059

5. pp. 1063–1064

6. pp. 1070–1072

7. pp. 1070–1072

8. p. 1074

Discussion and Analysis

1. pp. 1038–1041

2. pp. 1042–1044

3. pp. 1048–1050

4. pp. 1059–1061

5. pp. 1063–1070

What if

1. pp. 1040–1047

2. pp. 1063–1070

Crossword Puzzle

CHAPTER 31

POWER AND POLITICS SINCE 1974

American society during the 1980s and 1990s became disillusioned. The Vietnam debacle and the Watergate scandal bred cynicism in the American public and, coupled with anxiety regarding the economy, many lost faith in their own political leaders. There was a growing feeling that the government simply did not work anymore. The presidencies of both Gerald Ford and Jimmy Carter were undermined, in part, by their constituency's lack of trust in them.

After winning the election in 1980, Reagan's conservative advisors set about crafting a broad political coalition of their own. Although he spoke out against big spenders and budget deficits, his administration rolled up an extraordinary record of deficits and spending of its own. Many of the new jobs created were low paying and offered few, if any, benefits. Economic growth was not evenly distributed. The minimum wage, when measured in constant dollars, fell throughout the decade of the 1980s. Gradually Reagan's popularity began to fade. Militant conservatives and the religious right increasingly criticized him for failing to support their agendas vigorously. Economic problems led to calls for more leadership from the White House.

The political culture of the 1990s was characterized by uncertainty. During the Bush presidency, Soviet communism collapsed, and the international order experienced the greatest transformation since the end of World War II. Bush and his advisors spoke of creating a new world order but could not explain just what they meant. The old political standby—containment of the Soviet enemy—had disappeared. The unanticipated disintegration of Bush's popularity and the ascension of Bill Clinton to the White House in 1992 foreshadowed congressional elections two years later with the surprising triumph of conservative Republicans. These political upheavals suggested that the nation had become deeply suspicious of national leaders and declined to remain loyal to a specific political party.

The first Clinton administration seemed to lack clear direction or follow-through. The controversies surrounding military intervention in international affairs and the federal government's role in directing economic policy revealed fundamental uncertainties about America's role in the post-cold war world. In both foreign and domestic policy, winds of change were sweeping through American life, but their prevailing direction was hardly clear. As the economy strengthened in the mid-1990s, however, domestic issues seem less divisive, and this worked to Clinton's advantage.

LIBERTY, EQUALITY, POWER

The last years of the 20th century brought changes to American politics and to foreign affairs. The liberty, equality, and power of minorities and women, as evidenced by the increasingly visible

269

positions they hold in America's representative government, continue to develop and expand. The power base of America and of the world is changing rapidly, and Americans still are debating the proper relationship among liberty, equality, and government power.

OBJECTIVES

After studying this chapter, a student should be able to

1. Evaluate the administrations of Ford and Carter in economic matters and how serious economic problems affected those administrations.

2. Analyze foreign policy under Ford and Carter.

3. Describe United States relations with Iran from Carter through Bush.

4. Compare the campaigns of 1980 and 1984.

5. Contrast Reagan in his first and second administrations as to his personal style and domestic policies.

6. Analyze the end of the Cold War and its effects on the United States and its foreign policy.

7. Evaluate the different manner in which Carter and Bush handled problems in the Middle East.

8. Describe the use of the military for peacekeeping missions under Reagan, Bush and Clinton.

9. Compare the ideology and views on social issues of Presidents Carter, Reagan, Bush, and Clinton.

10. Describe the changes in political alignment and philosophy that took place in the last years of the 20th century.

CHRONOLOGY

1970s Public support for welfare state ventures began to die out, and the United States entered a new, more conservative era in social policy. Liberals continued to discuss how to improve, and even expand, welfare initiatives, but conservatives advocated a radical reduction in government-spending programs.

As a consequence of economic changes, large numbers of workers had to settle for low-paying, short-term jobs that offered no benefits, and many Americans were unable to find work in any form. Economists termed this "long-term joblessness," unemployment that lasts for a year or longer, a condition affecting more and more Americans after 1970.

1974 In **September**, President Ford granted a presidential pardon to former

President Nixon. This proved to be one of Ford's most controversial decisions.

1975   The antiwar mood in Congress, and in much of the nation, made military support of the South Vietnamese government impossible. Sensing victory, North Vietnamese armies moved rapidly through South Vietnam in **March**, and communist victories occurred throughout that country. In early **April**, Khmer Rouge forces in Cambodia drove the American-backed government from its capital and, on **April 30**, North Vietnamese troops took control of Saigon, South Vietnam's capital.

In May the Khmer Rouge boarded the American ship, the *Mayaguez*, and seized the crew. President Ford ordered a military response to secure the release of the ship and its crew.

1976   In **November**, Jimmy Carter of Georgia and his running mate, Walter Mondale of Minnesota, narrowly won a presidential victory over Ford. Carter's win resulted from a diverse, transitory coalition. This election witnessed the lowest voter turnout since the end of World War II.

1977   Unemployment stood at slightly over 7 percent and inflation at just under 6 percent. Three years later, stagflation still plagued the economy that had almost stopped expanding, with unemployment rising, and inflation topping 13 percent.

1978   Carter's strength as a diplomat and his personal skill as a facilitator emerged in the Camp David accords. Relations between Egypt and Israel had been strained for five years, so Carter brought Menachem Begin and Anwar Sadat, leaders of Israel and Egypt, together at the Camp David presidential retreat. After thirteen days, the three leaders emerged and announced the framework for a negotiating process and a peace treaty between the two countries.

Carter adroitly managed public and congressional relations to obtain ratification of treaties that granted Panama increasing jurisdiction over the Panama Canal—with complete control after the year 2000.

1979   The Carter administration also worked on relations in Asia and Africa. Building on Nixon's initiative, Carter expanded economic and cultural relations with China and finally established formal diplomatic ties with the People's Republic on New Year's Day.

The overthrow of Iran's Shah Reza Pahlavi by an Islamic fundamentalist revolution in **January** accompanied a massive rejection of U.S. influence. When the Carter administration bowed to political pressure to admit the Shah into the United States for medical treatment in **November**, a group of Iranians took sixty-six Americans hostage at the U.S. embassy compound in Teheran and demanded the return of the Shah in exchange for their release.

Criticism of Carter intensified during the hostage crisis. The Soviet Union invaded Afghanistan in **December**. Many Americans interpreted the invasion as a sign that the Soviets saw the United States as too weak to mount any effort at "containment."

1980   Jimmy Carter struggled to gain his party's nomination in 1980, so it was not surprising that former actor and California Republican Governor Ronald Reagan mounted a successful presidential challenge by winning slightly more than 50 percent of the popular vote.

1981   Reagan fired the nation's air traffic controllers when their union refused to halt a strike. Overall, union membership continued to decline as both the Reagan administration and many large businesses pursued anti-union strategies.

The Reagan tax plan significantly reduced taxes for higher income taxpayers.

1981–1986   After a short recession in 1980–1981, the worst since the Great Depression of the 1930s, the economy rebounded and entered a period of noninflationary growth. Between 1982 and 1986, eleven million new jobs were added to the economy, and, by 1986, the GNP was climbing steadily while the rate of inflation dropped to less than 2 percent.

1981–1982   Farmers in the Midwest were battered by the recession as falling crop prices made it difficult for them to make payments on high-interest loans contracted with banks during the inflation-ridden 1970s. The value of farmland, farmers' only real asset, plummeted, and a series of mortgage foreclosures hit farm states, leading to financial ruin for many small-town businesses.

1982   The Reagan administration displayed a new willingness to use military force abroad. Reagan sent a "peacekeeping force" of 1,600 American marines to restore stability to Lebanon. Muslim fighters turned their wrath against Americans. A suicide commando mission into a U.S. military compound killed 241 American marines.

1983   If Lebanon had raised questions over Reagan's judgment, they were forgotten temporarily after military success in Grenada. In October, two thousand U.S. troops were ordered to the tiny Caribbean island to overthrow the socialist government and install a regime friendly to U.S. interests.

1984   The most controversial aspect of Reagan's foreign policy involved Central America. United States–backed regimes were implicated in widespread abuses of human rights, not only against their own people, but also against American nuns, journalists, and human-rights workers. Congress broke with the president's policy and denied further military aid to the *contras*.

Reagan proposed the development of the Strategic Defense Initiative (SDI) or "Star Wars" program. The proposed space-based shield against incoming missiles was the most expensive defense system in history.

Representative Geraldine Ferraro of New York was the first female Democratic candidate for vice president.

In the **November** election, Reagan and the Republicans overwhelmed Mondale and the Democrats, with Mondale carrying only his home state of Minnesota and the District of Columbia.

1985   Mikhail Gorbachev became General Secretary of the Communist Party, and, realizing that his isolated country faced economic stagflation and an environmental crisis, he championed a major political transformation. He proclaimed a policy of *glasnost* (openness) and began to implement *perestroika* (economic liberalization).

1986   As militant Islamic groups escalated the use of terrorism against Israel and western powers, the United States launched air strikes in an attempt to destroy Libyan leader Muammar Qaddafi's power.

In **November**, the story broke that the Reagan administration was selling arms to Iran as part of a bargain to secure the release of American hostages being held by parties friendly to Iran's regime. During the Iran-contra hearings, Reagan maintained a remarkable display of forgetfulness.

William Rehnquist became Chief Justice of the Supreme Court.

1987   Reagan and Gorbachev signed a major arms treaty that reduced the number of intermediate-range missiles held by each nation and allowed for on-site verification. The following year, as part of his attempt to end the isolationism and scare tactics that protected communism in the Soviet Union, Gorbachev scrapped a policy that forbade any nation under Soviet influence from renouncing communism.

1988   Vice President George Bush won the office of president over Michael Dukakis. The voter turnout in the election was the lowest it had been since 1924, and polls suggested that a majority of voters considered neither Bush nor Dukakis worthy of the office of president.

1989   Congress authorized a comprehensive "bailout" of insolvent savings and loans, designed to save some institutions and to provide a means of transferring the assets of failed S&Ls to those that were still solvent. However, as taxpayers began paying for this expensive plan, considerable corruption was already taking place.

The pro-Soviet East German government fell in **November**, and Germans hacked down the Berlin Wall, the twenty-eight-year-old symbol of the cold war.

In a military incursion called Operation Just Cause (aired live on television throughout the world), U.S. marines landed in Panama and arrested alleged drug lord and Panamanian leader General Manuel Noriega. This incursion raised questions of international law and provided a new model of post-cold war action. In **April 1992**, an American court convicted Noriega of cocaine trafficking. Fifty percent of the federal judiciary had been nominated and confirmed during Reagan's two terms in office.

1990–1991 On **August 2, 1990**, President Saddam Hussein of Iraq ordered his troops to occupy the small neighboring country of Kuwait. In response to this act of aggression, President Bush mobilized an international military force and convinced the Saudi government to harbor western troops. In Operation Desert Shield, 230,000 troops were sent to protect Saudi Arabia. By **mid-January 1991**, the situation had escalated into Operation Desert Storm as the United States launched an air war on Iraq; ground troops began an offensive in late **February**.

1990 Bush broke his campaign promise of no new taxes. This was the issue on which conservatives judged his worthiness as a Reagan successor.

1991 In **December**, the Russian parliament ratified a new government with eleven former Soviet republics as members. The United States was faced with the task of setting up new embassies and establishing diplomatic relations with the new countries.

1992 Public dissatisfaction with the establishment carried over into the presidential election, vaulting Democrat Bill Clinton into executive office. He became the first Democratic president in twelve years.

In **December**, President Bush pardoned the six former Reagan administration officials who had been involved in the Iran-contra affair.

1993 A historic agreement between Israel and the PLO took place on **August 28**. The PLO recognized Israel's right to exist, and Israel agreed in principle to Palestinian authority over the Gaza Strip and over Jericho on the West Bank, a first step toward self-rule in Israeli-occupied territories.

In **December**, Clinton was able to muscle the North American Free Trade Agreement (NAFTA) through Congress by a close vote. NAFTA proposed to cut tariffs and eliminate trade barriers between the United States, Canada, and Mexico over a fifteen-year period. However, not until Clinton added certain safeguards on labor and environmental issues did NAFTA gain the necessary support for passage.

1994 The CIA was shaken by a scandal when, on **February 22**, a high-ranking officer, Aldrich Ames, and his wife were arrested for selling information to the Soviets over the past decade. Their activities contributed to the deaths of other CIA agents.

In **February**, the United States ended its nineteen-year trade embargo against Vietnam.

In **August** Kenneth Starr became a special prosecutor to investigate "Whitewater," a failed land development that involved the Clintons.

In **September**, Congress passed an anticrime bill that provided funds for more police officers and more prisons.

On **September 19**, the first 3,000 of a projected force of 15,000 troops landed in Haiti, allowing the return of elected President Jean-Bertrand Aristide. Last-minute negotiations by Jimmy Carter cleared the way for Aristide to assume power without resistance.

The socioeconomic changes that were transforming American life and lowering real wages bred anxiety and a feeling that the national government simply did not work anymore. In 1958, 73 percent of Americans thought that government generally did the "right thing"; by **November 1994**, only 13 percent felt that way.

In congressional elections in **November**, Republicans secured control of both houses of Congress for the first time in forty years.

1996   Congress passed the Personal Responsibility and Work Opportunity Reconciliation Act, which reorganized child-care programs. It also ended the welfare system that had been in place since the New Deal.

Helped by the growing economy, Clinton won reelection over Republican Robert Dole.

1997   President Clinton and congressional Republicans cooperated to pass legislation to cut taxes and phase in reduction of the federal deficit.

1999   In **February**, Republicans failed to remove President Clinton after a month-long trial.

In **March**, Clinton supported a bombing campaign by NATO in Kosovo. Clinton insisted that this use of the military was necessary to protect the Albanian Muslims.

2000   Plan Colombia was undertaken to combat drug cartels and guerrilla fighters in that country using the American military.

In the **November** election, there was a relatively light turnout on election day, but a controversy developed over the outcome of the presidential election. Governor George W. Bush defeated Vice President Al Gore in this close controversial election.

GLOSSARY OF IMPORTANT TERMS

born-again Christian One who made a personal commitment to Jesus Christ or who renewed that commitment. Usually these people are evangelical Christians.

contras	Opposition military force in Nicaragua that was trained and financed by the United States. It opposed the Nicaraguan socialist government led by the Sandinista Party.
détente	An easing of tensions among countries; usually leads to increased economic, diplomatic, and other types of contacts between former rivals.
Georgia mafia	Small group of President Carter's advisors from Georgia who believed that Carter's image as a political outsider would continue to serve him well. This group included Press Secretary Jody Powell and domestic advisors Hamilton Jordon and Bert Lance.
glasnost	Russian term; described increased openness in Russian society under Mikhail Gorbachev.
globalization	Clinton's policy to lower trade barriers and expand global markets. He suggested that it would increase prosperity.
long-term joblessness	Unemployment that lasted for a year or longer.
perestroika	Russian term describing economic liberalization that began in the late 1980s.
post-Vietnam syndrome	Failure of the government to act strongly in foreign affairs; passivity and loss of will for strong action.
supply-side economics	This economic theory held that tax reductions would stimulate the economy by putting more money in the hands of investors and consumers.
Teflon president	Term applied to Ronald Reagan. Critics complained that nothing ever "stuck" to the president, for no matter what problems beset his administration, he seemed to lead a charmed life.
UNESCO	Acronym for United Nations Educational, Scientific, and Cultural Organization.

WHO? WHAT? WHERE?

WHO WAS IT?

Complete each following statement (questions 1–16) by writing the letter preceding the appropriate name in the space provided. Use each answer only once.

    a. Bill Clinton
    b. Geraldine Ferraro
    c. Hillary Rodham Clinton
    d. J. Danforth Quayle
    e. James Watt
    f. Jimmy Carter

   g. Madeleine Albright
   h. Monica Lewinsky
   i. Muammar Qaddafi
   j. Nelson Rockefeller
   k. Newt Gingrich
   l. Oliver North
   m. Ross Perot
   n. Saddam Hussein
   o. Sandra Day O'Connor
   p. Zbigniew Brzezinski

_____ 1. The appointment of this leading liberal Republican to the office of vice president by President Ford angered many conservatives.

_____ 2. Presidential candidate who courted the youth vote by promising to pardon most of the young men who had resisted the draft during the Vietnam War.

_____ 3. Carter's hard-line anti-Soviet national security advisor.

_____ 4. First woman to sit on the Supreme Court.

_____ 5. Outspoken critic of environmental legislation who was appointed by Reagan as secretary of the interior.

_____ 6. First woman to be nominated for vice president by a major political party.

_____ 7. Leader of Libya who encouraged terrorist activities in the West.

_____ 8. Young lieutenant colonel who directed the contra arms deal.

_____ 9. Conservative young senator who was George Bush's running mate in 1988.

_____ 10. President of Iraq who ordered his troops to occupy the neighboring country of Kuwait.

_____ 11. Billionaire businessman who spent $60 million of his own money on an independent run for the presidency in 1992.

_____ 12. First presidential candidate to campaign on MTV.

_____ 13. First woman secretary of state.

_____ 14. Leader of the task force charged with designing a new system to provide health care for all Americans.

_____ 15. Chief spokesman of the Republicans after the 1994 election.

_____ 16. White House intern.

WHAT WAS IT?

Complete each following statement (questions 1–6) by writing the letter preceding the appropriate name in the space provided. Use each answer only once.

a. evil empire
b. *Mayaguez*
c. NAFTA
d. presidential pardon
e. Radio Martí
f. Whitewater

_____ 1. Granting this to former President Nixon was President Ford's most controversial decision.

_____ 2. An American ship boarded by the Khmer Rouge of Cambodia.

_____ 3. Term Reagan used to rally his supporters to a new battle against the Soviet Union.

_____ 4. Florida radio station beamed at Cuba and designed to weaken Fidel Castro.

_____ 5. Agreement that united Canada, the United States, and Mexico into the largest free-market zone in the world.

_____ 6. Failed land development in Arkansas in which the Clintons were involved.

WHERE WAS IT?

Complete each following statement (questions 1–11) by writing the letter preceding the appropriate name in the space provided. Use each answer only once.

a. Afghanistan
b. Florida
c. Grenada
d. Egypt
e. Haiti
f. Lebanon
g. New York City
h. Nicaragua
i. Panama
j. Somalia
k. Saudi Arabia

_____ 1. Major American urban area that faced bankruptcy in the 1970s.

_____ 2. One of the Middle Eastern countries involved in the Camp David accord with President Carter.

_____ 3. Small Central American country where the Sandinista revolution turned out a long-time dictator supported by the United States.

_____ 4. Country invaded by the Soviet Union in 1979; the invasion may have been sparked by fear of the growing influence of Islamic fundamentalists.

_____ 5. Middle Eastern country that was the first place the Reagan administration used military force.

_____ 6. Tiny Caribbean island that 2,000 American troops invaded in 1983.

_____ 7. Central American country invaded by the American military to arrest an alleged drug lord.

_____ 8. Largest oil-exporting country in the Middle East.

_____ 9. African country struck by a severe famine where President Bush ordered humanitarian supplies delivered.

_____ 10. Island country where American marines landed to reestablish the elected government in 1994.

_____ 11. The deciding state in the 2000 election.

CHARTS, MAPS, AND ILLUSTRATIONS

1. The large country adjoining Poland and Romania created out of the Soviet Union was

   _____.

2. The highest unemployment rate between 1952 and 2000 was _____.

3. The year with the highest poverty rate was _____.
   What ethnic or racial group had this rate? _____.

MULTIPLE CHOICE

Circle the letter that best completes each statement.

1. After the Kmer Rouge boarded a U.S. ship in May 1975, Ford and Secretary of State Henry Kissinger agreed it was time to assert pressure, and thus began bombing strikes against
   a. Laos.
   b. South Vietnam.
   c. North Vietnam.
   d. Cambodia.

2. After leaving government, Jimmy Carter reflected on his difficulties as president. Which of the following was not a statement made by Jimmy Carter regarding his presidency?
   a. "I had a different way of governing."
   b. "I was a southerner, a born-again Christian, a Baptist, a newcomer."
   c. "I was misunderstood."
   d. "As an engineer and a governor, I was more inclined to move rapidly and without equivocation."

3. Early in his administration, in response to an energy crisis, President Carter delegated James Schlesinger to put together a sweeping energy plan that included all of the following goals except
   a. promotion of the use of alternative sources of energy, especially coal and nuclear power.
   b. an increase in U.S. reliance on foreign oil and natural gas and the reduction of taxes to encourage use of gasoline.
   c. expansion of domestic energy production through new tax incentives and the repeal of regulations on the production of natural gas.
   d. fostering conservation by encouraging greater reliance on insulation and other energy-saving measures.

4. Although often criticized, the Carter administration broke new ground in foreign policy. One of their first victories was the final negotiation and ratification by Congress of the
   a. Portsmouth Treaty.
   b. SALT II Treaty.
   c. Hay-Pauncefote Treaty.
   d. Panama Canal Treaties.

5. Carter's faith in diplomatic solutions, and in his personal skill as a facilitator, again emerged in the Camp David accord of 1978, which involved
   a. Benito Mussolini and Winston Churchill.
   b. Menachem Begin and Anwar Sadat.
   c. Mao Zedong and Nguyen Van Thieu.
   d. Nguyen Cao Ky and Ngo Dinh Diem.

6. Carter's foreign policy became known for a new emphasis on
   a. human rights.
   b. weapons buildup.
   c. military intervention.
   d. Manifest Destiny.

7. When the Carter administration bowed to political pressure to admit Shah Reza Pahlavi to the United States for medical treatment, sixty-six Americans were taken hostage in
   a. Iran.
   b. Israel.
   c. Kuwait.
   d. Libya.

8. During the 1980 presidential campaign, Republican challenger Ronald Reagan stressed his
   a. promise to improve the economy.
   b. support for big government.
   c. opposition to nuclear weapons.
   d. support for a strong national defense.

9. Reagan touted a theory that held that tax reductions would stimulate the economy by putting more money in the hands of investors and consumers, thereby reversing the economic stagnation of the 1970s. Reagan's theory was called
   a. macroeconomics.
   b. microeconomics.
   c. efficient market hypothesis.
   d. supply-side economics.

10. In 1984, Reagan proposed development of the most expensive defense system in history—a space-based shield against incoming missiles. Officially known as the Strategic Defense Initiative (SDI), critics dubbed it
   a. Anti-Space Invaders.
   b. Star Wars.
   c. Luke Skywalker's R2D2.
   d. Darth Vader's light saber.

11. Which secretary of defense suggested that, as Soviets added to the burden on their own faltering economy in order to compete in the accelerating arms race, it might actually collapse under the economic strain?
   a. Caspar Weinberger
   b. Richard Cheney
   c. Les Aspin
   d. William J. Perry

12. The Reagan administration's willingness to use military power was first displayed as an American peacekeeping force of 1,600 was sent to restore stability in Lebanon. Muslim extremists sent a message of opposition to American involvement by
   a. concocting a failed plan to assassinate all leaders involved in the crisis.
   b. invading two refugee camps and slaughtering hundreds of unarmed Palestinians.
   c. carrying out a suicide commando mission into a U.S. military compound in Beirut, which killed 241 sleeping marines.
   d. meeting with an American delegation to arrange for the safe withdrawal of PLO forces and refugees.

13. In 1984, Congress broke with the president's policy and denied further military aid to the Nicaraguan *contras*, also known as Reagan's so-called
   a. crusaders for liberty.
   b. democratic soldiers.
   c. freedom fighters.
   d. Nicaraguan eagles.

14. Which of the following leaders advocated a domestic policy of *glasnost* (openness) and began to implement *perestroika* (economic liberalization)?
   a. Mikhail Gorbachev
   b. Ronald Reagan
   c. Joseph Stalin
   d. Boris Yeltsin

15. Many of Reagan's supporters were deeply disappointed by domestic events during his second term. The two most important pieces of legislation enacted during the second term, which seemed more symbolic than substantive, were
   a. the Glass-Steagall Act and the Agricultural Adjustment Act.
   b. the Pure Food and Drug Act and the Meat Inspection Act.
   c. the Gramm-Rudman-Hollings Act and the Family Support Act.
   d. the Tax Reform Act and the Clean Air Act.

16. Which of the presidential candidates in 1988 pledged his commitment to a "kinder, gentler America"?
   a. Michael Dukakis
   b. Lloyd Bentsen
   c. Robert Dole
   d. George Bush

17. Which of Bush's domestic policy promises came back to haunt his administration as critics refused to overlook the "broken promise" and used it to stain the rest of his term?
   a. supporting an increased minimum wage
   b. setting up employment quotas
   c. keeping prayer in schools
   d. no new taxes

18. Which of the following events did not occur as a result of the "melting" of the cold war?
   a. The anticommunist labor party in Poland, Solidarity, ousted the pro-Soviet regime.
   b. The pro-Soviet East German government fell, and Germans hacked down the Berlin Wall.
   c. The Baltic countries of Latvia, Lithuania, and Estonia declared their independence.
   d. The governments of Czechoslovakia, Hungary, Romania, and Bulgaria resisted change in political affiliation.

19. Former Soviet provinces assumed self-government and, in August 1991, the new state of Russia put down a coup by hard-line communists. This move increased support and popularity for Russian president
   a. Boris Yeltsin.
   b. Mikhail Gorbachev.
   c. Nelson Mandela.
   d. Manuel Noriega.

20. In August of 1990, President Saddam Hussein of Iraq ordered his troops to occupy the small neighboring country of Kuwait. Bush mobilized an international response based in Saudi Arabia and launched Operation
   a. Just Cause.
   b. Desert Shield.
   c. Rolling Thunder.
   d. Overlord.

21. Which of the following statements inaccurately portrays Clinton's presidential campaign of 1992?
    a. The press revealed that Clinton had avoided service in Vietnam and had participated in antiwar demonstrations.
    b. Clinton highlighted his affinity for rock-and-roll music and became the first presidential candidate to go on MTV.
    c. Clinton supported positions on issues that departed from the Democratic Party's familiar agenda.
    d. Clinton avoided economic issues but pledged to decrease government spending for job creation.

22. The first of a series of anticrime measures endorsed by Clinton instituted a five-day waiting period for the purchase of handguns and was known as the
    a. Brady Bill.
    b. Victim's Bill.
    c. Reagan Bill.
    d. Hinckley Bill.

23. Temporary Assistance to Needy Families, which effectively ended the welfare system that had been in place since the New Deal, was controversial for all of the following reasons except
    a. it ignored the difficulty that people without job skills faced.
    b. it did not consider its impact on the daily lives of children.
    c. it gave states control over medicalcare programs.
    d. it would cost the states too much local tax money.

24. Clinton committed U.S. troops to Haiti in an effort to reestablish the elected government and to restore power to exiled leader
    a. Anastasio Somoza Debayle.
    b. José Napoleon Duarte.
    c. Ferdinand Marcos.
    d. Jean-Bertrand Aristide.

25. The candidate of the Green Party in the election of 2000 was
    a. Ralph Nader
    b. Richard Cheney
    c. Ross Perot
    d. Margaret Albright

ESSAY

Description and Explanation (one- to two-paragraph essay)

1. Describe how economic problems undermined the presidencies of Gerald Ford and Jimmy Carter.

2. Explain why Carter and the Democrats lost in the election of 1980.

3. Discuss the principles of supply-side economics. Did this economic theory work? What were its results?

4. Describe the ways that Ronald Reagan and the New Right changed Americans' perception of many traditional political terms, such as liberal and conservative.

5. Describe how conservatives viewed Reagan's second term. Just how conservative was Reagan in his views of social issues?

6. What were the weaknesses of the candidates of both major parties in the election of 1988?

7. Discuss the causes, purposes, and success or failure of the Persian Gulf War.

8. Describe the candidates in the election of 1992 and how they conducted themselves.

9. Describe the role of the United States in United Nations peacekeeping missions. Do you think this role will expand in the future?

Discussion and Analysis (class discussion or one- to two-paragraph essay)

1. Discuss the events involved in the Iran-contra affair, including the role of President Reagan and his administration's ideological basis regarding its activities in the affair.

2. Compare Presidents Carter, Reagan, and Bush as to their views of social issues and domestic programs. How successful was each with his domestic programs?

3. Evaluate the foreign policies of the last four presidents. How were they the same or different? Which was the most productive or successful? Could you say that any was especially successful?

4. Discuss why Clinton's personal reputation was so low while his political status continued so high.

What If (include an explanation of your position)

1. If you had an opportunity to spend a day with one of the following former presidents, Ford, Carter, Reagan, or Clinton, which one would you select?

2. If you were serving in the Senate during the impeachment trial of President Clinton, how would you have voted?

3. If you were ordered to serve on one of the peacekeeping expeditions, would you go freely? Where would you prefer to be assigned? Do you think it would be important and necessary?

Crossword Puzzle: Power and Politics since 1974

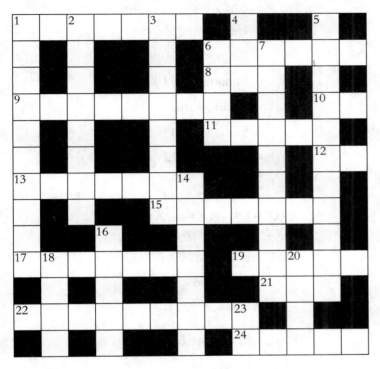

ACROSS

1. U.S. troops were killed here in 1993 while providing humanitarian aid.
6. Wall tumbled down here in 1989.
8. Nation that boycotted 1980 Olympics
9. Carter granted amnesty to those who had resisted becoming ____.
10. Short for Gulf state
11. U.S. restored President Aristide to power here in 1994.
12. State abbreviation and word
13. Nation where Reagan shocked Gorbachev with offer of nuclear disarmament.
15. Reagan sent 2,000 troops here in 1986.
17. People in nation invaded by Soviets in 1979
19. Whitewater special prosecutor
21. Anger
22. Chief Justice appointed by Reagan in 1986
24. Camp David nation in 1978 treaty

DOWN

1. ____ revolution toppled dictator Somoza in Nicaragua.
2. U.S. ship seized by Cambodian Khmer Rouge in 1975
3. Arrangement by which Social Security benefits increase along with inflation.
4. Affirmative
5. Ross Perot for one
6. He pledged "a gentler, kinder, America."
7. Florida source of anti-Castro information (2 wds.)
14. Severe
16. Carter established formal diplomatic ties with nation January 1, 1979.
18. Part of NAFTA
20. Organization of Colin Powell
23. Chemistry or music term

ANSWER KEY

WHO? WHAT? WHERE?

Who Were They?

1. j.   Nelson Rockefeller, p. 1080
2. f.   Jimmy Carter, p. 1082
3. p.   Zbigniew Brzezinski, p. 1084
4. o.   Sandra Day O'Connor, p. 1090
5. e.   James Watt, p. 1091
6. b.   Geraldine Ferraro, p. 1091
7. i.   Muammar Qaddafi, p. 1095
8. l.   Oliver North, p. 1096
9. d.   J. Danforth Quayle, p. 1097
10. n.   Saddam Hussein, p. 1100
11. m.   Ross Perot, p. 1103
12. a.   Bill Clinton, p. 1103
13. g.   Madeleine Albright, p. 1104
14. c.   Hillary Rodham Clinton, p. 1104
15. k.   Newt Gingrich, p. 1105
16. h.   Monica Lewinsky, p. 1108

What Was It?

1. d.   presidential pardon, p. 1080
2. b.   *Mayaguez*, p. 1080
3. a.   evil empire, p. 1094
4. e.   Radio Martí, p. 1094
5. c.   NAFTA, p. 1110
6. f.   Whitewater, p. 1104

Where Was It?

1. g.   New York City, p. 1083
2. d.   Egypt, p. 1085
3. h.   Nicaragua, p. 1085
4. a.   Afghanistan, p. 1086
5. f.   Lebanon, p. 1095
6. c.   Grenada, p. 1095
7. i.   Panama, p. 1100
8. k.   Saudi Arabia, p. 1100
9. j.   Somalia, p. 1102
10. e.   Haiti, p. 1112
11. b.   Florida, p. 1114

CHARTS, MAPS, AND ILLUSTRATIONS

1. Ukraine, p. 1099
2. 14%, p. 1106
3. 1967; black, p. 1106

MULTIPLE CHOICE

1. d   (p. 1080)
2. c   (p. 1082)
3. b   (p. 1083)
4. d   (p. 1084)
5. b   (pp. 1084–1085)
6. a   (p. 1085)
7. a   (p. 1085)
8. d   (p. 1086)
9. d   (p. 1087)
10. b   (p. 1094)
11. a   (p. 1094
12. c   (p. 1095)
13. c   (p. 1095)
14. a   (p. 1096)
15. c   (p. 1092)

16. d   (p. 1097)

17. d   (p. 1097)

18. d   (p. 1098)

19. a   (p. 1098)

20. b   (p. 1100)

21. d   (p. 1103)

22. a   (p. 1104)

23. a   (p. 1107)

24. d   (p. 1112)

25. a   (p. 1113)

ESSAY

Description and Explanation

1. pp. 1080, 1083–1084

2. pp. 1086–1087

3. p. 1087

4. p. 1092

5. p. 1092

6. pp. 1097

7. pp. 1100–1102

8. pp. 1102–1103

9. pp. 1110–1113

Discussion and Analysis

1. pp. 1095–1096

2. Chapter 31 *passim*

3. Chapter 31 *passim*

4. p. 1109

What If

1. Chapter 31 *passim*

2. p. 1109

3. pp. 1110–1113

Crossword Puzzle